Monographs
of the Rutgers Center of Alcohol Studies
No. 7

Monographs of the
Rutgers Center of Alcohol Studies

Under the editorship of MARK KELLER

This monograph series was begun as "Monographs of the Yale Center of Alcohol Studies" and Numbers 1, 2 and 3 in the series were published at Yale. Beginning with Number 4 the series has been continued as Monographs of the Rutgers Center of Alcohol Studies. The change conforms with the transfer of the Center from Yale to Rutgers University. The works published in this series report of original research in any of the scientific disciplines, whether performed at Rutgers or elsewhere.

No. 1. Alcohol and the Jews; a Cultural Study of Drinking and Sobriety. By CHARLES R. SNYDER.

No. 2. Revolving Door; a Study of the Chronic Police Case Inebriate. By DAVID J. PITTMAN and C. WAYNE GORDON.

No. 3. Alcohol in Italian Culture; Food and Wine in Relation to Sobriety among Italians and Italian Americans. By GIORGIO LOLLI, EMIDIO SERIANNI, GRACE M. GOLDER and PIERPAOLO LUZZATTO-FEGIZ.

No. 4. Drinking among Teen-Agers; a Sociological Interpretation of Alcohol Use by High-School Students. By GEORGE L. MADDOX and BEVODE C. MCCALL.

No. 5. Drinking in French Culture. By ROLAND SADOUN, GIORGIO LOLLI and MILTON SILVERMAN.

No. 6. American Drinking Practices; a National Study of Drinking Behavior and Attitudes. By DON CAHALAN, IRA H. CISIN and HELEN M. CROSSLEY.

No. 7. Problem Drinking among American Men. By DON CAHALAN and ROBIN ROBIN.

No. 8. Problem Drinkers Seeking Treatment. By EILEEN M. CORRIGAN.

No. 9. Drinking, Community and Civilization; the Account of a New Jersey Interview Study. By HAROLD FALLDING, with the assistance of CAROL MILES.

No. 10. The Beer Gardens of Bulawayo; Integrated Drinking in a Segregated Society. By HARRY F. WOLCOTT.

Problem Drinking among American Men

Distributed by

COLLEGE & UNIVERSITY PRESS · *Publishers*

263 CHAPEL STREET   NEW HAVEN, CONN.

Problem Drinking among American Men

BY
Don Cahalan and Robin Room

PUBLICATIONS DIVISION
RUTGERS CENTER OF ALCOHOL STUDIES
NEW BRUNSWICK   NEW JERSEY

Copyright © 1974 by
Journal of Studies on Alcohol, Incorporated
New Brunswick, New Jersey

Library of Congress catalog card number: 72-619570
ISBN: 911290-38-9   ISSN: 0080-4983

MANUFACTURED IN THE UNITED STATES OF AMERICA BY
UNITED PRINTING SERVICES, INC.
NEW HAVEN, CONN.

Contents

List of Tables

List of Figures

Foreword

This monograph reports the findings from two national surveys conducted in 1967 and 1969 and from a community survey of San Francisco in 1967–68, which were undertaken with the central purpose of describing in detail the many ways in which some men get into trouble in relation to their drinking of alcoholic beverages. The research mission was not directed toward detection of the characteristics of those who may be suffering from the "disease" of alcoholism. The findings of detailed descriptive surveys such as these, however, are necessary to provide foundations for a better understanding of problems related to misuse of alcohol, recently termed one of the four major public health problems in the nation.[1]

The surveys were conducted as part of a program of research on the drinking practices of the general population. The research program, initiated in 1959 under the sponsorship of the National Institute of Mental Health, had three general objectives: (1) To describe drinking behavior in detail, including "normal" and "deviant" drinking. This objective already has been largely fulfilled in the publication of a monograph in 1969 (20) and in a series of articles and papers.[2] (2) To carry out short-term measures of changes in drinking behavior and to measure drinking-associated problems. Some of these objectives have been realized in the publication of a book in 1970 (19) and various articles on problem drinking in the

---

[1] From the statement of the Honorable Jacob K. Javits, hearings before the Special Subcommittee on Alcoholism and Narcotics of the Committee on Labor and Public Welfare, U.S. Senate (144, *p. 20*): "The U.S. Public Health Service and the Crime Commission have described alcoholism as the Nation's fourth most serious health problem, ranking behind heart disease, mental illness, and cancer. Alcoholism afflicts an estimated 5 million Americans and roughly 250,000 persons become alcoholics each year."

[2] Many of the articles and papers will be referenced in this monograph. For a full list, see Appendix B in Cahalan (19).

general adult population. Detailed information of the correlates of drinking problems among men aged 21 to 59 is presented in the current monograph. (3) To complete longer-term measurements of changes in specific types of potential problems and their apparent consequences in the lives of individuals. Work on this objective will be completed during the 1970s, thus rounding out a longitudinal research program spanning nearly 15 years.

All the studies conducted under this research program have been based on personal-interview surveys with randomly selected samples of adults in the household population. The program was begun in 1959 under the aegis of the California State Department of Public Health, with Wendell Lipscomb as Principal Investigator and Ira H. Cisin as Research Director. In 1962, Cisin initiated a series of national surveys conducted by the Social Research Group of The George Washington University, while Genevieve Knupfer continued as Principal Investigator for the San Francisco Bay Area series of studies; these studies were conducted for a time under the sponsorship of the Mental Research Institute of Palo Alto. Don Cahalan joined the Washington group in 1964 as project director. In 1968, the two series of studies were reunited, with Cisin as Principal Investigator and Cahalan moving to Berkeley to direct the program. The final stages of the research program, supported by grants from the National Institute of Mental Health, are now being carried out under the sponsorship of the School of Public Health, University of California, Berkeley, with Cahalan as Principal Investigator and Robin Room as Senior Analyst.

The perspective for the research analysis in this monograph might be characterized as "descriptive epidemiology," concentrating first upon the delineation of about a dozen specific types of problems related to alcohol, then presenting prevalence rates in various subgroups and, finally, exploring the interrelationships between the various types of problems and their connections with many sociocultural and personality characteristics. The population chosen for study was narrowed down to the 1960 population of 41 million men aged 21 through 59 to concentrate upon the higher-risk group which does much of the heavy drinking, constitutes a majority of the working population and holds a large share of economic and political power in the United States.

Data from the parallel national and San Francisco community surveys are analyzed in this monograph, drawing upon the distinctive features of each type of study as appropriate. Primary emphasis is given to the findings of the 1969 national sample of 978 men aged 21 to 59, and to the findings of the combined 1967 and 1969 samples of 1561 men aged 21 to 59. The 1967–68 San Francisco survey of 786 men aged 21 to 59 is also drawn upon whenever its more qualitative approach can be helpful in putting the quantitative findings of the national study into better perspective, and whenever the community survey's superior availability of collateral community ecological data, external validation tests and better data on the time-ordering of respondents' life events are found useful.

A long-term research program of this sort benefits from the heritage of research concepts and leadership provided by a generation of social scientists. A special note of appreciation is due to the following persons who have been associated with the program:

The methodological principles and the epidemiologic perspectives of the research program were originally envisioned by Wendell Lipscomb, Ira H. Cisin and Genevieve Knupfer, all of whom have continued to make contributions throughout the course of the various studies.

Earlier San Francisco studies, directed by Knupfer with the assistance of Walter Clark, Robin Room and Selma Monsky, provided the groundwork for the San Francisco 1967–68 survey here reported and much of the conceptual and content underpinnings for the national surveys. Selma Monsky's West Coast Community Surveys provided the fieldwork for the San Francisco survey.

Helen M. Crossley made many contributions to the planning of the content and analysis for the national surveys here reported.

Nathan Rosenberg, research psychologist at the National Institute on Alcohol Abuse and Alcoholism, provided helpful suggestions on research content and analytic procedures. Richard Jessor, Institute of Behavioral Science, University of Colorado, helped make it possible to replicate in our analysis some of the principal features of his triethnic Colorado community survey (61).

Ellen Cahalan provided essential (and unpaid) editorial and analytic assistance at many points.

Appreciation is due also to the members of our Advisory Board for their helpful suggestions: Jeanne Block, Jack Block, Joel Fort, William Gaffey and Glen Mellinger. In addition, Anne M. Seifert, who is writing her doctoral dissertation on the association between religious affiliation and drinking behavior and problems, contributed useful counsel in that portion of the analysis.

Among the many staff members of the Social Research Group of The George Washington University, who assisted materially in the gathering and processing of the data for the national surveys, special appreciation is due Ben Owens, field director, Celia Pavis, coding supervisor, and Editta Mannix, administrator.

The staff members in our Berkeley office who made substantial contributions on both the national and San Francisco surveys include Jennifer Carlton, Danielle Hitz, Mary Milos and Andrea Mitchell, research assistants; Janie Pasalich, data-processing supervisor, and her assistants Dan deGrassi and Kirk Beck; and Joyce Gordon, office manager, and her assistants Shelley Wheeler and Julia Hart, who prepared the tables and typed the final manuscript.

Don Cahalan
Robin Room

Berkeley, California
September 1973

Chapter 1

The National Surveys: Sampling Operations and Data Collection Standards

THE DESCRIPTION of problem drinking among American men aged 21 to 59 reported in this monograph is based on two sources of data: a national survey conducted in 1969 and a combination of the 1969 survey and a national survey of 1967. This pooling of the data permits detailed analysis of the characteristics of persons who reported one or more of a dozen problems related to drinking within the last 3 years. Details of the sampling operations are provided in Appendix A. Following is a summary of the sampling procedures and standards:

1. A probability (random) sample of 2746 respondents representative of the adult household population was first interviewed in 1964–65 (hereinafter referred to as the National 1 or N1 survey). Results of this survey, conducted throughout the United States (exclusive of Alaska and Hawaii), were reported in a descriptive monograph on drinking practices published in 1969 (20). The questions on specific drinking problems were asked in a second stage, conducted in 1967, when a subsample of 1359 respondents were reinterviewed and the findings reported in several articles and a 1970 book (19) (hereinafter referred to as National 2 or N2). This sample size was adequate for the purpose of reporting general prevalence rates of specific types of problems. However, the 583 persons in the high-risk group of men aged 21 to 59 needed to be supplemented by an additional sample in order to permit sufficiently detailed analysis of the correlates of specific types of drinking problems.

2. A national supplementary sample of 978 men, aged 21 to 59, was therefore surveyed in 1969 (subsequently referred to as National 3 or N3); the interview replicated all of the key features of the 1967 survey. The data from the N2 and N3 samples were then pooled to yield the total N of 1561 men aged 21 to 59, the base for many of the analyses of the national data presented in this monograph. This 1969 supplementary survey entailed additions or revisions of content stemming from our prior experience with the other national and Bay Area studies, including additional coverage on certain types of drinking problems and more extensive coverage on certain variables cor-

1

related with problem drinking. Data obtained only on the supplementary 1969 sample of 978 men are presented separately, where appropriate.

Both the 1967 National 2 and 1969 National 3 surveys were conducted in accordance with strict principles of probability sampling, in which all households within 100 Primary Sampling Units were prelisted and every Nth one selected (by the survey office staff, not the interviewers) for interviewing. Interviewers called at the preselected households and enumerated the eligible persons (men aged 21–59) within the household; if there was more than one, the prospective respondent was preselected by a random-number device on the questionnaire specific for that household. Interviews were conducted in most instances by men, supplemented by women only when necessary to complete assignments. All interviewers were personally trained by regional supervisors from the Social Research Group's field staff and, in order to minimize problems of rapport, only nonabstainers were utilized. The rate of completed interviews was relatively high considering the sensitivity and length of the interview: 80% of those selected for reinterview in the N2 1967 survey[1] (of the 90% initially interviewed in the N1 1964–65 survey) and 73% of the eligible households (with one or more men aged 21–59) in the N3 1969 survey. The sampling and interviewing standards were such that the findings on the total N2 and N3 sample of 1561 can be projected with reasonable confidence against the total male population aged 21–59 in what the Census calls the "conterminous" United States (exclusive of Alaska and Hawaii).

Both the N2 and N3 portions of the sample of men aged 21 to 59 were selected so as to result in systematic underrepresentation of light drinkers and abstainers in N2, persons outside metropolitan areas in N3 and those living with other adult men (see Appendix A). To be fully representative of the national population of men aged 21–59, then, the results should

[1] These completion rates for the National 1 and 2 surveys were for the total samples, including both sexes and all ages. As noted in Appendix A, the N2 completion rate for the high-risk population of men aged 21 to 59 was not computed separately; it is assumed to be a few percentage points lower than for the adult population as a whole since younger men are harder to find at home.

be weighted to compensate for those underrepresentations. However, since comparisons of weighted and unweighted data showed no substantial differences in results (Appendix A), and since absolute distributions are of secondary importance to patterns of relationships in the present analysis, the results are presented in unweighted form throughout.

Chapter 2

Defining and Measuring
Drinking Problems

A. *General Issues in Defining Drinking Problems*

OUR GENERAL APPROACH to the definition of the drinking-related problems we wish to measure has been broadly inclusive rather than restricted to matters on which there is common agreement, and eclectic rather than confined to any one of the various conceptual models of alcoholism or problem drinking (131). This approach is in the spirit of Jellinek's later work in which he broke with the more unitary philosophy of his earlier statements to define the limits of his realm of discourse very broadly, as "drinking and . . . damage (individual or social, or both) incumbent upon the drinking" (60, *p. 1341*). It also follows the approach of recent workers who have been concerned with drinking problems in the general population, such as Plaut (35, *pp. 37–38*), "problem drinking is a repetitive use of beverage alcohol causing physical, psychological, or social harm to the drinker or to others," and Knupfer (66, *p. 974*), "a problem—any problem—connected fairly closely with drinking constitutes a drinking problem."

The general perspective governing the definitions of drinking problems is to be as inclusive as possible so as not to miss any potential problem which might be found in follow-up studies in this same series to have substantial long-term consequences for the individual. Thus several potential problems (notably "psychological dependence on alcohol" and "belligerence") were included merely because some writers have treated them as potential problems, not because they constituted obvious and immediate adverse consequences. As a result of this inclusive research strategy, it is possible that later follow-up studies will find certain types of potential "problems" to have only ephemeral consequences at most, and that other types of problems will be found to have such

4

severe consequences that they should be singled out for more intensive study than this analysis provides.

These surveys represent an early stage in the investigation of problem drinking. Additional longitudinal studies (including the current follow-up studies in the present series) will be necessary to determine more conclusively whether changes in behavior and life events are related to later changes in drinking behavior and its apparent consequences. This monograph presents certain findings on some modal patterns of sequences of experiences and behavior related to drinking. While these findings should be useful in modifying our concepts about the evolution of patterns of drinking behavior over time, they are interim in nature and subject to further modification and clarification when this longitudinal series of studies is completed.

We have thus sought to cover all major areas of content considered to be a part of alcoholism or problem drinking in any of the primary conceptual models. The specific or potential drinking problems covered in these surveys draw on considerable previous work. The proximate ancestry is the work of Knupfer (66), Clark (30) and Cahalan (19), and in line with this work we have made detailed distinctions in our measurements by the type and severity of the problem and its recency or relative timing. Earlier studies which were drawn upon include those of Mulford and Miller (93), Bailey, Haberman and Alksne (6), and Jellinek (58).

The aim has been to provide a set of drinking-problem measures in relatively unitary conceptual areas which can be used singly or in combinations for several different purposes. One purpose is to use the measures as "dependent variables" in the traditional survey research or epidemiological model of explanatory analysis, in which the object is to "explain" the variance in a dependent variable by means of one or more independent variables. For this, in the present report we use the individual problem measures, typological combinations in terms of content and timing, and over-all summary scales.

Besides this explanatory analysis, however, we shall also use the measures of drinking problems in studies of the patterning of drinking experiences in space and time. In this type of analysis, all variables are treated as of equal conceptual status; the aim is simply to describe empirically the clusterings and disjunctions to be found in a set of phenomena. And for yet another purpose, we examine the patterns of interaction of drinking-problem measures in studying alternative patternings of problems and "deviant case" analyses.

Although some attention was paid to patterns of empirical relations in the course of their construction, the basic criteria for forming the problem-drinking measures were a priori conceptualizations. We are convinced nevertheless that the resulting measures are more useful to our purposes than those derived by some more "objective" technique which would assume equality of status for all components or allow invisible computer-program parameters to make the decisions. The present aggregations were arrived at by a process of painful backing and filling involving many hands in several studies, but are certainly open to question and improvement. To aid the future efforts of others, we wish to make explicit the assumptions involved in the measures in their present form.

In general, the measures of drinking-related problems can be categorized into three broad areas: (1) the amount, patterning and style of drinking behavior; (2) the psychological loading the respondent attaches to the behavior; and (3) the physiological and social consequences of the behavior. The specific areas measured include the following:

Drinking behavior: heavy intake; binge drinking; symptomatic drinking behavior.

Psychological involvement: psychological dependence on drinking; loss of control over drinking behavior.

Consequences of drinking: belligerence after drinking; problems with wife due to drinking; problems with relatives; problems with friends and neighbors; job problems; police problems; health problems and injuries; financial problems.

We shall discuss in some detail the content and connotations of each of these problem areas. The list of areas measured is similar to those in previous studies of the same series, although specific items used as indices have changed over time.[1]

---

[1] See Appendix B and Cahalan (19).

B. Models and Measures

Basically, alcoholism may be viewed as a vice, a disease or a social problem, and models of alcoholism tend to fall within one or another of these three general rubrics. Vice models put the primary emphasis on the drinking behavior, disease models emphasize the condition of the individual drinkers, and social-problems models emphasize the individual's relation with his social and cultural environment. All three general rubrics share some minimal agreements: (a) that the phenomena subsumed have enough in common to be regarded as an entity; (b) that the entity involved is a condition rather than an occurrence—that is, its manifestations are continuous or repetitive; (c) that the condition is abnormal (if not in actual fact and statistically, at least in comparison to some idealized criterion); and (d) that it is undesirable—something should be done about it.[2]

Within each of these general rubrics, which are themselves not often explicitly enumerated but which are fairly generally recognized, there are several alternative models for alcoholism. It is at this level that there is the maximum of confusion—different disease models often being confused both by their adherents and detractors—and the same is true in the arenas of vice and social problems.

There is a strong tendency for the adherents of each model to claim for it the entire territory of drinking problems. There is thus considerable disagreement in the field about the conceptual status of each of the "problem areas": whether the behavior or experience is a problem or potential problem or whether it is not really just a symptom of yet another underlying problem.

Thus, broadly speaking, the seat for vice models is the behavior itself—heavy intake, binge drinking and perhaps symptomatic behavior and belligerence. The seat for medical models is either the respondent's mind or his body—loss of control and psychological dependence for the one, primarily health consequences for the other. The seat for social problems mod-

---

[2] ROOM, R. G. Assumptions and implications of disease concepts of alcoholism. Presented at the 29th International Congress on Alcoholism and Drug Dependence, Sydney, Australia, February 1970.

els is the social consequences—problems with wife, friends, relatives, job, police and perhaps finances and belligerence. We would argue that the legitimacy of a specific "problem" or "potential problem" concept lies in its utility for research, therapeutic or policymaking purposes, and that each of the problem areas which we utilize is relevant to at least one of the common models of alcoholism.

As an indication of the conceptual backdrop to our problem-areas measures, then, we shall list here some of the current models. Siegler, Osmond and Newell (131) and Bruun (16) have published careful and in some ways more systematic attempts to differentiate models of alcoholism on somewhat different principles.

1. *Vice:* (a) The crime model, in which the bad behavior is dealt with by laws and other formal sanctions. (b) The "bad habit" model, in which the bad habit is to be dealt with by training the person toward self-control (107). There are great variations within this model in the degree of willingness with which the problem drinker undertakes the treatment as well as in the types of treatment, which range from moral suasion through various forms of positive and negative behavior therapy.

2. *Disease:* (a) The classical disease concept, in which compulsive drinking is considered a disease of the mind or the will. Its focal point is "loss of control," although its adherents often confuse the issue by looking for a physiological etiology and by using physiological consequences, such as delirium tremens and withdrawal, to "prove" the existence of a disease. As is explicit in Alcoholics Anonymous orthodoxy and many medical discussions, the primary method of treatment has been "moral"—often indistinguishable from methods of behavior therapy. The only specifically medical treatments (other than psychiatric) have been disulfiram or other aversive-therapy substances and treating the physiological consequences of drinking (see below). (b) The physiological–disease or medical-consequences model, which concentrates on such physiological sequelae of heavy drinking as cirrhosis and delirium tremens. This model receives the primary emphasis in French discussions of alcoholism.

3. *Social Problems:* There have been a number of discussions recently of three alternative sociological models for "deviance" (48, 108, 127). (a) Labeling theory: The primary emphasis is not on the person's initial behavior but on social forces which single out and label him. The individual may label himself as deviant or he may be labeled by others as a member of a deviant subculture. Applications of labeling theory to alcoholism have tended to function as arguments for the equivalence of one form of labeling with another (90). However, informal labeling of an individual by his associates, his labeling of himself and public

labeling by institutions may be very different in their meaning and consequences. (b) Anomie theory, of which there are at least two versions: conflicting norms produce deviant behavior, and an absence of norms produces deviance (61, 72, 88, 106, 133). Recent U.S. discussions of possible policies for the prevention of alcoholism have given considerable attention to the role of cultural ambivalence and confusion over norms in precipitating alcoholism (35, *pp. 48–49, 126–127*). (c) Social and cultural support for deviance, or the "differential association" hypothesis expounded by Sutherland (137), in which the permissiveness of the individual's subculture is considered to have a profound influence on his drinking behavior. An historical illustration is the temperance movement's focus on the saloon or tavern as the transmitter and sustainer of a subculture of heavy drinking.

C. Principles of Aggregation: Severity and Certainty

The basic data from which the measures of drinking problems are derived are approximately 100 questions asked of the respondent concerning his drinking behavior, his drinking experiences and his drinking motivations. Other studies have shown that there seems to be somewhat less minimization of drinking in the respondents' own reports than in those from other members of the same household (6), but there is no question that respondents are in general more likely to underestimate than to overestimate their drinking. Projections from our respondents' reports of their amount and frequency of drinking, for instance, account for between one-half and two-thirds of the alcoholic beverages sold in the United States (120). Our data should be regarded, then, as providing only minimum estimates of prevalence. But since our emphasis in the present report is on patterns of association rather than on raw prevalences, the existence of some underestimation should be tolerable.

Problems of aggregation start, of course, whenever at least two items of data are collected which are conceived to fall in the same conceptual area. In many general-population studies of drinking, problems of aggregation have not been a great issue, since usually there were only a few items, and the scarcity of positive responses to any one item practically dictated an aggregation in terms of alternatives (having positive response on any one of the components). Thus Manis and Hunt (86), and Bailey, Haberman and Alksne (6), inquiring primarily about social consequences of drinking, report their results in terms of each component item and in terms of a composite "any one of the above" criterion.

Prior to the present series of studies, the other technique of aggregation used most in general-population U.S. studies in the field has been the Guttman scale or modified versions of it (93; 136, *pp. 157–158*). Such a scale is appropriately used where the component items form an empirical hierarchy so that the existence of more "severe" (less common) items presupposes the existence of the less severe components. Guttman scales were used also in earlier reports in the present series, notably in the conceptual area referred to here as "psychological dependence." But the scales formed in the alcoholism field have never fulfilled traditional standards for Guttman scales (75, *p. 356*).[3] Such scales have thus no discernible advantage over additively or hierarchically formed scales, being measures which represent an uneasy compromise between these two methods.

A Guttman-type scale is predicated on the existence of an empirical hierarchy—so that each more frequent item occurs whenever a less frequent item occurs—whereas the existence of conceptual hierarchies which do not "scale" empirically is common in measuring drinking problems. For instance, a respondent may lose his job due to drinking without anyone at work ever advising him to cut down, but the former is indisputably a more severe consequence of his drinking than the latter. Thus we do not treat all the individual items in our inventory as being equal in conceptual status. In each conceptual area, we distinguish between the items used as components in measuring that entity according to what we regard as their intrinsic severity and the degree of certainty that they are in fact measuring a problem in the area.

Thus, as we have mentioned, we regard loss of a job as intrinsically a more severe job problem than someone at work suggesting the respondent cut down on his drinking. And we regard hospitalization as a result of drinking as intrinsically a more certain health problem than the respondent's feeling that

---

[3] ROOM, R. G. Notes on "Identifying problem drinkers in a household health survey" by Harold Mulford and Ronald Wilson. Social Research Group Working Paper F10, 1966.

drinking has harmed his health. To a certain extent, then, the scales that result may be regarded as measuring a mixture of the dimensions of degrees of severity and degrees of certainty that the respondent has a problem.

In formal terms, our drinking-problems scales are constructed by methods which allow for and assume three different types of relations among the components: (1) as hierarchically ordered, when the items are regarded as unequally severe or unequally certain indicators of the underlying conceptual dimension; (2) as alternatives, where the items are regarded as alternative manifestations, of roughly equal severity, of a presumed underlying dimension, and where the possession of both items does not indicate a substantially more certain or more severe problem, e.g., wife's complaint about drinking, and wife's suggestion that the respondent cut down; (3) as additive or multiplicative in their relationship, where the items are regarded as manifestations of roughly equal severity, but where their joint occurrence is regarded as substantially increasing the severity or certainty of a problem. The joint occurrence of taking a drink first thing in the morning and sneaking drinks when no one is looking, for instance, greatly decreases the possibility that the positive response of one of these items is a naïve or overscrupulous reporting of problems. A limiting case of the multiplicative relationship is where only the joint occurrence of two items is accepted as constituting an indicator.

In applying one or more of these principles to build the drinking-problem measure for each problem area, we distinguished as many levels of severity as seemed meaningful. In this report, however, these original differentiations on severity are, in some cases, partially telescoped so that each area measure was scored at no more than four levels of severity, in addition to "no problem." Furthermore, in cross-tabulations in this report, each problem-area measure is normally used in dichotomous form—but at what we considered the minimum meaningful level of severity when the maximum number of "positives" was needed for the analysis, and elsewhere cut at a higher level of severity—what we call the "high problems" level.

Three different versions were built of each problem index to provide the best attainable measure for each of several different purposes: (1) the N3 optimum measures, built on the N3 sample only (N = 978), to represent our "best estimate" of prevalence on the basis of the extended list of items available only for that sample. This N3 sample is the source for the aggregate rates of specific problems reported in Table 1 below. (2) The N2 and N3 measures, built on the N2–N3 sample (N = 1561), to provide exact comparability in the 2 studies. The measures differ from the optimum measures in the omission of items not asked on N2. These measures are used throughout the analyses of the relation between drinking problems and independent variables, since the larger number gives a greater reliability to the detailed cross-tabulations and multivariate analyses. (3) The N3 past–current comparable scales, built on the N3 sample (N = 978), to provide exactly comparable measures of past and current problems. The measures differ from the optimum measures in the omission of items for which full data on past occurrences were not asked. They are used in the analyses of incidence and remission and of time ordering (Chapter 3). A summary of the contents of the N3 problem-drinking scales appears in Appendix B of this monograph.

D. The Measurement of Time and Order

In the study of occurrences and causes, epidemiologists have long recognized that, as the title of an article on the subject put it, "time is of the essence" (29). Indeed, the basic epidemiological concepts of incidence and prevalence do not have any meaning in the absence of a specification of time.

In other traditions of research on which the present study draws, however, the issue of time has often not been so explicitly faced. In previous general-population surveys of alcohol problems time has usually not been specified beyond the choice of tense in the questions: drinking behavior normally in the present tense, consequences of drinking normally in "ever" terms, e.g., lifetime occurrence. Often a measure based on items asked in the present tense has been compared with one based on lifetime occurrences as potential alternative indicators of alcoholism, without any recognition of the disparity in time frame.

These two different time frames used in general-population studies of drinking reflect the fact that the questionnaire items are drawn from two different research traditions, each with its own assumptions and myopias about time. The tradition of sociological sample surveys of the general population, on which measures of drinking-behavior patterns were primarily formed, has tended, as we shall discuss below, to limit itself to current time in collecting data, though not in the assumptions made in the subsequent analysis.

In some items in the dimensions of intake and psychological dependence, as measured in the present study, the wording remains (for comparative purposes) simply in the present tense, without further specification of time, although the responses are taken as indicators of our current time period—the last 3 years in the national data. This is a fair approximation of recent behavior, but only an approximation, as we know from the occasional "current abstainer" who, when asked when he quit drinking, says "yesterday."

The items on consequences of drinking, on the other hand, have been drawn from the tradition of viewing alcoholism as a progressive and unitary disease, based primarily on the ideology of Alcoholics Anonymous and Jellinek's study conditioned by that ideology (56).[4] Such studies have commonly been quite specific in inquiring about time, since a major aim has been the arranging of a miscellany of "symptoms" into a time-ordering sequence presumed to reflect the phases of an underlying disease entity. "Once an alcoholic, always an alcoholic" has been a persistent underlying assumption of these studies, however; thus while they systematically inquired about the time of first occurrence, none has inquired about the time of latest occurrence. Timing was not considered crucial in establishing the nature or occurrence of the phenomenon studied, but simply as a useful tool in describing its natural history. Consequently it is understandable that general-population studies, borrowing questions from this tradition, strapped for questionnaire space and knowing there would be relatively few positive responses to any item no matter how worded, simply

[4] See Footnote 2 to this Chapter.

asked about lifetime occurrences—"did this ever happen?"

Such questions obviously render a time-specific prevalence estimate impossible and allow an incidence estimate only from longitudinal data and only with "relapses" excluded. Most seriously, in studying the process of getting into and out of drinking problems in longitudinal studies, they make no allowance for the possibility of remission, so that what might otherwise indicate remission must perforce be viewed by the analyst as simply evidence of respondent unreliability (7). On the other hand, as we have indicated, in current sociological practice surveys rarely include much retrospective data and hardly ever any systematic coverage of the same variable both contemporaneously and in retrospect.

There are, of course, substantial issues of response validity involved in the filtering of data through human memory. A substantial but scattered literature has by now accumulated, mostly attesting to the obvious: there are tendencies to underestimate or backdate discreditable attributes, to invent or date forward creditable attributes, to remember more important and more recent events better, to "round" estimates of time to the nearest 5 years or decade (18, 26, 45, 55, 97, 100, 146, 147, 148). These difficulties are real but some are not necessarily insurmountable. Retrospective data may, in fact, in some cases be more accurate than contemporaneous: "Wasn't I a bad boy then" is a more comfortable social posture than "Aren't I a bad boy now." Sometimes the general distribution of the retrospective data can be compared with independently derived data (64). In any case, the use or nonuse of retrospective data should be a matter of conscious judgment rather than of unconscious avoidance. Often the restriction of a questionnaire to contemporaneous data seems to reflect simply an assumption that the respondent is to be regarded as a passive experimental object, to which instruments can be applied to measure its present state, but which cannot be asked to narrate its history.

The choice between retrospective and panel data must be weighed against the loss of response validity in the retrospective design, the more-than-doubled cost of panel design, and the probability of only a small amount of change in short-term panels and a large sample loss in long-term panels. If there is no alternative but a single survey, adding retrospective data would seem likely to result in fewer errors in distinguishing between and assessing association, sequence and cause than even the most methodologically sophisticated analysis of purely contemporaneous variables. The historical antecedents for the method of reconstructing the past by a comparative study of the present (as in 19th-century unilinear social evolutionary theory) are not very encouraging.

At the outset of the present studies, then, we knew that we wanted to measure both current and lifetime "prevalences" of the various drinking problem areas; and by the time of the San Francisco 1967 and N3 studies, we also wished to distinguish "past" from "current" behavior and gather more exact data on timing (in the present study, "lifetime" problems are defined to include both "current" and "past" problems).

There are three principal procedures available in trying to establish the temporal sequence of events through asking respondents retrospective questions. Two of them were used in the current studies, and we plan to conduct trials with the third in the future:

(1) The method used in these national studies, asking about behavior and experiences during a certain period (such as the last 3 years) in comparison to some other period. This procedure is relatively insensitive to day-to-day or month-to-month changes in behavior but was adopted in the present study because of considerations of respondent fatigue and more research interest in usual states than in single events. An extension of this method is to ask about experiences within a series of periods in the respondent's life. Thus in both the Hartford studies (17, pp. 139–143) and in the 1971 reinterviews in San Francisco, respondents were asked about experiences in each decade of their life. (2) Attempting to locate specific events in time (at least as to year) by retrospective questions, and then sorting the various events into temporal order. This method was used in the San Francisco 1967–68 study and will be reported later in this monograph. It permits greater precision in ordering events than does the use of the 3-year span noted above. (3) Asking the respondent to report the occurrences of various types of events, and then attempting to put them into temporal order, such as through a card-sort approach. This method, which will be tested in our forthcoming follow-up studies, can establish the temporal sequence of first and latest occurrence of experiences and problems. The technique has the advantage of utilizing the respondent as the informant about the circumstances attendant upon the temporal order with which two or more events occurred, thus contributing to

our understanding of the dynamics of the interaction of the events. It has the disadvantage of providing cues to the respondent on how he might rewrite history by suggesting a more socially acceptable order of events (wife nagged me, so I got drunk) than the actual order (because I had often gotten drunk before, my wife nagged me, which provided sufficient additional motivation or excuse to get drunk again).

In the present studies, we tend to look at drinking problems as conditions rather than events. This is in line with the general assumption in all models of alcoholism that it is repetitive behavior rather than isolated events which is the object of interest. In order to make sense of a whole life history, we are necessarily imposing a summary view on a sequence of events which a more detailed view might not support. Many component items of our measures of drinking problems are by their nature either momentary occurrences or relatively short-term sequences. This is particularly true of the most severe manifestations—a wife's complaining may be a chronic condition, but obtaining a divorce is not. In our analysis, a penumbra of conditions is assumed to surround each event. Since some events are by nature periodic (one may not arrange divorces very frequently), our definition of "current" was stretched to give them a decent chance to occur. Thus a problem condition is regarded as "current" if there were manifestations anytime in the last 3 years. Again, our analysis of time ordering is predicated on the assumption that the respondent continuously "had" the problem being measured between its first and latest occurrence. Thus if his first binge was 10 years ago and his latest 2 years ago, he is assumed to be a "binge drinker" for the intervening 8 years, even though he may not have been on a binge at all in the interval.

Our definition of a "current" problem, then, is one that has occurred within the last 3 years, whether or not it also occurred before. Conversely, a "past" problem is one that occurred at any time before 3 years ago, whether or not it has also occurred in the last 3 years. A "lifetime" problem is one that has occurred at all, without reference to time. Thus lifetime problems at any given level are roughly equivalent to the union, mathematically speaking, of current and past problems at that level (they are slightly more than the union in additively and conditionally formed scales, where the value of an item in one time frame can be increased by the accession of another item in the other time frame).

Ideally, prospective studies should be conducted with continuous measurements over a span of time to obtain accurate assessment of the temporal order of life events, including drinking experiences and problems. Only a limited number of studies has been conducted on drinking behavior involving many measurements over a short space of time (78)[5] and these studies could be conducted over a period of only a year or so because of problems of respondent cooperation, expense, and the fact that repeated measurements have a Heisenbergian way of influencing the very behavior that is being observed. Prospective studies of drinking behavior covering a lengthy span are also few in number (62, 80, 110) and entail only two measurements.

The usefulness of the latter type of study is limited primarily to the important issue of measuring long-term outcomes of variables available from past records, such as school and delinquency records (110). The survey approach ordinarily can permit a more intensive coverage of the sequence of life events through repeated measurements, but usually over a relatively short space of time. Completion of the current series of follow-up surveys will permit a better assessment of temporal order in life events and drinking practices and problems because they will permit some comparisons of states at three points of time, thus enabling us to assess (on a nonretrospective basis) whether changes in states and events applicable between stages A and B are followed by changes in other states or events between stages B and C. For the time being, however, we must make do with the retrospective information we have at hand. While it can be contended that the prospective approach is also contaminated with selective memory factors, in that any event earlier than the present moment must by definition be reported retrospectively, there is no question that the retrospective information we now have on temporal order among drinking problems is not as definitive as will be the information from multistage prospective (or follow-up) studies which are now under way.

[5] EKHOLM, A. A study of the drinking rhythm of Finnish males. Presented at the 28th International Congress on Alcohol and Alcoholism, Washington, D.C., September 1968.

E. The Meaning and Measurement of the Problem Areas

The components of each scale can be found in Appendix B. We shall concern ourselves here with general principles of measurement and meaning. For each problem area, we also indicate the general prevalence of the "high problem" level on the current measure, as shown in Appendix B in this monograph.

1. Heavy Intake. This indicator measures regular intoxication or regular drinking of sufficient quantities to put the respondent at risk of intoxication. In the N2–N3 sample, data were available only for the current period, and the criterion is essentially the frequency of drinking the relatively low quantity of 5 or more drinks on an occasion or of getting "high" or "tight": 6% of the men aged 21 to 59 reported these patterns at least 4 days per week. In the N3 sample past data were also available, and the frequency of drinking larger quantities (8 to 11 and 12 or more drinks on an occasion) was also taken into account. Of this sample, 13% reported currently drinking 5 or more drinks at least 4 days per week, or 8 or more drinks at least weekly, or 12 or more drinks at least monthly (Table 1). The N3 intake measure can be regarded as an approximation to the frequency of attaining given blood alcohol levels similar to those which have recently been reported by Finnish researchers (15, 84). For a precise measure based on attained blood alcohol level, we would need to know also the respondent's weight, the length of the drinking occasion and variations in the size and alcohol content of the drinks.

The meaning of a measure of heavy intake varies according to the conceptual framework in which it is viewed. It can be regarded as a measure of "liver insult," as Ewing (42) terms it—that is, as an indicator of the risk of long-term physiological consequences of alcohol consumption. The rather sketchy data from mortality studies suggest that the "lumping" of alcohol consumption into amounts sufficient for intoxication which this indicator measures is more crucial than the total annual consumption (103, *p. 127*). Treating frequent intoxication as a surrogate indicator of potential health problems is attractive partly because the health consequences of drinking are difficult to measure directly. But it would leave us with all the interpretive problems of an indirect measure which indicates risk of occurrence rather than occurrence, and which is based on a series of assumptions about relationships only suggested rather than proved by the available data.

Alternatively, high intake can be viewed as a problem in its own right, as would be implied by conceptualizations of alcoholism as a bad habit (107) or by Temperance conceptualizations of the "drunkard." In such views, it is the repetitive behavior itself which is regarded as the defining characteristic of the situation, while the psychological motivations for and the consequences of the behavior are viewed as ancillary phenomena.

Both the classical disease model of alcoholism and labeling theories of alcoholism tend to regard amount of drinking per se as relatively unimportant, though for rather different reasons. In the disease model, the emphasis is on the phenomenon of loss of control over drinking behavior, irrespective of what that behavior might be. The slogan of "once an alcoholic, always an alcoholic" implies that a person will be considered an alcoholic even when he has been a total abstainer for several years. Studies of the phases and symptoms of alcoholism as a disease have therefore commonly not measured intake directly (114). Labeling theories, on the other hand, emphasize the role of societal reaction and of the individual's perceptions in defining deviance, and the resulting secondary deviance of the individual reacted to. Thus little significance is attached to an "act of primary deviance," such as amount of drinking, "except insofar as others react towards the commission of the act. To them deviance is not a quality of the act, but instead is produced in the interaction between a person who commits an act and those who respond to it" (48, p. 874).

Another view of measures of heavy intake, which we use at times in this monograph, is simply as a measure of behavior which puts the respondent at risk of psychological entanglement or social consequences. This allows us to shed light on such questions as whether the greater social consequences of drinking among the poor are a function of a greater frequency of intoxicated behavior or a greater vulnerability to experiencing consequences from a given behavior.

2. *Binge Drinking.* Of our N3 respondents, 6% reported that they had stayed intoxicated for several days at a time within the last 3 years, the criterion for a current "high" binge problem. A total of 26% had ever either done this or stayed "high" or "tight" for more than a day at a time. Inevitably some unreliability accompanies such reports because individuals may vary in their definitions of what constitutes being on a binge or being "high" or "tight." Even though the level may be understated, it is nevertheless clear that binge drinking thus defined is not a characteristic behavior even in a sample of young men. We measure it as a separate dimension partly because of the prominent role assigned to "benders" (as the major symptom initiating the "chronic phase") in Jellinek's description of the phases of alcohol addiction (58) and in studies drawing on this model. The measure is clearly an indicator of behavior, of the prolonged ingestion of a large amount of alcohol. But the emphasis is not on the consumption itself, but rather on the fact that the respondent is making drinking his primary occupation, to the exclusion of other business or pleasures, for an extended period of time. Binge drinking, then, measures behavior which, however sporadic, is an indication that the respondent is prepared to treat drinking as a serious and single-minded pursuit rather than an incidental occurrence.

3. Psychological Dependence. This measure is constructed from items indicating a reliance on alcohol to change moods, as a "mind-bender"; e.g., "to forget my worries," or "because I need it when tense or nervous." While a majority of respondents answered positively to at least one of such items, only 9% of the N3 sample attained what we denominated the current high level on the additive score. Items such as these have been used in most U.S. studies of general-population drinking behavior, under various designations—"personal reasons" for drinking in Riley, Marden and Lifshitz (109), "definitions of drinking" scale in Mulford and Miller (92), "escape reasons for drinking" in Cahalan, Cisin and Crossley (20). The items are usually asked in a context of social and inconsequential reasons for drinking.

In past studies, these items have been asked only in the present tense, except of ex-drinkers. Thus, the N2–N3 measure of lifetime psychological dependence differs from the "current" measure only in including the retrospective responses of ex-drinkers. In N3 and the San Francisco 1967 survey, for the first times we attempted to measure some of these items also for the past. In the scales for these two samples, then, we have for the first time given some systematic data on past psychological dependence. Respondents appeared able to give meaningful answers to such questions, but obviously problems of response validity are particularly acute for retrospective data on past states of mind.

Psychological dependence is the drinking-problems area most like traditional psychiatric notions of neuroses and similar psychiatric impairments. As used here, psychological dependence refers to a reliance on the psychoactive effects of alcohol, and does not include dependence in the sense of loss of control over drinking behavior. Whether the acknowledgment of mood-changing reasons for drinking should be treated as a drinking problem in its own right is a matter for argument. To regard it as a drinking problem is to subscribe to some degree to a Calvinist asceticism, setting up an ideal of "a systematic self-control" which allows no time off from moral responsibilities (150, *pp. 115–119*).

A credible response to this is that it is a matter of degree: a little relaxation is different from continual recourse to a drug for escape or oblivion. It should be recognized, however, that this answer is grounded on esthetic or moral considerations with the assumption that the individual, his associates, the State or society in general would be better off if the person were denied an anodyne.

As measured by a respondent's self-report, psychological dependence necessarily has two special characteristics. Its existence is conditioned on the respondent's acceptance of the idea that he has states of mind and that they vary. But some people, especially men, tend to reject the whole notion of moods being relevant to them. The measure also depends on some degree of introspection by the respondent on his reasons for drinking and will probably miss people who are hard-pressed to assign reasons to anything they do.

4. Loss of Control. This measure was newly built for the present studies, from new items and from items previously dealt with as part of symptomatic drinking behavior. It represents an attempt to measure directly the heart of the classical disease concept of alcoholism as presented by Jellinek (59, *pp. 41–42*) and Keller (63, *pp. 312–313*)—inability to abstain from drinking or inability to stop once started. As with psychological dependence, treating loss of control as a problem involves moral considerations about preferred states of mind rather than judgments in terms of intrinsic tangible behavior or consequences. Again, as with psychological dependence, the measure requires some self-awareness on the part of the respondent. It has been cogently argued that loss of control is a meaningful concept only to the extent that there have been attempts at control (99). If it is conceptually possible to lose control of one's drinking without recognizing it, it at least is not included in this measure.

Loss of control of drinking is usually treated in the alcohol literature as an all-or-nothing phenomenon, and as a condition rather than an occurrence. So far as we are aware, there have been no discussions relating the concept to the possibilities of impaired rather than lost control, or of variation in time and by occasion of the degree of control. In the general population, however, these possibilities are commonplace realities. Analogies with control of other behavior may be instructive. On occasion, many people become so angry that they may be described as no longer in full control of their behavior, and they may commit an assault they would not even contemplate at other times. The fact of such a temporary impairment of control is probably associated statistically with the occurrence of repeated incidents, and also with the incidence of murder. But an assault is not a murder, and an incident is not a condition; and a majority of those who have committed assault when angry do not commit an assault whenever they are angry, and never commit a murder. Similarly, items drawn directly from the classical definitions of loss of control of drinking, when used in general-population samples, are probably measuring primarily a variable impairment of control rather than an invariant loss of control.

Since loss of control is the underlying concept in the classical disease model of alcoholism, many of the problem areas we treat separately have been relegated by others to the status of indirect indicators of a presumed underlying loss of control. Thus the Jellinek formula turns the prime medical complication of prolonged excessive drinking, cirrhosis mortality, into an indirect indicator of the prevalence of alcoholism characterized by loss of control. Similarly, Keller (63, *pp. 316–317*) has argued for treating indicators of social problems of drinking, e.g., drunken-driving arrests, as measures of an alcoholism defined by loss of control. At this stage of research on the interrelations of drinking problems, we regard such assumptions of equivalence as obfuscating more than they reveal. A greater understanding of drinking problems will be gained by turning, as Knupfer has argued, such assumptions into hypotheses to be tested (66, *pp. 975–977*).

Loss of control is weakly defined in the N2–N3 sample because of the relatively few items available. In the N3 sample, this variable is considerably stronger because of the use of more (and better) items: 5% of the respondents attained a current "high" score. Results on this measure should therefore be interpreted with unusual caution.

5. *Symptomatic Drinking Behavior*. The items in this index (e.g., blackouts, skipping meals when drinking, sneaking drinks) are drawn from the classical symptomatology of Alcoholics Anonymous as analyzed by Jellinek in the *Grapevine* study (56). Previous researchers, attempting to break down Jellinek's list of symptoms into conceptually unified subsets, have used similar sets of items under the rubrics of "Preoccupation with Alcohol" (53), "Addictive Symptoms" (66) and "Index of Possible Addiction" (30). To some extent, the list is a residue of the original *Grapevine* list after indicators of the respondent's moral history and of social and medical consequences of drinking have been stripped off. Of the N2–N3 respondents, 8% reported a current high score.

The face value of the items is reasonably clear: they are descriptions of behavior and short-term physiological consequences associated with heavy drinking. Several items are also conditioned on the lack of a social environment supporting the respondent's behavior: one only needs to sneak drinks, for instance, if there is someone around to watch disapprovingly. It is interesting to note that changes in the social climate surrounding smoking are now producing reports of similar behavior by "hidden smokers" (152).

However, the meaning of the items that measure drinking problems is not so clear. There seem to be three separate possible levels of meaning which the respondent can intend in answering these items positively.

(*a*) There are likely to be many "naïve" positive responses to any item. A respondent who tells us that he awakened the next day after drinking unable to remember some of the things he had done while drinking may merely be referring to a New Year's Eve when he became unconscious and does not remember how he was put to bed—hardly the classical notion of the "alcoholic palimpsest." Such respondents are unlikely to answer positively to many items. Since the scale is built additively, they are not a significant problem if the cutting-point for analysis is set at several items rather than just one.

(*b*) There is the straightforward level of meaning in which the respondent describes the occurrence of certain behavior and physiological consequences of intoxication. At this level, the scale is a mere description of behaviors. The analyst is at liberty to construe them as symptomatic of addiction or loss of control over drinking, but this construction is the analyst's and not necessarily the respondent's.

(*c*) That there is a third level of meaning is apparent from the provenance of these items. They are drawn from the orthodox A.A. description of the natural history of alcoholism, which in turn derives from the folk wisdom of what may be regarded as the subculture of heavy drinkers. They are, then, a crystallization of an ancient and arcane folklore of "bad signs" widely known among "serious drinkers."

Since their crystallization in A.A. orthodoxy, the items have taken on a new status and are now widely disseminated among the general public in the form of innumerable lists of "warning signs" in medical articles in the popular media. Fear that this destroys their validity as indicators has led to proposals for new lists to be kept somehow hidden from the public.[6] Such proposals, however, ignore the fact that the primary target population of "serious drinkers" has known about the items all along.

In addition, the A.A. orthodoxy has tended to view a claim of alcoholism as false unless the claimant has "been through the mill" of recognized symptoms. Jellinek accordingly found some evidence of overclaiming of such symptoms in descriptions of past behavior by A.A. members (59, p. 38).

To the "serious drinker," then, at least, the symptomatic items carry considerable connotations beyond their face value. Responding positively to them is also an admission of "having a problem" with alcohol, so that the scale's meaning to some degree becomes the admission of a drinking problem. This provides at least a partial explanation of the high correlation of the scale with loss of control and psychological dependence, and of its status as the highest-loading component on the general factor formed in a factor analysis of the current problem scales. Of course, an alternative explanation of these results would be provided by those who, like Mulford and Miller (94), tend to regard a scale of these items as the best direct measure of alcoholism as a disease. In our view, however, the scale is undoubtedly measuring aspects crucial to any addictive model of alcoholism, but its exact denotation remains equivocal.

6. *Belligerence after Drinking.* This measure is an additive score composed from the respondent's report of feeling aggressive or cross and getting into fights and heated arguments after drinking. Of the N3 respondents, 9% attained a current high score. MacAndrew and Edgerton (79) have recently reemphasized the importance of variations in behavior while drinking, particularly variations in violent behavior, in determining the potential for social disruption of a given amount of drinking. Belligerence after drinking can be viewed, then, as a social problem at the collective level, but it is not necessarily a social problem for the individual. In some contexts, belligerent behavior after drinking is tolerated or even encouraged, so that there are no social consequences for the individual.

7. *Problems with Wife over Drinking.* This and the succeeding indicators of other interpersonal, job and police problems are aimed at the heart of models of alcoholism as an individual social problem, in terms,

---

[6] EWING, J. and ROUSE, B. A. Identifying the hidden alcoholic. Presented at the 29th International Congress on Alcoholism and Drug Dependence, Sydney, Australia, February 1970.

for instance, of "spoiled identity" (47). They seek to measure the extent to which alcohol has interfered with the respondent's performance in the adult male's most significant roles. Included in problems with wife are respondents' reports that their wives actually left home, or threatened to, because of their drinking, or became angry over their drinking; 14% of the N3 men qualified as having a current high score on this problem. It is recognized that in some instances the disagreement over drinking may have been an indirect reflection of serious marital maladjustment over issues having nothing necessarily to do with alcohol. However, later findings in this study (Table 4) show that in about 8 of 10 instances of a respondent's having a significant score on trouble with their wives over their own drinking, there was evidence that the respondent had an average of 3 additional problems (such as with the police, friends or neighbors, the job) in fairly marked form.

8. *Problems with Relatives.* These include a report of a relative being very displeased with the respondent's drinking or indicating he should cut down; 8% of the N3 sample had a high score. A weak indicator of problems with other relatives was included with spouse problems in the previous report on the N2 sample (19). In N3 and the San Francisco 1967 survey problems with relatives were more systematically covered and are treated as a separate problem area in measures for these samples. In the N2–N3 sample, relatives have been omitted altogether since the coverage was so poor on N2.

9. *Problems with Friends or Neighbors.* These included the loss of friendships because of one's drinking, friends or neighbors suggesting that he cut down on his drinking, or the respondent's opinion that his drinking had harmed his friendships and social life: 7% of the N3 sample qualified for a high current score on such problems. This index of problem drinking is a conservative measure of the extent of alcohol-related alienation or friction vis-à-vis friends or neighbors because the heavy drinker often has the option of gravitating toward a set of friends and neighbors who will condone his heavy drinking.

10. *Job Problems.* These include losing or nearly losing a job because of one's drinking on or off the job, drinking leading to quitting a job or hurting one's chances for promotion, having people at work suggest that one cut down on one's drinking, being intoxicated on the job or missing work because of a hangover: 6% reported such job problems within the last 3 years and 13% as occurring at some time in their lives. Whether one has problems on the job is contingent upon whether the job almost "requires" drinking, whether the person can organize his life so as not to interfere too much with his drinking, and whether he is retired or otherwise outside the labor force and thus has no job to jeopardize. However, the level of responses on job problems necessary to qualify as having a high score was set so that relatively few qualified; therefore we believe that this index is a conservative indicator of

the existence of job problems. Job problems were very frequently associated with other problems: only 2% who qualified with a high score were found not to have a high score on any other problem.

11. Police Problems over Drinking. These problems included trouble with the law about drinking, whether or not driving a car was involved. Such police problems were reported as occurring in about the same proportion as problems on the job: 4% currently (within the last 3 years) and 12% at some time in their lives. The prevalence of police problems will be shown to be definitely related to differences in ethnic origin, age and socioeconomic status; however, the meaning of these relationships are ambiguous since police appear to be more likely to arrest or to question members of minorities, younger men and those so poor that they have few opportunities to practice their heavy drinking in private. Regardless of the causal relationships between drinking and police problems, however, it is self-evident that those who do get into problems with the police are therefore more likely to be put at a disadvantage in their future interpersonal relationships, whether or not their drinking actually might have warranted the attention of the police.

12. Problems with Health or Injuries Related to Drinking. A high score on this index is based on a physician's warning to reduce drinking, and the respondent's conclusion that drinking had harmed his health, or that he had given up drinking because of health reasons. Injuries in accidents due to drinking are also included. Within the last 3 years, 7% had high scores on this problem and 11% had had this type of problem at some time in their lives.

It could be argued that the conclusion that drinking is harming one's health may be more of a potential solution than a problem if it signifies that the respondent may intend to take remedial action. However, 76% of those with a high score on the health-or-injuries index also had a high score on one or more other problems.

Health-related consequences of drinking, short of hospitalization, are particularly difficult to measure by the respondent's self-report. Either one asks for a doctor's judgment, in which case one is measuring as much as anything the vagaries of the health-care delivery system, or one asks for the respondent's own assessment, in which case one gets a considerable dose of folk hypotheses and private fantasies and fears mixed in with any verifiable physiological consequences. In the present studies we used both approaches, but with greater emphasis on the doctor's assessment. The problem is, of course, not peculiar to our methods: the list of potential physiological consequences of chronic excessive drinking, besides liver cirrhosis, is now changing in medical circles; and the consequences in general are long-term, often ambiguous and sometimes only apparent at autopsy.

In the N3 study alone, some information was also collected on more severe and certain health consequences of drinking—having an illness connected with drinking which kept the respondent from normal functioning for a week, or being hospitalized for drinking. Between 1 and 2% of the sample had experienced each of these in the last 3 years.

13. *Financial Problems Related to Drinking.* A high score on this index was applicable when the respondent reported that drinking was harmful to his financial position: 7% reported having such problems within the last 3 years and 16% reported having had such problems within their lifetime. Responses are, of course, related to socioeconomic status: expenditure of any money for drink by the poor might deprive them of essentials. Responses may also be affected by some free-floating anxiety about spending money in general for anything. Of those reporting financial problems over drinking, however, 97% also reported having other drink-related problems (Table 4). In the N3 study, the respondent was also asked whether he had spent money on drinking which was needed for essentials like food, clothing or payments; 4% responded that they had done so in the last 3 years. We regard such specific lines of inquiry as promising for future approaches.

F. Summary Measures of Drinking Problems

A number of combined and summary measures are derived from the basic problem-area scales and used where appropriate later in this monograph. Their methods of construction and rationale vary considerably, according to their purpose.

1. *Summaries of Drinking Patterns.* To study the interaction of behavior and social consequences, we needed an over-all summary of problematic (potentially troublesome) drinking which would encompass both regular fairly heavy drinking and infrequent very heavy drinking. The N2–N3 high-intake measure is deficient for this purpose since it does not systematically measure heavy consumption occurring less than once a week. Accordingly, a measure denominated "heaviest intake" was used, composed of those who fulfill the minimal-severity criterion on either heavy intake or binge drinking.

Another partitioning of the heaviest-intake group was made to study the correlates of different patterns of drinking (Chapter 6). To compare the correlates of steady fairly heavy and intermittent very heavy drinking in the N3 sample, the frequency of consuming 12 or more drinks was detached from the frequency of drinking 5 or more and treated along with binge drinking as the dimension of at least occasional very heavy drinking.

2. *Social Consequences and Tangible Consequences.* A "social-consequences" score was constructed from the scores in the problem areas of wife, friends, job and police (and relatives for N3), with a weight of from 1 to 4 points according to severity in each area. This score may be regarded as the most direct measure of drinking as a social problem at the individual level.

A "tangible-consequences" score was constructed by adding to the social-consequences score the scores in the areas of finances and health. Essentially, this tangible-consequences score measures the general area encompassed by the second half of Jellinek's definition: "damage (individual or social or both) incumbent upon . . . drinking" (60, *p. 1341*). The score includes all the consequences of drinking which are at least in principle verifiable by someone other than the respondent.

3. Over-All Problems Score. This score was constructed on the N2–N3 sample by the same principles as described in *Problem Drinkers* (19), using all the problem-areas scores. With a few adjustments, the scoring scheme for each area is 6 points for a severe problem, 3 for a moderate, 1 for a mild. The cutting point on the over-all problems score used in this report (score of 7+) is equivalent to (*a*) having problems in two or more areas with at least one problem scored as "severe"; or (*b*) having problems in three or more areas with at least two problems "moderate" or more severe; or (*c*) having problems in five or more areas with at least one problem "moderate" or more severe; or (*d*) having at least slight problems in seven or more areas. The general scoring scheme derives from Knupfer's work on the San Francisco 1964 sample.[7] The N2–N3 score differs in detail from the N2 score used previously because of slight differences in the allocation of items and construction of problem-areas scales. The correlation between the two versions in current form was .96 in the men aged 21–59 of N2.

The over-all problems score serves as an indicator of a respondent's drinking problems. It is often a convenient tool in analysis, providing a single ordinal scale to use as a yardstick in data-dredging procedures. There are, however, some problems associated with the scale's use, primarily with the interpretations it invites: (*a*) By its nature it tends to imply a unity in the phenomena it comprehends; that is, an inclusive and eclectic definition of alcoholism. As we have outlined above, we consider that this field of phenomena may be better viewed in terms of a number of different dimensions. (*b*) Particularly when used in dichotomized form, it invites settling on an essentially arbitrarily defined level of severity as a prevalence estimate for alcoholism in the general population. There are already too many such arbitrary estimates floating around as justifications for one or another public policy.

We regard over-all problem scores, then, as useful tools for prospecting for and summarizing patterns of relationships in the data, and not as useful estimates of the prevalence of anything.

4. A Typology of Drinking Problems. A typology of drinking problems possesses advantages not shared by either the single problems or the over-all problems score, since the single-problems approach generates data that are too diffuse and the over-all score can mix apples and oranges, thus concealing potentially important inter-

[7] KNUPFER, G. Ex-problem drinkers. Presented at the 4th Conference on Life History and Psychopathology, St. Louis, Missouri, November 1970.

actions between types of problems in analyzing subgroup correlates. A number of typologies have been utilized in earlier studies of this same series: Clark (30, *p. 663*) used "excessive intake," "self-perceived drinking problems," "interpersonal problems" (including problems with police, work, spouse, friends, or aggressiveness), and "possible addiction or coping." Knupfer (66, *p. 978*) used "social consequences" (much like Clark's "interpersonal problems"), "dependence" (self-perceived problems, use of alcohol for coping and addictive symptoms), and "excessive intake" (prolonged drinking sprees and frequent high intake). Cahalan (17) had similar typologies in the Hartford study and N2, where he used the following mutually exclusive six categories: nondrinkers during the prior 3 years; drank but had no problems; those exhibiting only psychological dependence; those scoring high on "implicative drinking" (frequent intoxication, binge drinking or drinking symptomatic of addiction); those with "interpersonal problems" (with spouse or relatives, friends or neighbors, on the job, with police or involving accidents); or those with high scores on both "implicative drinking" and "interpersonal problems" (19, *pp. 50–51*).

The typology used in the present analysis is a somewhat simplified version of the one used in *Problem Drinkers*, reduced from six to five categories in the interest of simplicity. The data presented (Table 13) are from the combined N2–N3 samples. A summary of the five categories in the typology is as follows: (*I*) Nondrinkers during the last 3 years (15% of the total); (*II*) Drinkers who had no problems qualifying them for the three categories below (38%); (*III*) At least a minimal severity in some problem area but not in categories IV or V, thus primarily defined by psychological dependence, loss of control, symptomatic drinking or belligerence (21%); (*IV*) Relatively high score on heavy intake or binge but not on tangible consequences (12%); (*V*) Relatively high score on tangible consequences (14%).

This typology has the advantage of separating the rather disparate groups of nondrinkers, drinkers without problems and the catch-all category of those with problems other than heavy intake, binge or tangible consequences. It also singles out those who had high heavy intake or binge scores but did not have tangible consequences, thus making it possible to draw inferences on which subgroups of men appeared to be "getting by" with fairly heavy drinking without necessarily getting into discernible difficulty over it. Group V, with high scores on tangible consequences (14% of the total), was made up of 6% who had a high qualifying score on consequences but not on heavy intake or binge, plus 8% who qualified on both consequences and heavy intake or binge. Thus it is legitimate to contrast groups IV and V by saying that group IV consists of quite heavy drinkers who have not gotten into marked verifiable difficulty during the last 3 years, whereas group V consists of those who did get into verifiable difficulty. But it must be remembered that more than half of the latter group consisted of persons who also had rather high scores on heavy intake and binge.

Chapter 3

Interrelationships of Drinking Problems

A. *General Research Strategy*

AS WE HAVE INDICATED, there are well-recognized disagreements over what is legitimately included within the definition of drinking problems. There is also a lack of agreement over the degree of severity of those problems which should constitute the minimum definition. This is most obvious at the extreme positions: prohibitionists tend not to recognize any distinction between drinking and alcoholism, while the alcoholic-beverage industry tends to refer to alcoholics (if at all) as a tiny minority of all drinkers. In scholarly discussions of prevalence based on general-population data, however, the statistics have also varied quite widely, according both to the properties of the data cited and the predilections of the writer. Thus the Washington Heights study (6) found a prevalence rate of "probable alcoholics" of less than 2%, while Hayman (50, *p. 591*) interpreted some previously published data on pattern and amount of drinking to argue for a 36% prevalence rate of problem drinkers and alcoholics. If we accepted a positive response on a lifetime basis to any of the drinking problem component items as our criterion, more than two-thirds of the present sample would qualify. Conversely, as Mulford (90) has shown, one runs out of cases altogether (the prevalence is zero) if the criterion is a literal application of Jellinek's description of his Greek-letter species, requiring the presence of all the attributes Jellinek described. Defining a prevalence or incidence rate of "alcoholism," or even of a list of drinking problems areas, is therefore not a primary concern of this study; our concerns are rather with patterns of association of variables in a general-population segment especially rich in drinking problems.

Accordingly, in this chapter we shall be concerned with making comparisons between and probing the empirical interrelations of the conceptually defined problem-area measures described in the previous chapter. By the form in which we

29

asked the questions (e.g., dichotomizing the time spans into "current" and "past"), and by the summarizations entailed in the process of aggregation, we have already lost much of the abundant detail of the life history of a respondent's relation with alcohol. Even so, the possible patterns of relationships which remain to be sifted are numerous, given more than a dozen measures, each defined in three time periods and for several levels of severity. While there are everyday expedients available for sifting some of these relationships, for others there is no exact precedent to follow. Our procedures are therefore a mixture of the standard and the provisional. Our results thus provide more a series of beginnings than a definitive conclusion. Our general strategy is to separate analytically the different dimensions of patterning and association, rather than, for instance, to throw everything without further ado into a scrambled midden of factor analyses. We shall start with a series of comparisons of the problem measures in terms of the frequency of their occurrence by level of severity, and investigate the patterns of association between the problem areas at a given time. We shall then move on to an investigation of patterns of change over time, comparing incidence and remission rates, then analyzing the time-order patterns between the problem areas, and finally the patterns of association over time.

B. Patterns of Prevalence

In *Problem Drinkers*, reporting on the N2 sample, it was shown that the population which is the object of the present study (men aged 21 to 59) was by far the richest portion of the total population in drinking problems of all types (19, *Tables 1 and 3*). Table 1 presents data on the prevalence among men aged 21–59 of the drinking-problem measures as we have defined them, by two levels of severity and two time frames, current (within the last 3 years) and lifetime.

The data are drawn from the N3 survey only, because many of the N3 problem indices provided more comprehensive coverage of various components than did the N2 survey. Keeping in mind that, as we have mentioned, the definition of levels of severity is essentially an arbitrary judgment, substantial variations in prevalence were found between problem areas in this population. In each comparison, for instance, heavy intake appears

TABLE 1.—*Current and Lifetime Prevalences of Drinking Problems among Men Aged 21 to 59, in Per Cent*[a]

| | CURRENT | | LIFETIME | |
	At Least Minimal Severity	High Problems	At Least Minimal Severity	High Problems
Heavy intake	24	13	41	26
Binge	8	6	18	15
Psychological dependence	24	9	35	13
Loss of control	14	5	23	10
Symptomatic drinking	14	8	30	20
Belligerence	9[b]	9	20[b]	20
Wife	21	14	29	21
Relatives	12	8	19	15
Friends, neighbors	9	7	16	15
Job	10	6	21	13
Police	6	4	15	12
Health, injury	16	7	32	11
Financial	15	7	27	16
Summary social consequences score[c]	31	14	47	27
Summary tangible consequences score[d]	38	19	60	34
At least one problem at stated level of severity	50	36	72	55

[a] N3 optimal scales; $N = 978$. The rows are cumulative rather than mutually exclusive: Lifetime includes Current (within the last 3 years); At Least Minimal Severity includes High Problems. For summary of scoring procedures and definitions see Appendix B.
[b] No separate minimal severity level differentiated.
[c] Problems with wife, relatives, friends, neighbors, job, police.
[d] Social consequences plus health, injury or financial problems.

considerably more common than binge drinking, and wife problems are more common than police problems.

Table 1 provides further evidence of the wide variation in plausible measures of the over-all prevalence of drinking problems. As can be seen in Appendix B, even the "minimal severity" level as we have defined it falls short of including all responses which could possibly be (and have been in the literature) regarded as problematic: in each of the first six areas other than binge drinking, the questionnaire items could be used to distinguish milder levels of severity than that which we have defined as minimal severity. In nearly all the problem areas we can also distinguish in our data higher levels of severity than the level we have taken as "high problems." Even on our minimal severity definition, nearly three-quarters of all men aged 21 to 59 have attained a minimal-severity problem in at least one area during their lifetime. On the other hand, if one took a current high degree of problem on loss of control as an estimate of the prevalence of the classical disease concept of alcoholism, the "rate" even in this population becomes only 5%. By applying the ideal-type characterizations which abound in the clinical literature on alcoholism, it is easy to arrive at still smaller prevalences, although such measures are not of much further utility in studies of the general population.

In studies of the occurrence of "symptoms" of alcoholism, which under the classical disease concept cover much the same territory as is covered by our problem-areas measures, at least a majority of institutionalized alcoholics have normally reported having had the problem covered by each item.[1] It is evident that this pattern does not hold true in the general population, even with measures which (like ours) generally increase the chances of a positive response by combining several items in a single measure. At either level of severity and in either time frame, the proportion of those in the general population with any problem at that level who also have a problem in any particular problem area rarely reaches one-half, and is generally much below that. In general, the chances of those with any problem having one specific problem will decrease as the time frame is narrowed and the level of severity increased. We will examine the question of overlap and association more closely below; but Table 1 at least provides some evidence that it is quite common in our subject population to have had some kind of problem with drinking, but much less common to have had any specific kind of problem with drinking.

Although there are considerable variations by severity and problem area, Table 1 suggests that roughly twice as many people as report a current problem will report having ever had a problem in any area. This would seem to imply a rate of

---

[1] ROOM, R. G. Assumptions and implications of disease concepts of alcoholism. Presented at the 29th International Congress on Alcoholism and Drug Dependence, Sydney, Australia, February 1970.

fluctuation of drinking problems in the general population far greater than could be accounted for by the efforts of any formal agencies of intervention. We will explore issues of change in greater detail below, merely noting for the moment that the findings cast doubt on characterizations of drinking careers in the general population in terms of an irreversible progression or "snowball effect" (36, *p.* 973).

C. Interrelations of the Problem Areas at a Given Time

In Table 2 we turn our attention from comparisons of the patterns of occurrence of the problem-drinking measures to the question of their patterns of joint occurrence. Table 2 shows two correlation matrices for the 13 N3 drinking-problems areas, with each area dichotomized at the high-problems level. The semimatrix above the diagonal refers to lifetime problems, that below the diagonal to current problems. For purposes of comparison we computed other analogous matrices, not shown here, varying the time frame and level of severity of the dichotomization. In all variations, the correlations were uniformly positive, and at what might be described as moderate to high levels (ranging from .11 to .55) particularly considering the constraints on the maximum size of the coefficient imposed by dichotomous variables with differentially skewed distributions. When the coefficients for each pair of drinking problems across these matrices are compared, the following patterns emerged: (*1*) In all comparisons (one of them being the matrices of Table 2) both lifetime and past correlations are higher than current correlations about four-fifths of the time. Over-all, past correlations are nearly evenly matched with lifetime correlations (56% show past higher on the minimal-severity matrices). (*2*) Minimal-severity level correlations are generally higher than moderate-level correlations, again about three-quarters to four-fifths of the time.[2]

[2] These patterns are not evenly distributed across the measures from which the correlations are formed. For correlations involving relatives and psychological dependence, the current correlation is as often the higher one as is the lifetime correlation. This is true of wife problems in the comparison of current with past. Past correlations are more often higher than lifetime when binge, loss of control, wife problems, belligerence and financial problems are involved, while the reverse is true of psychological dependence and job problems. For correlations involving wife, job, friends and belligerence, the correlations at the two levels of severity are more evenly matched.

Generally speaking, then, the wider the time frame and the more lenient the severity level taken as constituting "a problem," the higher the general level of correlation. Having a problem at all and at any time is more likely to be associated with having any other problem at all at any time than is having a severe problem at a particular time likely to be associated with having any other severe problem at a particular time.

The correlations in Table 2 suggest that in both time frames there is a clustering of variables with distinctly higher correlations among themselves than the general level of correlations. This clustering includes problems with wife, relatives, friends and neighbors, job and finances, loss of control and symptomatic drinking. On the other hand, the lowest correlations in the matrices generally involve belligerence, police, and health and injury problems. A principal-components factor analysis of the current high-problems matrix revealed a strong first factor, accounting for .35 of the communality, and the loadings of the scores on this factor confirmed the pattern we have described (Table 4, first column).[3] The analysis also found a weak second factor (.08 of the communality), primarily related to health and injury problems and lack of belligerence.

These findings might be taken as suggesting that, whatever our conceptual qualms, the territory of our drinking-problems scores can in fact be adequately covered empirically by a single unidimensional score. However, we do not think that such a conclusion is fully warranted, although we recognize that such a score is often a serviceable analytical tool. The extent of clustering of a set of measures like our problem-area scores is to a certain extent a function of the field of vision in which we are viewing them. The smaller their fraction of the total field of vision, the more clustered they appear to be. A considerable part of the strength of the correlations shown in Table 2 is contributed by the considerable fraction of those who have no problems at all. Correlation coefficients, like all such measures of association in common usage in the social sciences, do not distinguish between a "positive match" and a "negative match"; that is, the members of the much larger group who have

---

[3] Factor scores based on this first factor correlated .75 with the N2–N3 current over-all problems score in the N2 sample.

TABLE 2.—*Intercorrelations of Current (Below the Diagonal) and Lifetime (Above the Diagonal) High Problems*[a]

	1	2	3	4	5	6	7	8	9	10	11	12	13
1. Heavy Intake	–	.41	.28	.29	.37	.30	.33	.30	.30	.26	.24	.18	.33
2. Binge	.27	–	.28	.37	.44	.36	.25	.25	.31	.38	.29	.26	.34
3. Psychol. dependence	.26	.28	–	.31	.31	.22	.27	.24	.32	.33	.18	.21	.30
4. Loss of control	.22	.32	.26	–	.48	.31	.35	.44	.45	.43	.25	.34	.44
5. Symptomatic drinking	.34	.36	.41	.33	–	.40	.40	.40	.44	.40	.33	.25	.43
6. Belligerence	.24	.30	.24	.18	.30	–	.34	.36	.33	.30	.41	.21	.36
7. Wife	.29	.23	.26	.28	.33	.30	–	.37	.43	.34	.25	.22	.41
8. Relatives	.31	.25	.26	.40	.37	.27	.38	–	.42	.35	.36	.30	.41
9. Friends, neighbors	.31	.31	.31	.28	.39	.26	.36	.39	–	.46	.29	.32	.44
10. Job	.23	.28	.30	.36	.35	.28	.28	.35	.46	–	.29	.31	.54
11. Police	.19	.26	.16	.15	.27	.17	.20	.23	.25	.25	–	.22	.36
12. Health, injury	.17	.18	.18	.31	.23	.11	.19	.30	.31	.32	.18	–	.29
13. Financial	.30	.31	.31	.39	.40	.29	.36	.42	.39	.49	.27	.31	–

[a] N3 optimal scales; N = 978. Dichotomized at the high-problems level (Appendix B). The coefficient is thus also a phi coefficient.

neither problem are each counted equally with the members of the smaller group who have both problems toward a positive correlation. But, just as anthropologists studying the association of traits in a sample of cultures (22, *p. 21*) or taxonomists classifying specimens by comparing characteristics (134, *pp. 128–131*) have found, the fact of not having either of the traits we are comparing is not particularly decisive in understanding the relation between the traits. As Adkins (2) and Winer (151) have pointed out, the size of the "negative match" group is rather indeterminate; perhaps we should exclude abstainers, for instance, in our calculations, since they are by virtue of a single characteristic excluded from the possibility of a problem on any of our measures. This aspect of the problem is, of course, analogous to the problem of defining the "population at risk" which epidemiologists face in constructing a denominator for incidence rates.

There is no tidy and generally accepted solution to the problem of whether and how much to deemphasize the negative matches. Sokal and Sneath (134, *pp. 129 ff.*) demonstrate schematically the large number of solutions that one or another taxonomist has used, and the even larger number of potential solutions. For the present data, to demonstrate the importance of the issue, we recomputed the correlation matrix for the current high problems, drastically restricting the field of vision in which the clustering is to be observed by using only that portion of the sample (36%) which reported at least one current problem at the high level (Table 3). Each of the correlations, it will be observed, is much diminished, and there are even a few negative values in relationships involving health and injury problems.

In a factor analysis of this matrix, the proportion of the communality accounted for by the first factor has dropped to .24. The loadings on the factor are shown in the second column of Table 4; it will be seen that the range of loadings is now much increased, so that five measures load less than .40 on it.

In considering the degree of association of the drinking-problems measures in the total sample, it should also be borne in mind that they all are derived from items asked in a single interview, and in fact the bulk of the content at the high-problems level, except for heavy intake, binge, and psychological

TABLE 3.—Intercorrelations of Current High Problems with at Least One Current High Problem[a]

	2	3	4	5	6	7	8	9	10	11	12	13
1. Heavy intake	.12	.06	.09	.17	.02	.02	.13	.15	.06	.05	−.02	.13
2. Binge		.17	.24	.26	.18	.06	.14	.21	.19	.19	.07	.21
3. Psychological dependence			.16	.29	.08	.05	.11	.18	.19	.05	.04	.18
4. Loss of control				.25	.07	.15	.33	.19	.30	.07	.23	.32
5. Symptomatic drinking					.16	.15	.26	.28	.25	.18	.10	.30
6. Belligerence						.09	.12	.11	.15	.06	−.06	.15
7. Wife							.21	.20	.13	.06	−.01	.20
8. Relatives								.28	.25	.13	.18	.31
9. Friends, neighbors									.38	.16	.19	.28
10. Job										.17	.23	.42
11. Police											.09	.18
12. Health, injury												.20
13. Financial												

[a] N3 optimal scales; $N = 351$. Dichotomized at the high-problems level (Appendix B).

TABLE 4.—*General Measures of Overlapping at the High-Problems Level*[a]

	LOADINGS[b]		CURRENT[e]			LIFETIME[e]		
	Total Sample[c]	At Least One Problem[d]	N with High Problem	Mean No. of Problems	% Only One Problem	N with High Problem	Mean No. of Problems	% Only One Problem
Heavy intake	.53	.26	127	3.9	24	256	4.6	17
Binge	.56	.48	59	5.1	12	142	5.8	5
Psychological dependence	.55	.40	87	4.4	15	132	5.3	11
Loss of control	.59	.58	44	5.8	5	98	7.0	3
Symptomatic drinking	.68	.60	80	5.3	5	190	5.8	4
Belligerence	.50	.29	92	4.1	18	194	5.2	8
Wife	.58	.34	132	4.0	21	205	5.2	12
Relatives	.66	.58	80	5.2	10	149	5.9	9
Friends, neighbors	.67	.61	72	5.4	1	145	6.2	4
Job	.66	.65	58	5.8	2	123	6.4	2
Police	.44	.35	42	5.0	21	115	5.9	4
Health, injury	.48	.35	68	4.4	24	108	5.5	9
Financial	.70	.67	72	5.7	3	151	6.3	3

[a] N3 optimal scales; $N = 978$. Dichotomized at the high-problems level (Appendix B).
[b] Correlations with first principal-components factor.
[c] From an analysis of the correlations below the diagonal of Table 2.
[d] From an analysis of the correlations of Table 3.
[e] The columns should be read as follows: the 127 persons with a current high heavy-intake problem had an average of 3.9 current high problems, including heavy intake; and 24% had a current high problem only on heavy intake.

dependence, comes from two sequences of items: "experiences while drinking" and areas of his life the respondent felt his "drinking has been harmful to." Part of the association between the problem areas, therefore, is likely to be an "admission" factor—respondents who admit one potentially discreditable occurrence will be more likely to admit others. Perhaps the most damaging admissions, in terms of self-esteem, are the expressions of being unable to help oneself in the loss-of-control dimension; thus it may be due partly to this general admission factor that loss of control emerges with the highest loading on the first factor in the factor analysis. Like the inflation of negative matches, however, this admission factor is at least partly neutralized in an analysis like that shown in Table 3, which excludes all those who do not admit anything.

Two further statistics bearing on the degree of aggregativeness of the drinking-problems measures are shown in the last columns of Table 4. The first of these shows the mean number of problems at the high level among those who have each particular problem at the high level. The value of 3.9 on current heavy intake thus means that those with high heavy intake had an average of 2.9 other high problems, of the 12 possible other problems. This is the lowest value on any problem, so that there is generally a substantial amount of overlap between the problem scores; on the other hand, on no current problem does the average number of extra problems exceed two-fifths of the theoretically attainable. As for current problems, the highest proportion of "isolated" problems occurs on heavy intake, and health and injury problems, and the lowest on job, friends and neighbors, and financial problems. The very low proportion on job problems tends to support the intimations in the literature that such problems rarely occur in isolation from other problems. The only lifetime problem area in which more than one-eighth had only that problem is heavy intake.

The general conclusion must be that some overlapping at the level of high current problems is more common than no overlapping—in fact, only two-fifths of those with at least one current high problem have only the one problem. As our previous analysis would suggest, the degree of overlap appears to decrease as the time frame is narrowed and the severity level increased: recalculation of the statistics in Table 4 shows that the average number of problems over-all among those who have at least one is 2.9 for current high problems, 3.6 for current minimal-severity problems, 3.7 for lifetime high problems, and 4.5 for lifetime minimal-severity problems.

These trends in the general population toward a diminishing overlap as the criteria are stiffened are in considerable contrast to findings in populations of institutionalized alcoholics, where the degree of overlap among even very severe problems is commonly very high (56).[4] This leads to the suspicion, which we intend to follow up in further study, that a distinguishing feature of the institutionalized is the very multiplicity of their problems, so that the proportion of the uninstitutionalized population who can be matched with them in the over-all breadth and depth of their drinking problems may be smaller than is commonly thought. For instance, only 4.8% of our sample had current high problems in as many as six of the problem areas.[5]

So far in our analysis of the static interrelations of the problem areas, we have viewed them as of equal conceptual status. They can be fruitfully viewed also in terms of the model of regression analysis, in terms of a criterion and predictors, to test which problem measures and which combinations of measures best predict the measure we have taken as the criterion. We take here as our criteria measures of the two general types of tangible consequences: the full social-consequences score and physiological consequences, as measured by the full health-and-injury-problem measure. The analytical question thus is, which of the measures of behavior and dependence best predict these types of tangible consequences? We shall use two analytical methods in devising an answer to this question, a stepwise multiple regression and the Automatic Interaction Detector (AID) analysis-of-variance-based procedure developed by Sonquist and Morgan (135).

Stepwise Multiple Regression. The stepwise regression in this analysis utilizes the procedures described by Draper and Smith (39), in which the one independent variable which accounts for the most variance on the dependent variable is sin-

---

[4] See also Table 1 in Room, cited in Footnote 1 to this Chapter.
[5] Some preliminary data on the question are included in Room (114).

TABLE 5.—*Multiple Regressions of Drinking Behavior and Dependence Measures on Social Consequences and Health*[a]

A. *Criterion: Full Current Social Consequences Score*

	Raw Correlation with Criterion	Regression with Belligerence:		Regression less Belligerence:	
		MCC	Partial Correlation	MCC	Partial Correlation
Loss of control	.60	.60	.35	.60	.35
Symptomatic drinking	.60	.69	.25	.69	.28
Belligerence	.43	.72	.24		
Heavy intake	.51	.74	.20	.72	.22
Psychological dependence	.49	.75	.14	.73	.16
Binge	.44	.75	.05	.73	.08

B. *Criterion: Full Current Problems on Health and Injury Score*

	Raw Correlation with Criterion	MCC	Partial Correlation
Loss of control	.39	.39	.22
Symptomatic drinking	.34	.43	.11
Heavy intake	.31	.44	.11
Psychological dependence	.31	.45	.09
Binge	.22	.45	−.02
Belligerence	.15	.45	−.01

[a] N3 optimal scales; *N*=978. The criteria and predictors are used with their full range (Appendix B). The predictors are listed in order of entry into the stepwise regressions. The Raw Correlation is the initial zero-order correlation of each predictor with the criterion. The MCC is the multiple correlation coefficient at the regression step where the listed predictor has entered the regression. The Partial Correlation for each predictor is defined after the last step of the regression.

gled out and set aside, and then the next variable which accounts for more of the remaining variance than any other remaining variable is identified and its contribution to explanation of variance is cumulated to the variance accounted for by the first variable, and so on until the combined contributions of all independent variables have been assessed.

The results (Table 5) show the predictors in the order in which they entered a stepwise regression, their raw correlations with the criterion, the multiple correlation coefficient at each step, and the final partial correlations of each predictor with the criterion. Both the criterion and the predictors were used in full rather than in dichotomized form.

Loss of control proved the strongest predictor of each criterion and retained a strong contribution to the predictive power in the final partial correlations. On the social consequences regression, belligerence also figured strongly; in view of its somewhat ambiguous conceptual relationship to the criterion, the social-consequences regression was also recalculated excluding belligerence. On both criteria, the indicators of dependence generally provided a stronger prediction than the indicators of drinking patterns, although heavy intake did contribute some to the predictive power of the other variables. On the other hand, heavy intake and binge drinking by themselves provided a fair prediction at least of social consequences, as can be seen from the raw correlations.

About 56% of the variance of social consequences is accounted for by the full regression, and about 20% of the variance of health and injuries. The social-consequences regression is thus notably more successful. This may be partly because the social-consequences measure probably has greater reliability and validity than do health and injury problems (the latter index is discussed in Chapter 2). But it is also probably a reflection of real differences in the predictability of the criteria: we can fairly safely predict that someone who drinks in a given fashion will sooner or later experience social consequences, but ending up with a health problem from a given pattern of drinking seems to be considerably more variable.

Though at least the social-consequences regression equation must be regarded as fairly strong, it should be recognized that a disproportionate share of its power derives from the prediction of nonproblems by nonproblems, a pattern we discussed above. The alternative method of analysis to some extent alleviates this difficulty by eventually isolating the "no problems at all" cases in a separate group.

Automatic Interaction Detector Analysis. This procedure of Sonquist and Morgan (135) is a nonparametric cross-tabulation procedure based on an analysis-of-variance model. It has the advantage over the stepwise regression technique in that it makes no assumptions about linearity; as its name implies, it detects interactions among variables that cannot readily be shown through regression methods. It has advantages over the traditional cross-tabulation approach in that it "hunts" rather efficiently for optimum combinations of cross-tabulations. Sonquist and Morgan (135) have described the essential features of the technique:

> Given the units of analysis under consideration, what single predictor variable will give us a maximum improvement in our ability to predict values of the dependent variable? This question, embedded in an iterative scheme is the basis for the algorithm used in this program. . . . The program divides the sample, through a series of binary splits, into a mutually exclusive series of subgroups. Every observation is a member of exactly one of these subgroups. They are chosen so that at each step in the procedure, their means account for more of the total sum of squares (reduce the predictive error) than the means of any other equal member of subgroups (*p. 4*).

This analytic procedure is similar to procedures developed earlier by Belson (9, 10) for analysis of survey data.

Figure 1 shows the results of AID analyses of the same criteria and variables as are reported in Table 5. The results show that one can isolate groups of respondents with a high concentration of positive scores on the criterion, but that the groups are very small. The analysis is notably successful, however, at ruling out the possibility of problems on each criterion, forming large groups with a low concentration of positive scores on the criterion.

The AID analysis accounts for essentially the same amount of the total variance on social consequences as the multiple regression, but for slightly more of the variance on health and injury. None of the predictors have substantial reversed relationship with the criterion in subdivisions of the sample formed in the AID tree. There are some differences between the two techniques, however, in the detail of the results. Binge drinking plays some part in both AID trees, though without substantially reducing the unexplained variance, while it played the least substantial role in both the regressions. Psychological dependence plays a more important role in predicting health and injury, but the least important role in predicting social consequences. Heavy intake and symptomatic drinking also play no substantial role in the AID analysis of the health and injury score.

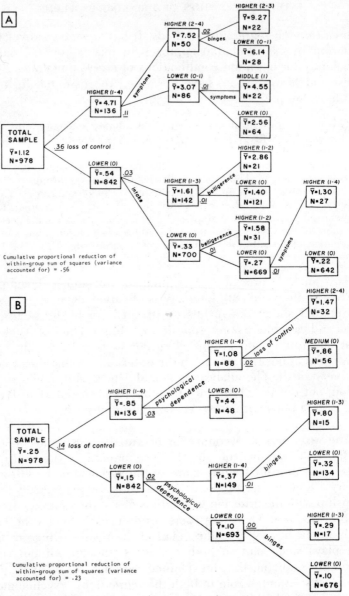

FIGURE 1.—*AID Analyses of Scores on Current Social Consequences (A) and Health and Injury Problems (B) with Drinking Behavior and Dependence Measures as Predictors.* N3 Optimal Scales, full scores, $N = 978$. For each split of a group, the splitting predictor and the proportion of the over-all variance accounted for are shown. For each resulting group, the codes on the splitting predictor, the mean value on the dependent variable ($\bar{Y}$) and the number of cases in the group are shown.

D. Patterns of Change

Our analysis so far has been essentially static, in that the comparisons and interrelations of the drinking problems have been for a given period of time. Only in our comparison of patterns of prevalence and association in different time periods did we catch a refracted glimpse of the patterning of the drinking-problem measures in time.

The establishment of a temporal sequence of events or states is usually a most important consideration in describing the interrelationships between variables in social research. In studies of relationships, the patterns of the relationship of the elements in time are intrinsically an important part of comprehending the patterns of association. In considering the "entitativity" of a set of observations—the degree to which they may be regarded as parts of some whole—appropriate criteria (in addition to proximity, similarity and "pregnance, good continuation or good figure") would include "common fate: elements that move together in the same direction, and otherwise in successive temporal observations share a 'common fate' " (22, *pp. 17–18*). Even more important is the issue of establishing whether hypothesized "independent" and "intervening" variables actually preceded the dependent variable or outcome in point of time: though temporal order is no proof of a causal relationship, the establishment of a temporal order is an essential precondition to understanding how variables interact.

This issue of temporal order is particularly crucial in clinical medicine and epidemiology, which place great emphasis on the differentiation and definition of disease entities on the basis of exhaustive circumstantial observation and history taking. Medical history has shown that descriptive studies of temporal sequences of events, besides serving as a foundation for etiological studies, can be of immediate practical utility in intervention in the disease chain: many diseases have been cured, controlled or prevented by methods suggested by descriptive studies long before the mechanisms of their causation were understood.

Others, notably Jellinek (56), have gone to considerable pains to attempt to demonstrate that there is a fairly uniform sequence of events or "symptoms" in the development of alcoholism; and this search for uniform sequences is often coupled with the categorization of alcoholism as a disease. We do not wish to enter, at this point, into the controversy over whether alcoholism is a disease, but a recent detailed review by one of us of past research rather clearly indicates that there is little evidence to support the contention that alcoholism ordinarily follows a fairly uniform sequence of events or symptoms.[6] In any case, the issue of whether problem drinking follows a uniform pattern of development is not necessarily central to the issue of whether alcoholism is a disease. However, the issue of the sequence of events in problem drinking is highly relevant to the process of understanding the forces which encourage or discourage the development of drinking problems—a process of understanding which is essential to accurate description of drinking phenomena, as well as to ultimate control over the more adverse effects of heavy use of alcohol.

Epidemiologists have long recognized the crucial importance of measures of incidence—the rate at which new cases of a disease occur in a population—as opposed to measures of the prevalence of cases of the disease at any given time. It is well recognized, also, that patterns of incidence and prevalence become increasingly disparate when a chronic rather than a short-term or acute condition is at issue. The corollary of this, that patterns of incidence and remission will also tend to diverge in chronic conditions, has been less explicitly recognized. Remission rates are often computed in evaluating treatment effectiveness, but they are rarely related to the incidence rates in a discussion oriented round an understanding of the condition.

Our measure of remission is reasonably close to those used in conventional evaluation studies. The denominator constitutes those who had a "high" problem at any time prior to 3 years ago; the numerator consists of those who have remained free of the problem at the high level for the last 3 years. The normal evaluation-study recovery or survival rate is for a period of time immediately following a particular event—release from a hospital, surgery, etc. An analogue to our measure would be rather to take those who had ever experienced the event and calculate their "recovery" or survival rate over a particular calendar period. This method would of course ex-

6 See Footnote 1 to this Chapter.

clude those who had died between the event and the beginning of the time period. This would be a serious defect in a
cancer survival study, for instance, but is less of a problem
in ours, particularly as we are interested in comparative rather
than absolute values.

Our measure of new cases is not a traditional incidence rate,
but is designed to be a complementary analogue of our remission
rate. We call it the accession rate. The denominator is those who
have had a "high" problem in the last 3 years (i.e., the numerator of the current prevalence rate), while the numerator is those
who had not had a high problem in the same area prior to 3 years
ago. Unlike traditional incidence measures, it bears no statistical relation with the prevalence rate, since it is based on the
prevalence rate's numerator. Like our prevalence measure, the
traditional incidence measure would depend on our essentially
ad-hoc decisions on level of severity and is therefore not as
well-suited to the present comparative purpose in which we
wish to examine general issues of the extent and nature of
changes in problem-drinking status. A more traditional 3-year
incidence rate could be derived from Table 6 by multiplying
our rate by the number (N) with current high problems and
dividing by 978 minus the N with past high problems. Our
measure of accession, then, is a proportion of new arrivals
among those who are now "there," as our remission rate is a
proportion of recent departures among those who were "there
in the past."

Table 6 shows the bases on which our measures are defined,
the measures of accession and remission and their orderings
among the 14 measures included, and a characterization in general terms of the measures, according to the criteria mentioned
in the key. Remissions are uniformly higher than accessions,
as we should expect from the great disparity in the mean span
of time of the current and past periods. Nevertheless, there
are interesting variations in rates from 1 measure to another, so
that accessions and remissions are almost evenly matched on
wife problems, but the remission rate is 5 times as high as the
accession rate on financial problems (the latter could be partly
a reflection of the fact that both the N2 and N3 interviews were
done in a period of rising prosperity).

Taken together, the two measures allow us to compare the

TABLE 6.—*Accession and Remission of High Problems*[a]

	N Current	N Past	ACCESSION % of Current Only	Rank Order	REMISSION % of Past Only	Rank Order	Charac- ter of Pattern[b]
Heavy intake	114	196	43	1	67	2	V
Binge	59	124	29	6	66	3	V
Psychological dependence	112	171	23	7	50	11	L
Loss of control	104	167	13	11	46	13	S
Symptomatic drinking	80	168	23	8	63	4	E
Belligerence	92	180	12	12	55	8.5	E,S
Wife	105	111	42	2	45	14	L
Relatives	80	135	18	9	51	10	S
Friends, neighbors	38	60	29	5	55	8.5	
Job	42	89	12	13	58	5	E
Police	42	101	33	4	72	1	V
Health, injury	37	48	38	3	52	9	L
Financial	36	76	11	14	58	6	E,S
Summary tangible consequences score	152	243	16	10	48	12	S

[a] N3 past–current comparable scales. Dichotomized at high-problem level (Appendix B).
[b] V = Variable–high rank on both accession and remission; sum of ranks <12. S = Stable–low rank on both accession and remission; sum of ranks >18. E = Early–rank on remission at least 4 lower than rank on accession. L = Late–rank on accession at least 4 lower than rank on remission.

properties of our scales on two dimensions: (1) The relative amount of the turnover—whether the accession and remission rates taken together are relatively high or relatively low. Since the rates are defined as a proportion of those having the condition at a given time period, a low proportion of turnover indicates a relatively high degree of chronicity. (2) The tendency of accession to predominate over remission, or vice versa. This tendency could be interpreted to mean that the problem area in question was becoming more prevalent or conversely was dying out. In the present context, however, it seems more reasonable to interpret the dimension as indicating a tendency of the problem area to occur relatively early (high remission) or late (high accession) in the problem drinker's drinking career.

By the "Character of Pattern" standards of Table 6, binge drinking, police problems and particularly heavy intake show a high turnover; and tangible consequences, problems with finances, relatives and particularly loss of control show a low turnover.

The finding of a high degree of variability on measures of drinking patterns agrees with the pattern shown in a longitudinal comparison on the N1 and N2 studies (19, *p. 115*), whereby less than one-third of those who showed a high score in either interview on a measure combining heavy intake and psychological dependence showed a high score in both interviews. Again, the finding on loss of control may be seen alternatively as the result of an "admission" factor or as an argument for chronicity in line with the classical disease conceptualization of alcoholism.

In relative terms, remission tends to predominate on symptomatic behavior, belligerence, job problems and finances, while accession tends to predominate on wife and health and injury problems and on psychological dependence. In our follow-up studies we are putting these general presumptions of earliness and lateness to test with more direct comparisons.

One alternative method of comparing the relative earliness and lateness of the different drinking problems areas is to analyze the patternings by age of those in our sample who report a current high problem. Table 7 accordingly shows the mean and standard deviation of ages of those having a current high problem in each area, and also the prevalence of each problem in each 5-year age group. Since adequate numbers are at a premium in this analysis, the combined N2–N3 sample and measures are used.

This involves treating the different age cohorts in a single cross-sectional survey as if they were successive samplings over the lifetime of a single cohort. That is, it confounds possible historical changes between succeeding age cohorts with changes in the course of the individual life cycle. This is a general problem for cross-sectional surveys using contemporaneous data; for the moment we are ignoring the retrospective aspects. On the other hand, since it is independent of retrospective data, the method does provide a means for a convergent validation of our results using retrospective data.

As Jellinek (56, *pp. 22–25*) demonstrated, a comparison of mean ages of occurrence is not a satisfactory demonstration of a sequence of conditions, so long as occurrence of the condi-

TABLE 7.—Specific Current Problems by Age, in Per Cent[a]

	N with High Problems	Mean Age (±SD)	21–24 (N = 147)	25–29 (204)	30–34 (186)	35–39 (216)	40–44 (226)	45–49 (201)	50–54 (199)	55–59 (182)	Total (1561)
Heavy intake	87	38.3±11.3	7	7	5	7	6	3	5	6	6
Binge	50	35.7±12.3	10	3	3	3	1	2	4	2	3
Psychol. dependence	63	39.0±10.6	5	4	4	4	4	5	4	3	4
Loss of control	86	37.8±11.5	12	5	4	5	7	5	4	4	6
Symptomatic drinking	147	35.8±11.4	26	11	8	7	6	10	9	3	9
Belligerence	128	35.4±10.2	15	12	10	8	7	8	6	2	8
Wife	181	36.6±10.9	19	17	15	10	9	9	11	6	12
Friends, neighbors	90	36.7±11.8	15	5	7	5	4	4	6	4	6
Job	77	38.6±11.1	10	4	3	5	5	5	6	2	5
Police	47	34.9±12.0	10	4	2	2	2	2	4	1	3
Health, injuries	88	40.8±11.7	8	4	5	6	4	6	8	6	6
Financial	67	36.1±11.7	11	4	6	4	3	2	4	3	4
Current over-all problems score	67	36.1±11.7	40	22	20	21	17	17	17	11	20

[a] N2–N3 sample, N2–N3 comparable scores.

tions is not universal in the population under study, and so long as all the conditions do not persist for exactly the same period. The mean age of those reporting a condition does provide some direct evidence, however, of a problem's tendency to occur relatively early or late in adult life and the standard deviation of the ages of occurrence does indicate differences in the tendency of different problems to cluster at particular life periods.

The range of mean ages of the 12 problems is only 6 years, out of a possible range of roughly 40; thus, while there are certainly tendencies for some problems to occur at earlier ages than others, they are not tremendously strong. The problems showing relatively earlier mean ages, police problems, belligerence, binge drinking, and those showing relatively later mean ages, health and injuries, psychological dependence, agree fairly well with the characterizations of Table 6. The most notable discrepancy is on job problems, which was characterized as "early" in Table 6, mostly because of its notably low accession rate.

The standard deviations of the mean ages are uniformly high (from 10.2 to 12.3 years, in a sample with a total age range of 40 years) suggesting that any tendency for a drinking problem to cluster at a particular age is relatively modest and that the general variability in the age of those having problems is much greater than any differences between problem areas in the degree of age clustering.

Many studies of American drinking behavior report that older men are less likely to drink or to drink heavily than younger men. The prevalence of current problems is at its highest among those in the youngest age group (21–24 years); and the proportion with a high current over-all problems score is almost twice as large (40%) in this age group as it is in any of the older groups. The disparity in rates is greatest on binge drinking, loss of control, symptomatic drinking, problems with friends or neighbors, police and finances, and not so great on psychological dependence or problems with health or drinking-connected injuries.

One might infer from the rapid decline in the rates of problem drinking between the 20s and 30s that much of the high rate of problem drinking among young adults is usually a temporary phenomenon, in keeping with society's permissiveness of young men's "sowing their wild oats." One can also infer from these rates that the seeds to longer-term serious problems with alcohol are probably usually sown by drinking behavior in the early 20s and not so much by habits acquired after age 40.

E. Ordering in Time

In the previous discussion, we have arrived at two different estimations of the tendency of drinking problems to occur relatively early or late in adult life. Such estimations can be used also as indirect evidence of the tendency of problems to precede or succeed one another in time. It seemed desirable, however, to use the more direct evidence available from our data to compare the tendency of pairs of problems to occur in a definite order.

In the analysis of surveys, the time ordering of variables has always been recognized as an important issue (46, *pp. 12 ff;* 52, *pp. 193 ff;* 64, *pp. 141–147*); however, it has primarily been regarded as a matter for a-priori assumptions rather than for the testing of hypotheses. General discussions of survey methodology universally assume that time ordering is of interest only in the establishment of causal chains, so that the issue is discussed only in the context of explanatory analysis.

When the determination of cause is at stake, it should be recognized that the establishing of time order is only one among the several conceptually distinct elements involved.

A coherent listing and discussion of such elements can be found in the report on smoking by the advisory committee to the U.S. Surgeon General (145, *pp. 182–189*): "to judge or evaluate the causal significance of an association . . . a number of criteria must be utilized no one of which by itself is pathognomonic or a *sine qua non* for judgment. These criteria include: (*a*) the consistency of the association; (*b*) the strength of the association; (*c*) the specificity of the association; (*d*) the temporal relationship of the association; (*e*) the coherence of the association."

Time ordering (at least, that the timing not be reversed) is a necessary but not a sufficient condition of causation. In the classical techniques of explanatory survey analysis, this relationship was implicitly recognized in the stress on defining

assumptions about time ordering of variables prior to considering the strength and nature of the relationships between them.
In recent years there has been a welcome tendency to turn time
ordering into a hypothesis to be tested rather than an axiom to
be stated. This tendency is apparent both in the form of discussions of direct measurement of time ordering and in elaboration
of sophisticated techniques, such as path analysis, for deciding
between competing causal hypotheses which would often involve opposite time orderings. Unfortunately, however, in both
of these traditions the distinction between time order and cause
has tended to be blurred. Discussions of the direct measurement
of time ordering have often identified it with the establishing
of cause, describing it, for instance, in terms of "detecting causal
priorities" (104). In path analysis, even though the conceptual
distinction may be recognized, the degree of time ordering is
in fact aggregated with all other dimensions of causation, at least
with cross-sectional data, in a single "path coefficient."

The direct determination of the time ordering of two variables
requires measuring the values of each for at least two points in
time (either retrospectively or through separate interviews as in
panels) and comparing the relationship of earlier A and later
B with the relationship of earlier B and later A. The logic of this
relationship was developed early in the history of panel surveys
in Lazarsfeld's discussion of the "sixteenfold table" (73, 76). The
logic has been applied occasionally by others (123), but the
technique was obviously not well adapted for data-dredging
operations which seek determinate time orderings in pools
of variables.

In the last decade a number of analysts started to use a technique, called "cross-lagged panel correlation," which yielded a
quickly and easily calculated summary of the time relationship
of pairs of variables in panel studies (23, 24, 104, 125). Initially
the comparison was simply of the correlation of earlier A with
later B and of earlier B with later A, but Pelz and Andrews (104)
also used partial correlation coefficients, and the weight of
later statistical opinion seems to be in favor of using either partial correlations (13), a "directly related" measure (34, *p. 452*),
unstandardized regression coefficients (11, 13, 14) or "triple
covariances" (74). Meanwhile, Rozelle and Campbell (126),
considering results with simple correlations, pointed out that

the comparison was in fact between the net effects of two pairs of competing hypotheses about causation, and suggested a model for the use of cross-lagged comparisons which sharply limits their general applicability.

The end result of this barrage of often highly technical literature is considerable confusion, at least for the present writers, but the moral is clear: a summary statistic to measure the cross-lagging needs to be chosen with care to be appropriate both to the kind of question being asked of the data and the nature of the data itself; there is no single statistic which will suit all purposes and situations. Thus Lazarsfeld (74) points out that "Campbell's approach deals with prediction: the difference between the two correlation coefficients defines what he means by relative effect," while Lazarsfeld himself has been interested primarily in "a structural analysis; the shift back and forth from consonant and dissonant positions" (pp. 11–12). Neither approach specifically measures the time ordering of variables other than as part of a general measure of the dominant association or preponderant "influence."

Although cross-lagged comparisons were developed for and have been used primarily on panel data, they are also potentially useful in cross-sectional studies if retrospective as well as current data are collected. The general burden of the literature is that a lack of differences in the correlations may result when there is in fact an inherent time ordering, rather than that the existence of differences may falsely indicate a time ordering. The cross-lagged correlation method, then, will offer us at least an underestimate of time ordering and, since it has been fairly widely used, it seems appropriate to offer the results of such an analysis.

The cross-lagged correlations are shown in Table 8. In this table, differences in pairs of correlations of 5 or more points are emphasized by printing the higher correlation of the pair in bold face. This is not to imply that a difference of 5 points is either statistically significant or important; but singling out differences of 5 or more points indicates which types of problems are more likely to precede other types.

Of the 78 pairs of correlations, 1 was 5 or more points higher than the other in 38 comparisons, or approximately half of the total comparisons. In short, the cross-lagged correlation com-

TABLE 8.—Cross-Lagged Correlations for Past versus Current Problems[a]

	2		3		4		5		6		7	
	C	P	C	P	C	P	C	P	C	P	C	P
1. Heavy intake	.27	.30	.34	.32	.29	.35	.32	.32	.33	.23	.23	.14
2. Binge			.38	.27	.21	.25	.32	.26	.28	.22	.20	.08
3. Symptomatic drinking					.32	.36	.38	.33	.35	.28	.26	.20
4. Psychological dependence							.36	.32	.27	.21	.24	.18
5. Loss of control									.30	.28	.27	.28
6. Belligerence											.19	.16
7. Wife												
8. Relatives												
9. Friends, neighbors												
10. Job												
11. Police												
12. Health, injury												
13. Financial												

	8		9		10		11		12		13	
	C	P	C	P	C	P	C	P	C	P	C	P
1. Heavy intake	.30	.24	.20	.22	.24	.24	.21	.19	.17	.11	.25	.22
2. Binge	.30	.21	.19	.23	.24	.22	.20	.22	.20	.13	.26	.20
3. Symptomatic drinking	.37	.27	.33	.27	.35	.27	.23	.28	.28	.24	.38	.33
4. Psychological dependence	.35	.20	.27	.23	.30	.25	.18	.19	.25	.25	.34	.30
5. Loss of control	.41	.33	.34	.31	.38	.31	.24	.26	.12	.28	.40	.38
6. Belligerence	.29	.21	.18	.20	.19	.19	.20	.25	.16	.16	.25	.26
7. Wife	.26	.28	.21	.19	.17	.19	.08	.15	.17	.26	.18	.24
8. Relatives			.29	.31	.28	.30	.26	.30	.24	.33	.27	.33
9. Friends, neighbors					.43	.37	.22	.26	.31	.37	.32	.29
10. Job							.20	.22	.34	.39	.39	.40
11. Police									.19	.26	.29	.18
12. Health, injury											.30	.25
13. Financial												

[a] N3 past–current comparable scores; N = 978. Left (C) correlation in each pair is Current vertical by Past horizontal; right (P) correlation in each pair is Past vertical by Current horizontal. The more interesting comparisons are in boldface. The full range of the past–current comparable scores is used.

parisons left a considerable degree of indeterminacy as to which of the paired variables occurred more often during the past 3 years or more often at an earlier time. This is in part a reflection of the lengthy time span chosen (3 years) as well as of the limitations of the correlation method itself. The comparisons were particularly indeterminate because this sample of men aged 21 to 59 had a relatively high probability of having both problems of any given pair during the 3-year interval, hence an indeterminate temporal order.

Some fairly definite findings do emerge from the cross-lagged correlation data, however, if we consider only the first few and last few of the 13 types of problems. It appears fairly clear that symptomatic drinking, binge drinking, psychological dependence and police problems tended to occur earlier than some of the other problems. Similarly, those problems which occurred relatively later than most others were certain interpersonal problems, such as relatives, wife and job. While not conclusive, the findings are fairly congruent with results from other methods of estimating temporal sequence on the same data, presented elsewhere in this monograph.

There are, in fact, several problems with applying cross-lagged correlations to our data and for our purpose, even beyond those mentioned in the general literature cited above. In the first place, there is the general problem with correlation coefficients when used on our variables: "negative matches" are quite common and consequently a strong though varying component of the coefficient, although they are particularly irrelevant to a discussion of the time ordering of the positive ends of our variables. Secondly, as we have stated, our variables are defined and measured as conditions, rather than events; they have a beginning and an end. The conditions of beginning and ending may not be the same and in fact may appear opposed to one another: thus if variable A is an indicator of a more severe state of variable B, the onset of A may always be preceded by the onset of B, but the remission of A may always precede the remission of B. There is a definite time ordering involved here, but a cross-lagged correlation will give us the net effect of the two patterns combined, so that the pair of correlations will show no difference. Cross-lagged correlations may fail utterly to find a time ordering when both of the variables being compared are conditions rather than events.

In the third place, the cross-lagged correlations technique gives a measure of the one-sidedness of the general degree of association of the two variables over time, rather than a specific measure of the time ordering of their occurrence. The question of the degree of association over time is of course interesting in its own right, but it is not the same question as time ordering itself. Only a relatively small fraction of our study population shows a determinate time ordering between two conditions, namely, those who have at one time or another had both of the conditions.

All of these problems boil down to the fact that the cross-lagged correlations are computed over the entire sample for all values of both variables at both times, when the statistics needed to measure time order of the onset and cessation of conditions should be confined to the subsamples which provide the only determinate information on time ordering. For specific time-ordering measures of conditions, we need an index of the direction and degree of precedence and an analogous one for succession, based only on the respondents for whom there is a determinate ordering. If our measures of timing were sufficiently fine, everyone who had ever had both of the variables being compared would have a determinate order. With measures in years, as in the San Francisco data analyzed later in this study, a large majority of those who had ever had both conditions would yield a determinate order. When, as in N3, however, we have two measures—before and after 3 years ago—only a fraction of those who ever had both problems yields a determinate order.

The cells of the Lazarsfeldian 16-fold table which yield cases with a determinate order are those with entries in Figure 2. The numbers on which our analysis is based are therefore quite small; but these are the only cases available for a determination of time order, and any statistic which includes other cells in the 16-fold table in its calculations is merely confounding the issue. Our measures of order of precedence and succession are, respectively, Precedence = $Pn/(Pn + Pd)$; Succession = $Sn/(Sn + Sd)$; or, simply stated, the proportion of those with a determinate time ordering on precedence (suc-

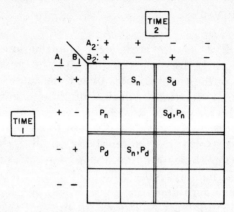

FIGURE 2.—*The Cells in the Lazarsfeld 16-Fold Table Yielding a Determinate Time Order*[7]

cession) whose ordering shows variable *A* prior to variable *B*.

A measure of precedence conceptualized in the same terms has previously been used by Park[8] and Kiviranta (65) in reporting on the time ordering of "classical symptoms" of alcoholism in a sample of 806 Finnish alcoholics.

Table 9 presents the data on the order of precedence. The top half of the table shows the proportions (limited to those with a determinate precedence) where one type of problem preceded the other (more than 3 years ago versus within the last 3 years). The bottom half of the table shows the (usually sparse) instances in which the paired comparison of temporal sequence can be made. In order to be able to make even these limited pairs of comparisons, levels for qualifying as having an indentifiable "problem" were set at minimal severity.

Before interpreting the findings of Table 9, we should repeat a few caveats about the use of the data. Again, the numbers are

[7] Figure 2 should be read as follows: If data on two dichotomous variables *A* and *B* are collected at Time 1 and again at Time 2, there will be 16 possible response combinations for each respondent. The Figure shows these 16 combinations; A_1+ means a positive response at Time 1 on variable *A*. P_n indicates the two cells entering both the numerator and denominator of our measure of precedence, P_d the cells entering only the denominator. S_n and S_d indicate the analogous cells for our measure of succession.

[8] PARK, P. A rough ordering of alcoholic symptoms. Presented at the annual meeting of the Society for the Study of Social Problems, San Francisco, August 1967.

TABLE 9.—*Order of Precedence of Drinking Problems*[a]

A. *Percentage with determinate precedence where the horizontal item preceded the vertical item*

	1	2	3	4	5	6	7	8	9	10	11	12	13
1. Heavy intake	–	27	48	30	32	31	57	42	56	50	59	74	38
2. Binge	73	–	67	67	64	67	94	43	67	82	60	100	56
3. Psychol. dependence	52	33	–	40	55	50	70	64	100	86	60	100	43
4. Loss of control	70	33	60	–	33	40	75	64	88	75	33	100	60
5. Symptomatic drink.	68	36	45	67	–	44	75	71	91	89	63	90	57
6. Belligerence	69	33	50	60	56	–	93	80	67	67	80	91	64
7. Wife	43	6	30	25	25	7	–	17	47	38	29	54	25
8. Relatives	58	57	36	36	29	20	83	–	86	64	50	82	40
9. Friends, neighbors	44	33	0	13	9	33	53	14	–	36	17	57	20
10. Job	50	18	14	25	11	33	63	36	64	–	33	83	44
11. Police	41	40	40	67	38	20	71	50	83	67	–	67	47
12. Health, injury	26	0	0	0	10	9	46	18	43	17	33	–	15
13. Financial	62	44	57	40	43	36	75	60	80	56	53	85	–

B. *Numbers with determinate order of precedence (one problem in pair occurred at least 3 years ago; the other occurred only in the last 3 years)*

	1	2	3	4	5	6	7	8	9	10	11	12	13
1. Heavy intake	–	15	23	23	28	16	42	24	18	20	17	23	26
2. Binge	15	–	6	6	11	9	18	7	3	11	10	13	9
3. Psychol. dependence	23	6	–	5	11	6	23	11	7	7	5	8	14
4. Loss of control	28	6	5	–	6	5	20	11	8	8	6	12	15
5. Symptomatic drink.	28	11	11	6	–	9	32	14	11	9	8	20	14
6. Belligerence	16	9	6	5	9	–	15	10	9	9	5	11	11
7. Wife	42	18	23	20	32	15	–	18	17	16	24	13	24
8. Relatives	24	7	11	11	14	10	18	–	7	11	14	11	10
9. Friends, neighbors	18	3	7	8	11	9	17	7	–	11	6	7	10
10. Job	20	11	7	8	9	9	16	11	11	–	12	12	9
11. Police	17	10	5	6	8	5	24	14	6	12	–	12	15
12. Health, injury	23	13	8	12	20	11	13	11	7	12	12	–	13
13. Financial	26	9	14	15	14	11	24	10	10	9	15	13	–

[a] N3 past–current comparable scores. All problems dichotomized at minimal severity level.

relatively small because we are considering only persons who have had a pair of problems with a determinate ordering within the broad dichotomy of more than 3 years ago versus 3 years or less. There is also an artifactual tendency for problems which are essentially occasional (rather than continuous) in nature (divorce, drunken driving, etc.) to be at a disadvantage in primacy of temporal order when compared to problems which are more subject to habit, such as heavy intake and belligerence.

(Periodic problems also would be less likely to appear later than habitual problems, simply because, by definition, they are less likely to appear at all.) It must also be borne in mind that the population on which one pair of problems is compared is not the same as the population on which another pair is compared. Table 9 and Figure 3 should not be taken to imply that we are directly measuring any progression over time through several variables in individual respondents. In fact, with our dichotomous measure of time, no respondent can contribute to both an arrow leading to and one leading from a particular variable.

Even so, if one picks out the top and bottom of the paired-comparison distributions, certain gross patterns of temporal order are discernible. These become more graphic in Figure 3, which is drawn from the Table 9 data to illustrate paired comparisons where one problem preceded the other in 65% or more of the instances. It can be seen that the social and health consequences of drinking tend to start later than other drinking problems. Health, friends and wife problems seem to occur latest; but even problems with relatives (which would include

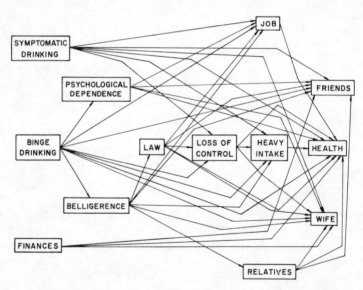

FIGURE 3.—*Order of Precedence of Earliest Occurrence of Drinking Problems* (Data from Table 9)

the complaining mothers of young men) appear to occur later than belligerence, symptomatic drinking, binge drinking and financial problems. Trouble with the law seems likely to precede other social consequences; on the other hand, it is shown as tending to be preceded by manifestations of belligerence.

The relatively late appearance of heavy intake appears odd, since one needs to drink in order to get into difficulty over one's drinking. However, heavy intake as here defined means simply relatively heavy and steady drinking—five or more drinks per occasion at least once a week. The nature of the problems which precede heavy intake in temporal sequence suggest that what we will later describe as the "Southern pattern" or "dry area pattern" (infrequent binges accompanied by belligerence and guilt feelings) may also be a young man's pattern. Certainly this theory fits the various findings of college and high-school studies: the young are often not in a position to make drinking a relatively steady activity.

In interpreting Figure 3 a certain arbitrariness of arrangement should be noted. By and large, problems at the same distance from the left margin of the diagram can be taken as being roughly of the same rank. Symptomatic drinking, however, could as well be shown on a slightly lower level, parallel with police problems, with belligerence or with psychological dependence. Financial problems could be on any of the levels except the very bottom; and either psychological dependence or problems with relatives could be parallel with police problems or loss of control. Thus the chart should be accepted only as a rough approximation of the actual relationships. An even more cogent reason for caution against reliance on these findings is that all were based on small samples (Table 9).

A separate issue from that of precedence is that of order of succession: which of any pair of problems occurred latest (within the last 3 years). These findings, shown in Table 10 and Figure 4, resemble those in Table 9 and Figure 3 in a general way, in that early-acquired problems appear to diminish soonest. Thus symptomatic drinking, belligerence, and binge drinking appear not only to start relatively early, but are relatively specific to younger drinkers. On the other hand, problems with wife, friends and relatives, which were shown in Figure 3, start relatively late, appear also to persist beyond other prob-

TABLE 10.—*Order of Succession of Drinking Problems*[a]

A. *Percentage with determinate succession where the horizontal item occurred later than the vertical item*

	1	2	3	4	5	6	7	8	9	10	11	12	13
1. Heavy intake	–	71	52	47	55	50	15	36	59	53	63	27	47
2. Binge	29	–	30	14	18	37	6	13	33	30	52	9	17
3. Psychol. dependence	48	70	–	53	61	52	22	6	50	47	68	44	45
4. Loss of control	53	86	47	–	76	67	0	35	64	53	71	39	50
5. Symptomatic drink.	45	82	39	24	–	45	3	19	27	38	75	27	27
6. Belligerence	50	63	48	33	55	–	12	17	40	40	68	39	32
7. Wife	85	94	78	100	97	88	–	73	88	82	91	79	80
8. Relatives	64	88	94	65	81	83	27	–	75	69	72	79	68
9. Friends, neighbors	41	67	50	36	73	60	13	25	–	36	80	60	27
10. Job	47	70	53	47	62	60	18	31	64	–	63	38	27
11. Police	37	48	32	29	25	32	9	28	20	37	–	38	20
12. Health, injury	73	91	56	61	73	61	21	21	40	63	63	–	44
13. Financial	52	83	55	50	73	68	20	32	73	73	80	56	–

B. *Numbers with determinate order of succession (one problem in pair occurred within the last 3 years, the other only before then)*

	1	2	3	4	5	6	7	8	9	10	11	12	13
1. Heavy intake	–	45	42	34	53	48	47	39	27	38	41	26	40
2. Binge	45	–	23	21	28	27	35	24	12	20	21	22	24
3. Psychol. dependence	42	23	–	15	23	23	23	17	14	17	19	18	20
4. Loss of control	34	21	15	–	21	24	17	20	11	19	21	18	18
5. Symptomatic drink.	53	28	23	21	–	29	33	31	15	21	24	22	30
6. Belligerence	48	27	23	24	29	–	25	24	10	20	28	18	28
7. Wife	47	35	23	17	33	25	–	22	16	22	34	19	25
8. Relatives	39	24	17	20	31	24	22	–	12	16	29	14	19
9. Friends, neighbors	27	12	14	11	15	10	16	12	–	14	10	5	11
10. Job	38	20	17	19	21	20	22	16	14	–	19	16	15
11. Police	41	21	19	21	24	28	34	29	10	19	–	16	25
12. Health, injury	26	22	18	18	22	18	19	14	5	16	16	–	18
13. Financial	40	24	20	18	30	28	25	19	11	15	25	18	–

[a] N3 past–current comparable scores. All problems dichotomized at minimal severity level.

lems—even beyond the cessation of the behavior which presumably precipitated these problems. This may indicate that there is a perceptual lag in which those who are closest to the drinker will tend to become anxious about his drinking early in his drinking career and persist in remaining anxious or censorious for some time after some of the more conspicuous problems have abated. Another possibility is that the respondent will tend to backdate problems of high social unacceptability (such as

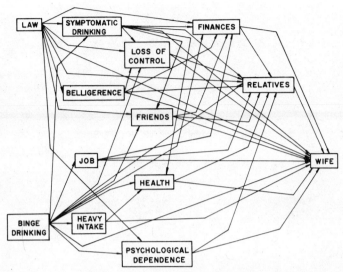

FIGURE 4.—*Order of Succession of Latest Occurrence of Drinking Problems* (Data from Table 10)

with the police, going on binges and admitting addictive symptoms) while conceding that some of his significant others are still concerned about his drinking.

F. Association in Space and Time: Predicting Current Behavior from Past

Part of our reservations about using measures like cross-lagged correlations as indicators of time ordering is that they attempt to measure a specific dimension of patterning with a summary statistic that confounds the dimension with several others. At least conceptually, although not always in practice, we have attempted in the previous analysis to treat separately the various dimensions of patterning and association. The measures of time ordering used in Tables 9 and 10, for instance, are statistically independent of the degree of association between the variables compared, at least when the association is measured in lifetime terms, since the time-order measures use only respondents who appear in a single cell of the table of lifetime association—the cell of those who have at one time or another had both of the variables in question.

TABLE 11.—*Partial Correlations and Multiple Correlation Coefficients from Regressions of Past Problems on Each Current High Problem*[a]

A. Regressions including past problems in the same area as the criterion

	1	2	3	4	5	6	7	8	9	10	11	12	13
1. Heavy intake	.22	.00	−.01	−.02	.00	.05	.02	.02	.00	−.03	.01	.03	.01
2. Binge	.02	.38	.01	.07	.01	.01	.01	.03	.00	−.07	−.01	−.01	.04
3. Psychol. dependence	.08	.06	.37	.01	.06	.03	.06	.08	−.01	.01	−.02	.02	.05
4. Loss of control	.05	.04	.01	.23	−.02	−.01	−.01	.07	.10	.08	.03	.11	.06
5. Symptomatic drinking	.00	−.11	.00	−.01	.26	−.01	.02	.01	.01	−.01	−.03	.01	−.05
6. Belligerence	−.02	.01	−.00	−.04	−.04	.46	.01	−.06	−.02	−.01	.00	−.07	−.01
7. Wife	−.03	.01	.09	.13	.08	.07	.42	.07	.10	.05	.02	.01	.02
8. Relatives	.09	.05	−.02	.04	−.02	−.05	.09	.43	.07	−.02	.06	−.03	.04
9. Friends, neighbors	.05	.05	.01	−.01	.01	−.01	−.05	−.02	.22	.11	.01	−.04	−.03
10. Job	.02	.01	.02	.06	−.07	−.02	−.04	−.06	−.02	.27	.01	.10	.02
11. Police	−.03	.07	−.05	−.01	.04	−.06	.06	.07	.05	−.02	.32	−.02	.06
12. Health, injury	−.07	−.03	.02	.08	.02	−.01	.06	.09	.09	.11	.04	.39	.09
13. Financial	−.02	−.05	−.03	−.02	.06	.02	.01	−.02	−.07	.05	−.03	−.02	.25
Multiple correlation coefficient	.41	.50	.50	.47	.47	.56	.55	.61	.46	.53	.42	.52	.49

B. Regressions excluding past problems in the same area as the criterion

	1	2	3	4	5	6	7	8	9	10	11	12	13
1. Heavy intake	—	.10	.07	—.02	.03	.10	.06	.03	—.01	—.03	.04	.00	.01
2. Binge	.08	—	.01	.09	.09	.03	.01	.00	.01	—.06	.00	.00	.02
3. Psychol. dependence	.13	.05	—	.05	.12	.01	.04	.08	.00	.02	—.02	.06	.07
4. Loss of control	.05	.08	.08	—	.00	.03	.03	.10	.11	.09	.05	.13	.11
5. Symptomatic drinking	.03	.01	.09	.01	—	.07	.03	.04	.04	.03	.01	.01	—.02
6. Belligerence	.01	.03	—.01	—.02	.00	—	.04	—.01	—.01	—.03	.06	—.08	.01
7. Wife	—.01	.01	.08	.15	.08	.09	—	.13	.10	.06	.00	.04	.03
8. Relatives	.10	.03	—.01	.07	.00	.00	.15	—	.09	—.02	.09	.03	.06
9. Friends, neighbors	.03	.06	.01	.01	.03	.01	—.03	.03	—	.18	.01	.03	—.01
10. Job	.03	.03	.02	.06	—.04	—.05	—.01	—.06	.04	—	.03	.13	.09
11. Police	—.02	.07	—.05	.00	.07	.04	.02	.10	.05	.00	—	.02	.07
12. Health, injury	—.09	—.02	.06	.09	.02	—.03	.09	.14	.12	.14	.07	—	.08
13. Financial	—.02	—.07	.01	.03	.09	.05	.03	.02	—.05	.12	—.01	—.03	—
Multiple correlation coefficient	.35	.34	.35	.42	.41	.35	.39	.48	.41	.48	.29	.37	.43

[a] N3 past–current comparable and optimal scores; $N = 978$. The predictors are the full past scores from N3 past–current comparable measures. The criteria are the N3 optimal current high-problems dichotomies (Appendix B). In each of parts *A* and *B*, each column represents the results of a regression on the current problem identified at the head of the column. The multiple correlation coefficient, and partial correlations after all the past problems variables have been entered, are shown.

While we would argue for the utility of looking at the various dimensions of patterning and association separately, we recognize that there is also considerable value in adding them back together to measure association in both space and time. At least from the viewpoint of preventive public health, an assessment in this framework is crucial. The analytical question now becomes, how well can we predict, and how can we best predict, future behavior on the basis of past behavior?

One solution is simple correlations of past behavior with present—the prediction half of the cross-lagged correlations (left member of each pair in Table 8). Comparing these past–current correlations with the analogous current–current correlations (Table 2, below the diagonal), we find that the prediction correlation on the basis of past behavior is higher than the correlation between current behaviors in one-third of the same problem pairs. The prediction correlations are as likely to exceed as to fall short of the current correlations when symptomatic drinking, police, health and injury, or belligerence problems are involved. On the other hand, the prediction correlations are almost uniformly lower than the current correlations when problems with wife or friends are involved. If it is true that "troubles seldom come singly," we might expect to find behaviors in the same time period uniformly more highly correlated than behaviors at different time periods, so that the substantial number of comparisons where this expectation is not fulfilled may be taken as underlining the importance of relationships in time in understanding drinking problems.

Another and somewhat more complex approach is to use each current problem as the criterion of a regression analysis in which the predictors are the past problems. This kind of analysis yields an estimate of the extent to which a given current drinking problem can be predicted on the basis of past drinking behavior and problems, and of the relative weighting, in terms of partial correlation coefficients, of the various past drinking problems to provide the best prediction of the current problem. Table 11 shows the summary results of two series of such analyses, one including and one excluding past problems in the same problem area as the current-problem criterion.

Uniformly, the strongest contribution to predicting a current specific problem is the respondent's score on past problems in the same area. This result is to be expected, partly on grounds of general principle (analogous, admittedly, to the one we just found to be violated) and partly because of the likelihood of response artifacts in a questionnaire in which past and current problem were inquired about separately but contiguously.

When past problems in the same area are included, the regression equations explain between 17 and 37% of the variance. Without the past problems in the same area, the proportion of variance explained drops to a range of 8 to 23%. Even when they are measured in the same interview, then, past problems in total provide only a moderate prediction of present problems.

When past problems in the same area are included, the partial correlation of any other past problem with the current problem criterion is no higher than .11. Though there are obviously variations in the contributions of other problem areas to the prediction, the partial correlation with any other problem area is relatively small compared with the partial correlation between past and current problems in the same area. When past problems in the same area are excluded, some moderately strong partial correlations appear; for instance, problems with friends predicting job problems, wife problems predicting loss of control, problems with relatives predicting wife problems, health problems predicting problems with relatives and job.

The prediction analyses attempted above are open to the objection we noted earlier, that correlation-type statistics are unsuited to the nature of our variables in paying too much attention to "negative matches." Table 12 accordingly presents prediction data in terms concentrating on the "positive matches": of those who had a particular problem in the past, what proportion has each kind of problem in the present? The numbers on the diagonal—the prediction of current problems among those with past problems in the same area—are, of course, the complementary percentages to the "remission rate" of Table 6 (i.e., 100 minus the remission rate).

In nearly all cases, past problems in the same area provide a better prediction than past problems in other areas of current problems. The only exception is on current heavy intake, which is about equally well predicted by past problems with friends or job. Any past problem elevates the chances of having any current problem above the marginal distribution for the current problem (bottom row); again, this result is partly due to the "negative matches" elsewhere in the total sample. In general, Table 12, along with Table 11 and our previous findings on concurrent associations, suggests that drinking problems as measured by our scales are relatively loosely associated, once those in the population who have never had problems are excluded. We regard the present analysis as raising such issues rather than settling them, but, in view of its practical implications, we consider it worth considerable further attention. For instance, current proposals to deny drivers' licenses to problem drinkers may well be predicated upon a greater overlapping of problems in space and time than we find in our data.

G. Summary

In this chapter, we have engaged in a long exercise in "taking apart the dependent variable to see how it works." In general, the results may be viewed as showing considerable variation in the comparisons between and patterns of interrelation of the drinking problem areas, according to the severity, timing and methodological frameworks being used. We have been enabled to make these kinds of detailed comparisons by the extensive measures we have employed in the area of the dependent variable. Our results caution against the kinds of assumptions that can too easily be made in interpreting the results of more limited measures of drinking problems. For instance, short lists of social problems caused by drinking commonly employ a single indicator in each area roughly as severe as what we have designated the minimal-severity level. It would be tempting for an analyst inspecting the correlation matrix of such measures to assume that this was an underestimation of the overlapping which would exist on more severely defined measures. In our general-population data, however, we found the opposite to be the case. Again, studies with fewer dependent-variable measures might well ignore the crucial finding which became so clear in our own analysis: that much of the strength of whole-sample measures of association like the correlation coefficient derives from the "negative matches"—the very

TABLE 12.—*Predicting Current Problems by Past Problems, in Per Cent*[a]

Past Problems	N	1	2	3	4	5	6	7	8	9	10	11	12	13
1. Heavy intake	197	33	16	25	25	20	24	20	22	10	10	9	7	10
2. Binge	125	29	34	28	33	25	26	22	26	11	14	13	11	13
3. Psychol. dependence	171	27	18	50	30	26	22	22	28	14	15	9	11	15
4. Loss of control	167	30	19	32	54	25	24	26	31	16	19	13	15	16
5. Symptomatic drinking	168	26	17	30	32	36	23	26	27	16	16	11	11	16
6. Belligerence	180	23	16	22	26	19	44	24	22	11	10	11	6	11
7. Wife	111	20	14	26	32	25	26	55	25	14	14	12	10	11
8. Relatives	135	27	16	23	33	23	21	28	48	15	16	15	12	13
9. Friends, neighbors	60	35	23	32	38	30	25	32	35	45	35	18	25	22
10. Job	89	33	20	33	36	25	20	29	30	26	40	12	21	24
11. Police	101	25	20	25	29	25	25	26	30	17	15	27	11	14
12. Health, injury	48	19	19	35	40	29	19	38	42	33	33	23	48	25
13. Financial	76	26	18	43	43	32	29	36	36	20	29	12	20	41
Total Sample	978	12	6	12	11	8	9	11	8	4	4	4	4	4

[a] N3 past–current comparable scales; $N = 978$. The measures are dichotomized at the high-problems level (Appendix B). The table should be read as follows: of the 197 persons with a high score on heavy intake in the past (more than 3 years ago), 33% qualified for the same level of intake currently (within the last 3 years).

substantial proportion of any general-population sample who do not have either of any given pair of drinking problems. The overlapping of problems diminishes when the base for the statistics is even moderately restricted, say, just to those who ever get drunk.

In spite of these variations, some relatively robust patterns of association emerged repeatedly with different methods. Drinking behavior generally showed more variability than the psychological loading which respondents placed on the behavior. Among the social consequences, police problems seemed to be particularly a hit-or-miss area, with low stability over time and low predictability. Health problems tended to emerge late, and again to be relatively less predictable. In general, the onset of heavy-drinking behavior preceded the social consequences; but, interestingly, there appeared to be a quite strong tendency for the social consequences to persist after the behavior had remitted.

These are, of course, but a sample of the more obvious findings, and the reader is invited to do some contemplation of his own. All the data used here were gathered at one point in time and thus are subject to the special hazards of retrospective information and response sets. We are now embarking on studies involving reinterviews with the same subjects so that in the course of time we will be able to answer at least partially such questions of temporal sequence as can be answered only by a longitudinal study.

Chapter 4

Problem Drinking and
Social Differentiations

NOW that the interrelationships between the specific types of drinking-related problems have been explored in a detailed but preliminary fashion, we shall investigate the patterns of association of demographic or socio-cultural variables with the various types of problems. The variables included under this rubric traditionally appear in broad differentiations of the general population: differentiations in terms of life cycle, such as age and family status; in terms of ecological variations, such as region and urbanization; in terms of cultural variations, such as ethnicity and religion; and in terms of general socioeconomic status.

These variables or their analogues are the minimum stock-in-trade of any descriptive social survey. Most such surveys begin, and many end, with a series of cross-tabulations of demographic variables against the variable which is the subject of the study. Why such tabulations should be of interest is usually considered to be sufficiently self-evident as to merit no discussion; that many of the cross-tabulations commonly show large associations is considered to be reason enough for the undertaking.

Much of the importance of these variables is that they in fact measure major bases of social differentiation without reference to the actual behavior of the individual being classified. This is most explicit in impersonal bureaucratic situations (most application forms for any purpose have a sprinkling of questions on these variables) but also applies even more clearly in traditional societies and situations. Unlike many sociological and psychological variables, they are differentiations which ordinary people recognize and use in everyday life. They make a measurable difference in innumerable life-chances—the price of insurance depends on the district of residence, the amount of income tax

71

depends on marital status: these kinds of differentiations stretch far beyond the now well-recognized differentiations on race, sex, religion and ethnicity. Some are easily visible (sex, age and race), while others are less determinate. There is a tendency for those who think a given differentiation to be specially important to invent perceptible differences (4, *pp. 130–137*) or to look for visible signs (wedding rings, business suits, Texas 10-gallon hats).

While all of this enhances the importance of the variables, it tends to make their analytical status ambiguous. Thus the full "meaning" of a finding of association between social status and mental health, for instance, is a far more implicative but far less determinable issue than the fact that there is an association. The fact of an association between ethnicity and drinking problems is unarguable, but the number of possible hypotheses about the meaning of this relationship has far outrun the capacity to test them.

One common characteristic of these variables—in fact, a characteristic intrinsically related to their social importance—is a relative lack of variation in them in an individual over time. People do change their religion or social class, of course, or learn to "pass" as of another ethnic group or age. The sociological discussion of the openness of American and other industrial societies has been concerned with this very issue of the amount of change. Nevertheless, for broadly defined categories, even in societies characterized as "open," change in status even between generations is less common than stability.

In our analysis, therefore, we will follow the common presumption, testing it where possible, that the demographic variables are logically prior to drinking problems, while the demographic variables are, for the most part, equal to each other in logical status. That is, the direction in influence is usually assumed to be from the demographic variable or whatever it represents to drinking problems, and the interrelation of any pair of demographic variables and drinking problems is viewed as a case of specification or replication in the Lazarsfeld tradition of analysis (46) and not explanation or interpretation. In general, we are assuming that the demographic characteristics are acquired at birth or in childhood, while drinking problems are acquired later.

This assumption will not always be true. Thus age-group correlates of problem drinking do not account for any heavy drinkers who died or dropped out of the household population prior to the survey; low socioeconomic status may be as much a reflection of drinking oneself into poverty as it is a predictor of problems; people may move from one urban area or region to another in pursuit of heavy drinking; whether one has a wife or children in the same household may be in part the outcome of one's excesses or moderation in drinking; and it even could be contended that the direction of influence over one's religion is not immutable—those who are born to a religion which frowns on heavy drinking may elect to drop out of it rather than face subsequent social pressures. To the meager extent possible, we will test for the operation of these reverse causations in the present analysis; a fuller test, however, must await the final stage in our longitudinal studies.

For the cross-tabulations which form the bulk of this chapter, we shall use the combined National 2 and National 3 sample (N = 1561) and the N2–N3 comparable problem scores, since the independent variables of concern to us here are available in full form in both samples and the larger numbers in the combined samples allow us to extend the analysis to test several variables at one time.

A. Age

As we noted above (Table 7), all drinking problems show their highest prevalence to a greater or lesser extent in the youngest adult group (aged 21 to 24) so that the proportion of this cohort with a high current over-all problems score is almost twice that in any other age group. At least through the mid-50s, the over-all level of prevalence remains fairly stable through the other age groups, though there are definite tendencies for some particular problems to be most prevalent early in life and others to be relatively more prevalent later.

Results by age on the current-problems typology are shown in Table 13. As previously noted in a partially overlapping sample (20, p. 22), the proportion of abstainers rises fairly regularly with increasing age. With the present sample and a 3-year time base for abstinence, the differences by age of abstainers are greater than previously shown among those aged under 60.

TABLE 13.—*Current Problems Typology by Age, in Per Cent*

Age	N	Non-drinker[a]	Drank: No Problems	Poten-tial Problems Only[b]	Heavy Intake or Binge: No Conse-quences[c]	High Conse-quences[d]
21–24	147	5	22	25	16	31
25–29	204	9	37	24	18	13
30–34	186	8	43	22	13	14
35–39	216	16	37	22	14	12
40–44	226	15	43	17	13	12
45–49	201	16	44	19	9	12
50–54	199	18	41	22	8	13
55–59	182	31	33	20	7	9
Totals	1561	15	38	21	12	14

[a] Did not drink in last 3 years.

[b] A problem of at least minimal severity in any one problem area except heavy intake or binge and with tangible consequences score of less than 3.

[c] At least minimal severity on heavy intake or binge and with tangible consequences score of less than 3.

[d] Tangible consequences score of 3 or more.

Other than among those under 25, the proportions of drinkers with no problems of even minimal severity, and with minimal-severity problems not qualifying them for the heavy-intake and tangible-consequences categories, remain fairly constant at all ages. Both the proportion with tangible consequences (problems with wife, friends, neighbors, on the job, with police, or health or financial problems) and the proportion without the consequences but with heavy intake decline regularly with age. The ratio of these two categories is a rough indicator of the risk of heavy drinking ending in tangible consequences. Men under 25 not only have a relatively high prevalence of heavy drinking without tangible consequences, but also have by far the highest likelihood of eventual tangible consequences. Otherwise the risk of tangible consequences does not appear to vary greatly by age, though there is some tendency for tangible consequences of a given behavior to be relatively higher in relation to heavy drinking among men over 45 than among men aged 25 to 44.

B. Life Cycle

Marital and family status are important variables in studying problematic behavior. In Durkheim's view (40, *p. 271*), marriage was a protection against suicide in men, but having children did not provide any extra protection. Obviously, marital status and age are intertwined to a considerable degree, so that it is always possible that a finding for young men will turn out to be specific to the single, or that a finding for the single will turn out to be general among young men. The two measures have accordingly been combined by Lansing and Kish (71) and others into a concept of position in the life-cycle as an important determinant of life adjustment.

It will be shown later in this monograph that the wife is an important influence in the amount and character of drinking. Accordingly, one might expect that men living with their wives and children would be less likely to have drinking problems, in part because heavy drinking sometimes is the occasion for being single or divorced.

Table 14 divides the N2–N3 sample into 3 groups: those living with wife and children, living with wife but no children, and not living with either. Each is further divided into four age groups. This presentation of 12 specific types of problems shows some highly particularistic patterns. For example, high intake is most common in those living with neither wife nor children who are in their 30s or 50s, but binge drinking is most common among single men in their 20s. Loss of control and symptomatic drinking are most common among younger respondents, particularly unmarried men in their 20s. Problems with one's wife are highest among men in their 20s, particularly if there are children at home. Problems with friends or neighbors or the police are commonest among single men in their 20s or 50s, but problems on the job are most common among those in their 30s with a wife but no children, and among single men in their 40s.

Some of these differences may be a function of chance variations because of small subsamples; but the differences are sufficiently varied to demonstrate the importance of utilizing life cycle as a concept in more detailed analyses in future studies.

In terms of the over-all score (last row of each section of Table 14) the pattern of association of drinking problems with life cycle is clear and reasonably regular. Among men at any age between 21 and 59, not being married is associated with an excess of

TABLE 14.—*Current High Problems by Family Status and Age,
in Per Cent*

	21–29	30–39	AGE 40–49	50–59	Totals
Living with wife and children					
	(N = 177)	(322)	(338)	(174)	(1011)
Heavy intake	7	5	5	4	5
Binge	3	2	1	2	2
Psychol. dep.	6	4	4	3	4
Loss of control	5	4	4	3	4
Symptomatic drink.	13	6	8	6	8
Belligerence	14	9	7	3	8
Wife	22	12	9	9	12
Friends, neighbors	10	4	4	3	5
Job	7	3	4	2	4
Police	4	2	1	2	2
Health, injuries	5	5	4	6	5
Financial	7	5	2	2	4
Current over-all problems	27	18	17	14	18
Living with wife, no children					
	(N = 89)	(30)	(53)	(167)	(339)
Heavy intake	7	10	2	4	5
Binge	5	3	2	3	3
Psychol. dep.	2	13	6	4	4
Loss of control	10	10	11	5	8
Symptomatic drink.	15	10	6	5	8
Belligerence	10	17	8	4	7
Wife	16	13	11	8	11
Friends, neighbors	3	10	4	5	5
Job	2	13	6	5	5
Police	6	0	4	1	3
Health, injuries	5	13	2	7	6
Financial	7	7	6	4	5
Current over-all problems	23	33	15	13	18
Living with neither wife nor children					
	(N = 85)	(50)	(36)	(40)	(211)
Heavy intake	7	12	3	13	9
Binge	13	8	8	8	10
Psychol. dep.	5	0	3	5	3
Loss of control	12	4	11	8	9
Symptomatic drink.	28	16	11	13	19
Belligerence	14	4	8	5	9
Wife	12	10	8	10	10
Friends, neighbors	13	10	6	13	11
Job	9	8	11	8	9
Police	13	4	6	10	9
Health, injuries	8	8	8	13	9
Financial	8	4	6	8	7
Current over-all problems	41	28	25	23	32

drinking problems; but among the married, having children at home makes few substantial differences. This effect is separate from and additive to the effects of age: in all family-status comparisons (except for one with a small *N*), the proportion with a high problems score is greatest among the young men and fairly constant (declining only slightly with increasing age) among the older men. Drinking problems are not, therefore, relatively specific to the unmarried among young men, nor to the young men among the unmarried.

Table 15 presents findings by the same life-cycle age groups on the five-category problem-drinking typology. Abstinence is less common among the unmarried than among either cate-

TABLE 15.—*Current Problems Typology[a] by Family Status and Age, in Per Cent*

	N	Non-drinker	Drank: No Problems	Potential Problems Only	Heavy Intake or Binge: No Consequences	High Consequences
Living with wife and children						
Age 21–29	177	8	32	25	16	19
30–39	322	13	44	21	10	12
40–49	338	17	43	18	11	12
50–59	174	21	43	19	9	9
Totals	1011	15	42	20	11	13
Living with wife, no children						
Age 21–29	89	8	33	26	21	12
30–39	30	3	10	37	37	13
40–49	53	11	38	28	11	11
50–59	167	29	34	22	5	11
Totals	339	18	32	25	13	12
Living with neither wife nor child						
Age 21–29	85	6	26	21	15	32
30–39	50	10	23	22	20	20
40–49	36	6	53	11	11	19
50–59	40	18	25	28	13	18
Totals	211	9	31	21	15	24

[a] Defined in Table 13 footnote.

gory of married men at most age levels. There does not appear to be any uniform relation between abstinence and age among the unmarried, such as we found among men generally. Distributions on the tangible-consequences criterion are analogous to those we found on the over-all problem score: consequences decline with marriage, and within each family-status category, with increasing age. There appears to be some tendency for having children at home to increase the chances of tangible consequences among the youngest group of married men. Table 14 shows that this surplus is concentrated in interpersonal (including wife) and job problems.

The ratio of heavy drinking without consequences to drinking with consequences is considerably higher among the married than among the unmarried, despite the fact that it is only the married who are "at risk" of wife problems, the most common tangible consequence. Heavy intake without consequences is especially common among young married men with no children, and this pattern forms a strong contrast with their unmarried age mates. We might surmise that the initial "influence of a good woman" is more to direct behavior into less consequence-prone channels than to cut it off completely. It may well be that the influence of wife on the husband's drinking patterns, and vice versa, is most direct among young newly marrieds since drinking may be more likely then to involve both the husband and wife than when there are children at home. Certainly, Table 14 shows that it is particularly in the more florid styles of drinking—binges, symptomatic drinking, belligerence—that the greatest nonconsequence differences between childless married and the unmarried among the the young are to be found.

In terms of drinking with no reported problems, even at the minimal-severity level, the pattern by family status does differ from the findings on other drinking measures. Over-all, and at all age levels above 30, the men living with wife and children are substantially more likely to manifest no problems at all than either the comparable married men without children or the unmarried.

C. Geographic Region

As Gusfield has shown (49), regional variations within the United States in attitudes toward drinking have a long history, and the temperance movement can be viewed as a "symbolic crusade" by one part of the country to validate its own life-style and values as normative for the entire nation. If we compare the nine general regions of the country as defined by the Census, we find a natural division between what we shall call "wetter" and "dryer" regions, when they are compared either on manifestations of temperance sentiment or on proportions of abstainers and relatively heavy drinkers (Table 16 and Figure 5). The comparisons on drinking patterns in general replicate Mulford's in his earlier national quota sample (89, *pp. 640-641*). That these findings are a continuation of historical patterns is clear from a comparison with temperance sentiment exhibited in a 1932 *Literary Digest* poll.[1]

FIGURE 5.—*Dry sentiment, 1932 and 1964.* ([a]For retention of Prohibition in 1932. [b]Reported "Nothing good about drinking" in 1964.)

[1] The Literary Digest poll suffered an eventually fatal debacle in its prediction of the 1936 presidential election, which one of us has examined in detail (21). This casts some retrospective doubt on the validity of its results in earlier polls; therefore we checked the proportions against repeal by states with the proportions voting against repeal in the elections for constitutional conventions on repeal held in 34 states in 1933 (57, *p. 30*). The Literary Digest result was, on the average, 1½ percentage points "wetter" (standard deviation = 6.3). This result suggests that the two sets of data are in close enough conformity to use the more easily applicable in making comparison between regions.

TABLE 16.— Regional Differences in Adult Drinking Patterns and Sentiments

	BEHAVIOR				SENTIMENT	
	% Current Abstainers 1964[a]	% Heavy Drinkers 1964[b]	Per Capita Consumption[c] 1968[d]	1940[e]	% "Nothing good" about drinking 1964[f]	% Against Repeal of Prohibition 1932[g]
Dryer Regions						
South Atlantic	42	7	2.42	1.11	41	35
East South Central	65	4	1.50	0.57	61	41
West South Central	38	6	2.08	0.88	36	38
West North Central	34	6	2.16	1.22	41	33
Mountain	42	8	2.54	1.33	41	30
Wetter Regions						
New England	21	13	2.94	1.72	29	22
Middle Atlantic	17	16	2.75	1.78	24	19
East North Central	25	12	2.58	1.75	31	24
Pacific	27	12	2.98	1.87	26	24

a From Cahalan, Cisin and Crossley (20, p. 38).
b High-volume–high-maximum drinkers, from Cahalan, Cisin and Crossley (20, p. 219).
c Gallons of absolute alcohol (population aged 15 and over).
d From Efron and Keller (41, p. 6).
e Recalculated from 1940 Census state populations and Jellinek (57, pp. 4, 15).
f Proportion volunteering "nothing good" when asked what are the good things to be said about drinking, from Cahalan, Cisin and Crossley (20, Table A-77).
g Percentage for retention of prohibition, Literary Digest poll, 30 April 1932.

Of course, in this differentiation we are not implying a uniformity of behavior within each region. The boundaries, like the boundaries of the states from which they are composed, are to a considerable degree arbitrary lines rather than straightforward reflections of topographical, economic and social distinctions within the U.S. population. If we could draw a detailed isometric map of the country according to drinking sentiments, we would no doubt find, for instance, downstate Illinois reapportioned to the "dryer" area and New Orleans to the "wetter." We will investigate some of the differentiations in more detail (Chapter 7). The existence of considerable variation at more detailed levels, however, does not nullify the importance of general regional comparisons. Whatever the local sentiment on drinking, sentiments at the statewide and areawide levels are also important components of the social climate in which individual drinking patterns and attitudes operate.

As the *Literary Digest* findings suggest, our wetter and dryer regional division is a fair reflection of the geographical divisions on the "liquor question" during the decades of political and moral ferment when this question figured so prominently. By and large, the wetter region encompasses the coastal and Great Lakes seaports (excluding the South). In many societies, border areas are traditional centers of tolerance of diversity. The wetter region also encompasses the largest cities which absorbed the bulk of the waves of immigration of the late 19th century, while the dryer region is the heartland of small-town old-stock fundamentalist America.

Table 17 shows that, when the regional comparisons are confined to men aged 21 to 59, there remains a tendency for the dryer regions to show a higher proportion with no drinking-related problems of even minimal severity (including abstainers); however, they do not appear to have a smaller prevalence of tangible consequences due to drinking. The dryer regions also show definitely lower proportions of heavy drinkers without consequences: thus heavy drinking appears more likely to get a man into trouble in dryer than in wetter areas.

The same pattern can be seen in comparing the prevalences of high current problems in the two general regions (Table 18, last two columns): the prevalences of indices of social consequences and disruptive drinking in dryer regions exceed or

TABLE 17.—*Current Problems Typology*[a] *by Region, in Per Cent*

	N	Non-drinker	Drank: No Problems	Potential Problems Only	Heavy Intake or Binge: No Consequences	High Consequences
Dryer Regions						
South Atlantic	156	28	30	19	12	12
East South Central	113	29	30	16	5	20
West South Central	188	23	40	17	5	14
West North Central	134	10	47	17	12	14
Mountain	61	21	33	26	3	16
Totals	652	22	37	18	8	15
Wetter Regions						
New England	89	7	43	33	11	7
Middle Atlantic	288	7	39	20	19	15
East North Central	353	13	41	22	13	12
Pacific	179	10	32	27	14	16
Totals	909	10	39	23	15	13

[a] Defined in Table 13 footnote.

equal those in wetter regions. In the wetter regions prevalences are higher only on problems associated with steady, relatively heavy consumption with medical rather than social consequences—heavy intake, psychological dependence and health and injury problems. When interpreting these findings, it should be borne in mind that intake appears especially likely to be underestimated in dryer regions (120). The conceptual issues raised by these patterns will be explored in greater detail in Chapter 7; for the moment we will simply note that the findings are consistent with results from social statistics showing that drunken-driving arrest rates are higher in towns in dryer states (98, 116), and with Christie's Scandinavian studies (28) in which he concludes that "a strict system of legal and organizational control of accessibility of alcohol seems to be related to low alcohol consumption, but also to a high degree of public nuisance" (*p. 107*). Room (117, *p. 94*) also concluded in a recent analysis of the 1964–65 National 1 data that the social pressures against drinking are generally stronger in rural areas than in the

TABLE 18.—*Current High Problems by Urbanization and Region, in Per Cent*

	CENTRAL CITIES			OTHER CITIES, TOWNS			RURAL AREAS			TOTALS	
	Wetter Region	Dryer Region	Totals	Wetter Region	Dryer Region	Totals	Wetter Region	Dryer Region	Totals	Wetter Region	Dryer Region
(N =)	(343)	(184)	(527)	(387)	(163)	(550)	(179)	(305)	(484)	(909)	(652)
Heavy intake	8	7	7	7	3	5	7	2	4	7	3
Binge	3	10	6	2	2	2	2	2	2	3	4
Psychol. dep.	6	4	6	4	1	3	4	3	4	5	3
Loss of control	5	11	7	4	6	5	5	5	5	4	7
Symptomatic drink.	11	20	14	7	8	7	7	6	7	9	10
Belligerence	11	13	12	7	7	7	5	7	6	8	8
Wife	15	17	16	8	8	8	13	11	12	11	12
Friends, neighbors	7	9	8	4	4	4	6	6	6	5	6
Job	7	7	7	3	3	3	5	5	5	5	5
Police	4	6	5	2	3	2	2	2	2	3	3
Health, injuries	8	8	8	5	3	5	5	4	4	6	5
Financial	6	7	6	3	2	3	3	5	4	4	4
Current over-all problems	27	32	29	16	16	16	16	14	15	20	19

city, and particularly in the rural South and on heavier drinkers in southern cities.

Substantial differences were also found between regions and urban–rural residence on amount of drinking among those who drank at all: men in rural areas were somewhat less likely than others to drink with their families—which is consistent with the finding of greater sex differences in rural drinking patterns (20, p. 41)—and more likely to drink with friends and in bars (117, p. 95). The dry area (especially southern rural) pattern of drinking shows up in the independent social statistics on alcohol: per capita consumption is lower but drunkenness arrests are higher in the southern region (117, p. 97). This pattern appears to parallel in many respects that in Scandinavian studies, where Finland was found to play the "southern" role of low per-capita consumption combined with high indices of social consequences:

"Ambivalent attitudes toward the consumption of alcohol have been characteristic of the Finnish culture up to very recently. These may have had their roots in strong religious attitudes that condemn drinking, on the one hand, and in the influence of the temperance movement on the other, both of which have been liable to reinforce people's feelings of guilt. . . . It has been claimed that alcoholism and the noxious effects of drinking are of particularly frequent occurrence in communities whose culture includes ambivalent attitudes toward the consumption of alcohol and where a great deal of guilt is associated with drinking. This hypothesis appears plausible, and Finland can be regarded as a country of which such attitudes are characteristic. . . . The alcohol consumption figures for Finland are low; at the same time, however, the figures indicating the deleterious effects of drinking . . . are among the highest in the world" (1 pp. 19–20).

D. Urban–Rural Differences

In line with the venerable theme of the sinfulness of cities, previous general-population studies in the United States (19, pp. 56, 60–61, 102; 89, p. 640) have found the prevalence of drinking problems to be substantially higher in large cities than elsewhere.[2] Tables 18 and 19 show the distribution of current high scores on specific problems and on an over-all summary problem measure by urbanization and region, with residence in the cen-

[2] The association of urbanization and high rates of drinking does not appear to be universal—see Swiecicki's report on Poland (138).

sus-defined central cities of Standard Metropolitan Statistical Areas (1960 Census) as the most urbanized group and residence in rural areas or in places of less than 2500 population as the least urbanized. Since the wetter and dryer regions as defined differ considerably in the extent of urbanization, Tables 18 and 19 also show results by urbanization in these 2 regions to enable us to gauge the mutual effects of the 2 broad ecological variables.

In all individual problem areas, and on the over-all "current problems score" (Table 18), the central-cities groups show the highest prevalence, whether the comparison is nationwide or regional. Between the rural and the other cities and towns groups, however, the differences tend to be smaller and not all in the same direction. The differences are generally not substantial enough to be reliable, but there seems to be some tendency for the rural areas, and particularly the dryer rural areas, to exceed the other cities and towns in the prevalence of consequences, but for the other cities and towns to be equal or higher on indicators of behavior and psychological involvement.

Combining urbanization with regional comparisons does not greatly change the general findings for region alone: the associations of drinking problems with urbanization seem to have considerable similarity in wet and dry areas. There appears to be some tendency for urban–rural differences in drinking problems, as measured by the over-all problems score, to be accentuated in the dryer regions.

The results by typology (Table 19) reveal some rather more dramatic effects of the interaction of region and urbanization. In the proportion of abstainers, the two variables operate in a strongly additive fashion in the direction which previous studies would have predicted: those living in rural areas are roughly twice as likely as others to be abstainers, as are those living in dryer regions; the two effects are cumulative. On urbanization the distinction is quite definitely between the other cities and towns and the rural areas. On the other hand, urbanization shows a strong direct effect on a high consequences score, but with the distinction between the other cities and towns and the central cities. This effect is additive with a weak reverse relation between consequences and the wetness of the region: in each of the urbanization groups, those living in dryer areas are slightly more likely to show consequences.

TABLE 19.—*Current Problems Typology*[a] *by Urbanization and Region, in Per Cent*

	N	Non-drinker	Drank: No Problems	Potential Problems Only	Heavy Intake or Binge: No Consequences	High Consequences
Central Cities						
Wetter region	343	9	30	26	17	19
Dryer region	184	14	32	20	11	23
Total	527	11	30	24	15	20
Other Cities, Towns						
Wetter region	387	8	44	21	16	10
Dryer region	163	16	44	20	9	11
Total	550	10	44	21	14	10
Rural Areas						
Wetter region	179	14	44	22	10	10
Dryer region	305	31	36	16	6	12
Total	484	24	39	18	7	11
Totals, wetter region	909	10	39	23	15	13
Totals, dryer region	652	22	37	18	8	15

[a] Defined in Table 13 footnote.

The ratio of heavy intake only to tangible consequences shows yet a third pattern. In all three urbanization groups heavy drinking seems more likely to result in consequences in dryer than in wetter regions; but the relation with urbanization is U-shaped, both over-all and in each region. It is the residents of the other cities and towns which seem to be the most protected against the consequences of a given behavior, with the rural areas and central cities roughly equal in this regard. Some possible explanations, in terms of social-class differences and differential community norms, will be discussed elsewhere in this monograph.

Place of residence is obviously one of the demographic variables most subject to change by the respondent himself. There is, therefore, a considerable possibility that residence in the city or in a particular region is a result rather than a cause of drinking problems. "Geographic escape" figures prominently in the conventional symptomatology of the classical disease concept of alcoholism (56, *p.* 5). Our data enable us to make some assessment of the relative importance, and possible interactions, of the urbanization of place of upbringing and the urbanization of the current place of residence. Unfortunately we cannot make the same test for movement between regions, but this seems less likely to be a crucial factor: the slight excess of consequences in dryer regions seems unlikely to be a result of immigration into these regions where emigration generally exceeds immigration, and which does not seem to offer any particular advantages to the heavy drinker.

To allow for sufficient numbers for analysis, the size of current place of residence was dichotomized at above and below 50,000 population. Size of place of upbringing was trichotomized so as to yield categories which indicate a definite move upward or downward in size of place of residence. Thus there are separate categories by dichotomous current urbanization for those brought up in places of under 25,000 population and for those brought up in places of over 100,000. An intermediate group with a defined current urbanization but an indeterminate change in urbanization is omitted from the present analysis.

In the country as a whole (third section of Table 20) abstinence is commoner in those brought up in places of small population, no matter what their current residence. Tangible consequences, on the other hand, are associated with the urbanization of present residence rather than with size of the place of upbringing. But the ratio of heavy intake without consequences to tangible consequences is greater among those brought up in large places, no matter what their current residence. The interaction of these patterns indicates a high probability of social consequences of a given behavior among those who were brought up in rural areas or towns but who now live in cities.

Specification by general area (first two sections of Table 20) shows that the patterns described generally hold true in both types of regions, but are muted in wet regions and correspondingly intensified in dry regions. Abstinence seems to be associated with both measures of ruralism in dryer areas, but only with ruralism of upbringing in wetter areas. The comparison between the two categories of changes on the ratio of behavior to consequences is particularly dramatic in the dryer regions.

TABLE 20.—*Current Problems Typology*[a] *by Size of Place of Upbringing and Present Residence, in Per Cent*

	Upbringing: <25,000		100,000+	
Residence:	<50,000	50,000+	<50,000	50,000+
Dry Region	(N = 380)	(91)	(47)	(64)
Nondrinker	28	19	11	6
Drank: no problems	39	29	40	38
Potential problems only	15	19	32	19
Heavy intake or binge:				
no consequences	5	4	13	20
High consequences	13	30	4	17
Wet Region	(N = 258)	(184)	(105)	(251)
Nondrinker	14	14	5	6
Drank: no problems	42	38	50	33
Potential problems only	22	20	18	27
Heavy intake or binge:				
no consequences	13	12	14	19
High consequences	9	16	13	16
Totals	(N = 638)	(275)	(152)	(315)
Nondrinker	22	15	7	6
Drank: no problems	40	35	47	34
Potential problems only	18	20	22	25
Heavy intake or binge:				
no consequences	8	10	14	19
High consequences	11	21	11	16

[a] Defined in Table 13 footnote.

These data suggest that whether one drinks at all, and perhaps also the general pattern of drinking, are related more to the character of the place of upbringing than to the place in which the respondent resides as an adult. The prevalence of tangible consequences of drinking, however, appears to be more related to the adult place of residence and to be particularly high among those in dryer regions who were brought up in the country but now live in the city. The data do not support a hypothesis that geographical mobility in general is associated with drinking problems, as Smith (132) and others have hypothesized in epidemiological studies of cardiovascular disease; rather, mobility in one direction (into the city) is associated with a higher rate of drinking problems, while mobility in the other direction is associated with a lower rate. This finding, of course, says nothing to the issue of cause: we still do not know if the moving produces the problems or if those already with problems gravitate to the city; perhaps both processes are at work. But we do know that the pattern seems much stronger in a region of the country characterized both by traditional temperance attitudes and, at least in the South, by recent rapid urbanization and industrialization. We are reminded of a further speculation by Achté et al. (1) on the determinants of Finnish drinking problems:

"Until recently the Finnish culture has had a predominantly rural character. Today, however, Finnish society is in a rapid process of transition from an agrarian and rural toward an industrial and urban type of culture. . . . At present only 27 per cent of the inhabitants [of Helsinki, the capital city] are persons born there. Urban culture is freer than rural culture. It permits more freedom, but it is also apt to create ambivalent situations of conflict for those accustomed to different kinds of norms" (pp. 50–51).

E. Socioeconomic Status

Many studies of drinking problems (e.g., 6, 19, 66, 89, 115) have found that problems are more prevalent among the poor than among the remainder of the population, even though drinking at all (and in some contexts drinking fairly regularly and heavily) is more prevalent among persons of higher social status (118; 122, Tables 3 and 4). The data in Table 21 confirm the past findings on each of the problem areas, using a summary measure of socioeconomic status based on Hollingshead's two-factor index of social position (ISP) (51).[3] On many of the problem areas, however, the relationship appears to be J-shaped rather than linear; i.e., it is only the lowest of the four ISP groups which shows results substantially different from the others in many problem areas. This result is mirrored in the distribution of the over-all problems score: the difference in prevalence between the two lowest ISP groups is twice as great as the other differences between adjacent statuses.

Table 22 (bottom section) shows that both drinking problems (particularly high tangible consequences) and abstinence are positively associated with lower ISP in the total population of

[3] The measure is aggregated from the respondent's education and main earner's occupation, with greater weight to occupation (in a ratio of 7:4), as described in Cahalan, Cisin and Crossley (20, p. 228).

TABLE 21.—*Current High Problems by Index of Social Position,*[a] *in Per Cent*

	Lowest ISP (60–77) (N = 281)	Lower Middle (49–59) (411)	Upper Middle (37–48) (401)	Highest ISP (11–36) (468)
Heavy intake	9	5	6	3
Binge	6	3	2	3
Psychological dependence	8	3	4	2
Loss of control	9	5	4	5
Symptomatic drinking	13	10	9	7
Belligerence	12	9	7	6
Wife	19	14	11	6
Friends, neighbors	13	5	5	3
Job	12	5	3	3
Police	6	3	2	2
Health, injuries	10	6	4	5
Financial	10	5	3	2
Current over-all problems	32	22	17	13

[a] From Hollingshead (51).

men aged 21 to 59. The converse of these findings is that drinkers without even minimal problems are over twice as common in the highest status group as in the lowest. As might be expected, the ratio of heavy intake without consequences to consequences is also strongly associated with ISP: the probability of consequences is relatively high in the two lower ISP groups, and particularly high in the lowest group. In the words of the old music-hall song, "It's the poor wot gets the blyme."

When age is controlled (first four sections of Table 22), the broad pattern is for a replication of the relation between low status and both abstinence and tangible consequences of drinking in each age group. All ISP groups also show their highest prevalence of consequences in the youngest age group. There are, however, some suggestive variations between status groups in the association of consequences with age: a relatively high level of consequences appears to persist into middle age in the lowest status group, while the lower-middle group matches the lowest in the prevalence of consequences in the youngest age group but shows a drastically reduced prevalence after age 30.

It remains true in each age group that the ratio of no-consequence heavy drinking to consequences is higher among those

TABLE 22.—*Current Problems Typology*[a] *by Age and ISP, in Per Cent*

	N	Non-drinker	Drank: No Problems	Potential Problems Only	Heavy Intake or Binge: No Consequences	High Consequences
Age 21–29						
Lowest ISP	39	15	18	13	21	33
Lower middle	106	5	26	25	12	33
Upper middle	119	9	33	29	19	11
Highest ISP	87	5	40	23	20	13
Totals	351	7	31	24	17	21
Age 30–39						
Lowest ISP	68	9	27	22	19	24
Lower middle	91	13	45	15	13	13
Upper middle	99	11	39	24	14	11
Highest ISP	144	14	43	24	10	8
Totals	402	12	40	22	13	13
Age 40–49						
Lowest ISP	78	19	23	13	13	32
Lower middle	112	21	44	16	8	11
Upper middle	99	10	49	18	19	4
Highest ISP	138	12	50	23	7	8
Totals	427	16	43	18	11	12
Age 50–59						
Lowest ISP	96	28	21	23	8	20
Lower middle	102	27	36	18	8	12
Upper middle	84	30	35	25	5	6
Highest ISP	99	12	56	18	8	6
Totals	381	24	37	21	7	11
Social Position Total						
Lowest ISP	281	19	22	19	14	26
Lower middle	411	17	38	19	10	17
Upper middle	401	14	39	24	15	8
Highest ISP	468	11	47	22	11	9
Totals	1561	15	38	21	12	14

[a] Defined in Table 13 footnote.

of higher status. Nevertheless, there are some interesting variations between status groups in changes of this ratio with age. The probability of consequences of a given behavior remains very high at all ages in the lowest status group. In the highest status group, however, there appears to be some tendency for the ratio to decline with age, so that heavy intake without consequences is relatively more prevalent in the youngest age group. This could be viewed as indicating that the protections of those with high status against the consequences of their behavior apply most strongly during a period of youthful sowing of wild oats; or, alternatively, as indicating that when the behavior itself is relatively rare, as it is among middle-aged persons of high status, it is somewhat more exposed to consequences.

Like place of residence, social status is a demographic variable subject to considerable change in adult life. Whether low social status is more a cause or a consequence has long been an issue, for instance, in discussions of the epidemiology of schizophrenia. Table 23 throws some light on the dimensions of this question for drinking problems in the comparison of intergenerational change in ISP, i.e., whether or not the respondent's ISP is lower than his father's as determined by the full-range ISP score (11 to 77 points). Table 23 suggests that those now of lower ISP who have moved down from their father's position may be a little more likely to drink at all and to have tangible problems with their drinking than all others of lower ISP. Thus downward social mobility appears to have some effect independent of the effect of the social position which is the result of the process. This does not tell us whether downward mobility is a cause or a consequence of drinking problems but tends to confirm that the question is of interest at least in the sense that there is a relationship to explain. The ratio of no-consequence heavy drinking to consequences is rather similar in the two low ISP groups, suggesting that vulnerability to consequences is more a function of current status than of prior social position.

The results of Table 23 also suggest some ambiguity, however. The relationship with social mobility is certainly weaker than the relationship with social position per se. And the relationship between consequences and mobility almost evap-

TABLE 23.—*Current Problems Typology*[a] *by Intergenerational Change in ISP among Respondents of Low ISP, by Age, in Per Cent*[b]

Respondents' ISP:	High	Low	
Change from father's ISP:[c]		Down	Other
Total Sample	(N = 302)	(181)	(495)
Nondrinker	13	14	18
Drank: no problems	44	29	30
Potential problems only	18	18	18
Heavy intake or binge: no consequences	12	16	12
High consequences	13	24	21
Age 21–39	(N = 157)	(91)	(245)
Nondrinker	12	8	10
Drank: no problems	38	24	28
Potential problems only	21	21	22
Heavy intake or binge: no consequences	13	19	16
High consequences	17	29	24
Age 40–59	(N = 145)	(90)	(250)
Nondrinker	15	20	26
Drank: no problems	51	33	33
Potential problems only	15	16	15
Heavy intake or binge: no consequences	10	12	8
High consequences	10	19	18

[a] Defined in Table 13 footnote.

[b] N3 sample only; N2–N3 typology measure.

[c] "Change down" is determined by comparing the respondent's and father's full ISP scores (range 11–77). Data on father's ISP are missing in 84 cases; these are included in the "other" category on change from father's ISP.

orates among middle-aged men. Since the social status reported of the father is probably as of his middle age, the possibility is raised that with further and more refined testing the relationship might evaporate.

Discussions of the relationship of social status and drinking behavior since Dollard's study (38) have tended to assume the existence of a simple relationship holding for all measures of drinking behavior and of status, and for all stages of the life cycle and places of residence. Recent probings of these assumptions have suggested their untenability: that there may be no single form of relationship that holds for all measures and in all situations (118, 122). Accordingly, it seems worth while to explore the interactions of socioeconomic status and the life-cycle and place-of-residence variables in their effects on the drinking-problems typology.

In Table 24 the relationships of the drinking-problems typology with social status are superimposed upon the relationships with age and family status. With a couple of small exceptions, low age, being unmarried and low ISP all contribute to the probability of consequences of drinking and a low ratio of heavy intake without consequences to consequences. Here socioeconomic status does not greatly affect the previously discussed relationships with abstinence, except that abstinence is particularly prevalent among older married men when they are of lower ISP.

The relationship of the drinking-problems typology with social status has a somewhat more complicated set of interactions with the previously discussed relationships with region and urbanization (Table 25). Abstinence is almost uniformly higher in those living in rural areas, in the "dryer" regions and of lower status, even after controlling for each of the other variables. The one exception is cities in dry regions, in which, as noted in a previous paper (122, *Table 3*), abstinence seems to be slightly more common among those of higher ISP. Generally speaking, however, region and urbanization seem to be more strongly associated with abstinence than is ISP.

Table 25 shows that the variations in prevalence of consequences by city size in each region appear to be almost totally specific to those of lower ISP. The differences by city size in consequences among those of lower ISP are very large; in both regions, the rate in central cities is over twice that in rural areas. In dry-area cities nearly half of those of low ISP had tangible consequences. In their effects on the ratio of heavy intake without consequences to consequences, region and ISP are roughly additive: the risk of consequences is increased by living in a dry region and also by being of lower ISP. The previously described U-shaped relationship with city size, however, almost disappears when ISP is added to the analysis: among those of high ISP, the degree of protection against consequence is directly proportional to urbanization, especially in the wetter regions; but among those of low ISP, the protection is least

TABLE 24.—*Current Problems Typology*[a] *by ISP, Age and Family Status, in Per Cent*

	N	Non-drinker	Drank: No Problems	Potential Problems Only	Heavy Intake or Binge: No Consequences	High Consequences
HIGH ISP						
Age 21–39						
Living with wife and children	284	12	44	24	11	9
Living with wife, no children	83	7	30	29	25	8
Living with neither wife nor children	82	7	30	24	20	18
Age 40–59						
Living with wife and children	279	14	49	19	11	7
Living with wife, no children	405	19	43	25	7	7
Living with neither wife nor children	36	11	56	25	8	0
LOW ISP						
Age 21–39						
Living with wife and children	215	11	35	19	14	21
Living with wife, no children	36	6	19	28	25	22
Living with neither wife nor children	53	8	21	17	13	42
Age 40–59						
Living with wife and children	233	24	36	15	9	15
Living with wife, no children	115	29	27	23	6	16
Living with neither wife nor children	40	13	23	15	15	35

[a] Defined in Table 13 footnote.

TABLE 25.—*Current Problems Typology*[a] *by ISP, Region and Urbanization, in Per Cent*

	N	Non-drinker	Drank: No Problems	Poten-tial Problems Only	Heavy Intake or Binge: No Conse-quences	High Conse-quences
High ISP						
Wetter Regions						
Central cities	154	8	35	28	20	9
Other cities, towns	269	6	49	23	15	7
Rural areas	93	11	46	26	9	9
Totals	516	7	44	25	15	8
Dryer Regions						
Central cities	112	15	38	24	12	11
Other cities, towns	86	14	44	23	9	9
Rural areas	155	28	43	17	5	7
Totals	353	21	42	21	8	9
Low ISP						
Wetter Regions						
Central cities	189	11	25	24	14	27
Other cities, towns	118	13	34	18	20	16
Rural areas	86	17	42	19	11	12
Totals	393	13	31	21	15	20
Dryer Regions						
Central cities	72	13	21	14	11	42
Other cities, towns	77	18	44	17	8	13
Rural areas	150	33	29	15	6	17
Totals	299	24	31	15	8	22

[a] Defined in Table 13 footnote.

for city dwellers in both regions, and is only small also for rural dwellers in the dryer regions. It is in the cities, then, and particularly in the wetter-region cities, that ISP most dramatically affects the chances of a given drinking behavior resulting in consequences.

F. Religion

Alcohol has played an important historical role in many religious rituals; and religions, as major agencies of social control in traditional societies, have commonly been sources of prescriptions and proscriptions concerning drinking. In the United States, the importance of the association also rests on the historical association between 19th-century fundamentalist and conservative Protestant revivals and the temperance movement (49).[4]

The continuation of these historical connections between religious affiliation and use of alcohol has been well documented, for example, in the first national survey in the present series (20, *pp. 55–61*): Among Catholics and liberal Protestants there were relatively few abstainers and many heavy drinkers, most Jews drank at least a little but few drank heavily, and conservative Protestant denominations ("conservative," that is, in terms of taking a strong stand in the past in favor of complete abstinence) show a fairly high percentage of abstainers. The second national study in this series found that Catholics had an above-average rate of problem drinking, and Jews a very low rate (19, *p. 103*).

This combined N2–N3 sample provides a sufficient number of interviews to analyze in some detail the association of religious affiliation with drinking problems in the relatively high-risk group of men aged 21 to 59. It should be borne in mind that while our data undoubtedly measure associations between religion and drinking problems, they should not be taken as indicating causality or even homogeneity within each religious category. For example, as we shall see below, there are considerable differences by ethnicity within each religious category.

Table 26 (bottom section) presents findings on the current-problems typology by the various religious denominations. Within this national sample of men aged 21 to 59, Catholic and liberal Protestant groups ("liberal," that is, in not taking a pronounced historical antidrinking stand) have about 90% who drink, and an above-average proportion with drinking problems. Among the latter, slightly more had a higher rate of heavy intake or binge potential problems as compared to consequences (largely interpersonal problems). In contrast, the conservative Protestants had a relatively high proportion (24%) who said

---

[4] A full discussion and probing of the relationship between religious affiliation and drinking problems is the subject of a dissertation, using the present national samples, by Seifert (129).

TABLE 26.—*Current Problems Typology*[a] *by Region and Religion, in Per Cent*

	N	Non-drinker	Drank: No Problems	Potential Problems Only	Heavy Intake or Binge: No Consequences	High Consequences
Wetter Regions						
Catholic	389	7	37	23	20	14
Jewish	34	3	62	27	6	3
Liberal Prot.	112	5	48	25	13	9
Conservative Prot.	268	18	35	22	10	15
No Religion	54	4	44	22	13	17
Other[b]	52	8	29	29	21	14
Dryer Regions						
Catholic	98	5	36	22	15	21
Jewish[c]	6	(2)	(3)	(1)	0	0
Liberal Prot.	108	16	36	23	13	12
Conservative Prot.	395	28	38	16	4	14
No Religion	30	10	37	17	17·	20
Other[b] [c]	15	(6)	(4)	(2)	(2)	(1)
Total						
Catholic	487	6	37	23	19	16
Jewish	40	8	60	25	5	3
Liberal Prot.	220	10	42	24	13	11
Conservative Prot.	663	24	37	19	6	14
No Religion	84	6	42	20	14	18
Other[b]	67	15	28	25	19	12

[a] Defined in Table 13 footnote.

[b] Other Religion includes Protestant, no denomination; Liberal Protestant includes Episcopalian, Presbyterian, Lutheran and other liberal denominations; Conservative Protestant includes Methodist, Baptist and Fundamentalist denominations.

[c] Unpercentaged because of small N.

they did not drink during the last 3 years, and a relatively lower ratio of heavy intake without consequences to tangible consequences. From this finding one may infer that the conservative Protestants may be subject to an above-average amount of social pressure against drinking and intemperate drinking. Those with no religious affiliation reported the highest prevalence of consequences.

The findings among Jews reflect the pattern discussed earlier, of a low rate of both abstinence and drinking problems. Of this small sample of Jewish men, 60% drank but without having any drinking problems within the prior 3 years.

Since both the historical temperance movement and reli-

gious fundamentalism were both specially strong in what we
have termed the dryer regions of the country (roughly the same
territory as covered by the term "Bible belt"), it seemed plausible that religious patterns might well vary by region (Table
26, top sections). Religious groupings are differentially distributed between the regions: 55% of the men in wetter regions are Catholic or liberal Protestant, but only 32% in the
dryer regions; 29% in the wetter regions are conservative
Protestant, but 61% in the dryer regions. Nevertheless, if we
standardize results on the problems typology in the two areas
to hold constant the proportion of conservative Protestants
(table not shown), the unstandardized results from each area
are not changed by more than a couple of percentage points
in any category. This is not to say that the fact that there is a
majority of Catholics and liberal Protestants in the wetter
areas, and a majority of conservative Protestants in the dryer
areas, may not set the tone for attitudes and laws about drinking in the two areas, affecting to a considerable extent the
conservative Protestants' behavior and attitudes in the wetter
areas and those of the Catholics and liberal Protestants in the
dryer areas.

The effect of region on religious patterns varies from one
religious category to another. Abstinence does not vary between regions among Catholics, but is increased in the dryer
region among both categories of Protestants. On the other
hand, region does not have a substantial relationship to the
prevalence of consequences in either category of Protestants,
but is higher in dryer regions among Catholics. The ratio of
heavy intake without consequences to consequences drops
in dryer regions among Catholics and conservative Protestants, but not, apparently, among liberal Protestants. The probability of consequences relative to heavy intake or binge drinking appears to be particularly high among conservative
Protestants in dryer regions, tending to bear out the hypothesis
that they are subject to even more social pressure against drinking and excessive drinking than are Catholics and liberal
Protestants.

G. Ethnoreligious Groups

As we have noted, the meaning of the association between
religion and drinking problems is considerably affected by the

ethnic mix of the religious categories in any population. The alcoholism literature commonly uses Italian and Irish patterns as contrasting examples, although both Italy and Ireland are predominantly Catholic. Conversely, when ethnicity is defined in terms of "which one nationality did most of your family come from?" in these U.S. national samples, Irish conservative Protestants are about as common as Irish Catholics, although their "Irishness" is in most cases filtered through many generations of residence in the rural South.

Table 27 shows results on the drinking typology in those groups jointly defined by religion and ethnicity for which there was a sufficient base for reporting. Ethnicity appears to be more or less secondary to religious affiliation in the two largest nationality groups, British and German. As we expected, religious affiliation is also clearly predominant in conservative Protestants who report Irish ancestry. Among Irish and Italian Catholics, on the other hand, ethnicity makes a great difference: the prevalence of consequences of drinking, and the probability of consequences of a given behavior, are both considerably greater in the Irish than in the Italians. Black conservative Protestants and Latin-American or Caribbean-origin Catholics both also show a considerably higher rate of consequences, and a higher probability of consequences of a given behavior, than is true for the average of their religious category.

These statistics should be treated with some caution in drawing conclusions. In the first place, the clustered-sampling technique on which our data are based cannot guarantee representativeness for segments of the population which are, like Black conservative Protestants and Latin-American Catholics, both a relatively small part of the total population and highly segregated and unevenly distributed geographically. It is thus possible that the sample of these groups we happened to draw is not representative of the whole population of men aged 21 to 59 in the group. On substantive grounds, also, the findings need to be viewed in context: both groups have, on the average, high proportions of persons with lower ISP, living in wetter-area cities, lower age and recent rural-to-urban immigration—all factors which we have found to be associated with a high rate of drinking problems.

TABLE 27.—*Current Problems Typology*[a] *by Ethnoreligious Categories,*
in Per Cent[b]

	N	Non-drinker	Drank: No Problems	Potential Problems Only	Heavy Intake or Binge: No Consequences	High Consequences
British: Catholic	34	12	35	27	18	9
Liberal Prot.	48	13	31	38	8	10
Conservative Prot.	204	20	39	22	3	16
Irish: Catholic	77	4	33	27	16	21
Conservative Prot.	74	27	46	15	3	10
German: Catholic	76	7	40	21	22	11
Liberal Prot.	86	12	47	24	9	8
Conservative Prot.	120	22	42	21	7	9
Italian: Catholic	64	5	52	14	23	6
Latin Amer.: Catholic	42	10	10	21	17	43
Jewish	40	8	60	25	5	3
Black: Conserv. Prot.	97	18	23	16	13	31
East. European: Catholic	71	6	38	21	21	14
Other: Catholic	114	7	42	26	11	13
Liberal Prot.	56	5	43	18	23	11
Conservative Prot.	158	34	35	15	8	8

[a] Defined in Table 13 footnote.
[b] Categories with small *N*s are omitted. Ethnicity is defined by religion for Jews, by race for Blacks, by "country most ancestors came from" for the remainder. Religious categories are defined as in Table 26 footnote.

Controlling in part for these factors (by comparing the proportion with high consequences in a subsample limited to
lower ISP persons living in wetter-region central cities, not
shown in Table 27), we found that half of the 24 Latin-American Catholics, 29% of the 38 Black conservative Protestants,
and 21% of the 127 other persons in the subsample reported
high consequences. The ethnoreligious differences remain,
but are considerably reduced by the increased prevalence in
the residual group, so that it is quite possible they would
disappear altogether if a comparison fully matched on "life
chances" could be made.

H. Cumulative Relations of Social Differentiation
and Drinking Problems

In the preceding section we have discussed the association
between drinking problems and social-differentiation vari-

ables taken one, two and three at a time. This procedure is illuminating in its own right, showing the nature and extent of relationships and the patterns of interaction between the social differentiation variables. But the analysis cannot be extended conveniently beyond a few variables at once, and there is no doubt that some of the same variance in drinking problems is being "accounted for" in the different analyses, since the independent variables are themselves interrelated. Percentage tables can provide neither a summary comparison of the power of different independent variables in "predicting" drinking problems, nor an estimate of the total variance in drinking problems accounted for by all the independent variables taken together.

Answers to such questions can be readily derived by using summary statistics such as the correlation coefficient or reduction-in-sum-of-squares measures and by applying methods of sequential multivariate analysis to yield estimates of the total variance explained and of the relative contributions of the different predictors—such as the stepwise multiple regression technique and the automatic interaction detector analysis referred to in the previous chapter.

In the present analysis, and in our extension of it in the succeeding chapter, we shall direct our analysis back to the N3 sample only and the N3 optimal scales, to allow using the additional data collected only from that sample. We shall concentrate our attention on two ordered dependent variables: problematic intake, which yields information on the correlates of relatively heavy drinking behavior, and the full tangible consequences score which is our best measure of the occurrence and severity of the social problems of drinking.

For the present, we confine ourselves to the general indicators of social differentiation with which we have been concerned in this chapter, seeking an answer to the question of how much of the variance in drinking behavior and consequences can be explained by these general dimensions of the individual's formal position in society. In Table 28, we show the interrelations of the social-differentiation measures to be used in this analysis, as measured by the correlation coefficient, and also the pairwise correlation of each measure with the two dependent variables. As we have noted, religion and

TABLE 28.—Intercorrelations of Social-Differentiation Measures and Drinking Criterion Scores[a]

	9	10	11	12	13	14	15	16	17	18	19	20	Tangible Consequences	Problematic Intake
1. British	-.16	.17	-.12	-.09	-.14	.01	-.12	-.01	.03	-.24	.02	.21	-.00	-.02
2. Irish	-.02	.06	.05	.02	.01	.04	-.07	-.02	-.04	.11	-.06	-.03	-.03	-.03
3. German	-.05	.14	-.06	-.10	-.09	-.04	-.08	-.04	-.06	-.04	.19	-.04	-.07	-.07
4. Italian	.07	-.22	.15	.11	.06	-.01	-.01	-.02	.01	.22	-.00	-.16	-.04	-.01
5. Latin American—Caribbean	.14	-.30	.04	.12	.19	-.09	.19	.02	.17	.22	-.07	-.11	.16	.19
6. Jewish	-.06	-.11	.11	.10	.07	.10	-.11	.02	-.05	-.12	-.06	-.13	-.05	-.05
7. Black	.16	.11	-.00	-.02	.17	-.03	.21	.17	.12	-.17	.08	.23	.14	.17
8. East. European	.05	-.15	.19	.15	.14	-.00	.06	-.02	.01	.23	-.04	-.21	.00	-.03
9. Father's isp low		-.13	-.10	.03	.00	.09	.43	-.07	.11	.11	-.16	.11	.12	.04
10. Father born in U.S.			-.21	-.33	-.24	-.18	-.06	.06	.00	-.29	.03	.30	.03	.01
11. Size of place of upbringing				.25	.47	-.15	-.16	.05	.01	.28	-.01	-.34	-.03	.08
12. Wet region of residence					.31	-.01	-.00	.00	.06	.31	-.12	-.30	-.01	.04
13. Urbanization of residence						-.10	.01	.18	.12	.24	-.08	-.26	.07	.18
14. Age							.10	-.06	-.22	-.03	-.01	.04	-.10	-.18
15. Isp low								.05	.22	.11	-.15	.09	.24	.15
16. Home-role instability									.11	-.09	.03	-.01	.13	.17
17. Work-role instability										-.03	-.05	.05	.26	.17
18. Catholic													.02	.11
19. Liberal Prot.													-.03	-.04
20. Conservative Prot.													.00	-.09

[a] Religion and ethnicity are dichotomized from the measures used in Tables 26 and 27. Isp constructed as in Table 21, but used here in full-range form (11–77). Size of place of upbringing used in 7-category form, urbanization of residence in 8-category form, with highest score for most urban on both. Age used in full (1-year steps) form. Home-role instability adds together a score on present marital and parenthood status (Tables 14, 15) with whether the respondent has ever had a divorce (highest score = not now married, has been divorced). Work-role instability adds together scores on job changes and unemployment in the last 3 years and whether the respondent has ever been out of work.

ethnicity are spread for this purpose into a series of dichotomies.

In general, the correlations between the indicators of social differentiation are quite modest. There are some predictable exceptions: several variables centering around a coastal city heartland division are highly correlated—urbanization, size of place of upbringing, wet region, being Catholic and not being conservative Protestant. Low ISP shows strong relationships with father's low ISP, being Black or Latin American and having a relatively unstable work history. There are also some strong connections between religion and ethnicity, as we discussed earlier in this chapter.

The correlations with tangible consequences are definitely highest on those variables just noted as intercorrelated indicators of disadvantaged status, including ISP, Black and Latin American ethnicities and work-role instability. These variables are also fairly highly correlated with problematic intake, as are home-role instability, urbanization and youthfulness.

As would be expected, variables from these lists show up early in the multiple regressions on tangible consequences and problematic intake (Table 29). In fact, in spite of their relatively higher intercorrelations, which might have led us to expect only one or two to appear early in the regressions, the variables with the high initial correlations with the criteria dominate the early steps of the regressions. The strongest predictions of tangible consequences of drinking, then, are made by variables indicating a disadvantaged status: under- and unemployment, low status and disadvantaged ethnic groups. In spite of their relatively high intercorrelations, each contributes separately to the prediction of tangible consequences of drinking. The only other variables entering the regression fairly early are home-role instability and age.

On the regression predicting problematic intake many of the same variables appear, although with different relative contributions, as can be seen from the partial correlations. Work-role instability disappears from the early steps of the regression, while a variable from the "urban wet" clustering, Catholic, enters. Over-all, the social-differentiation variables predict problematic intake a little better than tangible consequences. The total power of the variables in explaining the variance in either criterion (as measured by the square of the

TABLE 29.—*Multiple Regressions of Social-Differentiation Measures on Criterion Scores*[a]

	Including Role Histories		Excluding Role Histories	
	Multiple Correlation Coefficient	Partial Correlation	Multiple Correlation Coefficient	Partial Correlation
A. TANGIBLE CONSEQUENCES				
Work-role instability	.26	.17		
Isp low	.32	.17	.24	.20
Home-role instability	.33	.08		
Latin American–Caribbean	.34	.10	.29*	.12
Black	.35	.07	.30*	.10
Age (neg.)	.36	−.07	.27*	−.11
Entering all predictors	.37		.32	
B. PROBLEMATIC INTAKE				
Latin American–Caribbean	.19	.15	.19	.14
Black	.26	.15	.26	.13
Age (neg.)	.31	−.16	.31	−.16
Home-role instability	.33	.14		
Urbanization			.32	.12
Catholic	.35	.10		
Isp low	.36	.09	.34	.11
Entering all predictors	.39		.37	
C. TANGIBLE CONSEQUENCES (SUBSAMPLE)[b]				
Isp low	.30	.23	.30	.24
Work-role instability	.36	.20		
Size of place of upbringing (neg.)	.41	.10		
Wet region (neg.)	.42	−.07		
Catholic (neg.)			.36	−.15
Latin American–Caribbean			.38	.12
Liberal Prot. (neg.)			.39	−.10
Entering all predictors	.45		.42	

[a] See footnote to Table 28. Predictors are listed in order of entry into the regression, except at asterisk (*). Predictors for which no multiple correlation coefficients are shown do not enter that particular regression in the steps shown. The partial correlations shown are after the entry of the last predictor shown in the table for that regression. Variance numbers cited in the text, however, are derived from the square of the multiple correlation coefficient after all predictors used have entered the regression.

[b] Subsample with problematic-intake scores of 1 to 3 only ($N = 256$).

final multiple correlation coefficient) is not, however, very great—in the range of 10 to 15%.

Work-role and home-role instability have a somewhat ambiguous relation with the criteria. Of course, like some other social-differentiation variables, the direction of ordering between them and the criteria is not determinate. For instance, there is always a lively possibility in cross-sectional data that the drinking problems precede the low ISP rather than vice versa. The problems with using the role instability variables to predict consequences extend beyond this: the same sequence of events can sometimes figure in both the predictor and the criterion variable, since job and spouse problems form a part of the tangible consequences score.

Accordingly, the regressions were recalculated without these two predictors (Table 29-A and B, columns 3 and 4). The strength of the over-all prediction from the social differentiation variables drops somewhat, particularly for the regression on tangible consequences. Youthfulness appears earlier in this regression, but the first few steps are not substantially changed. On problematic intake, the main change in the early steps of the regression is the replacement of one "urban wet" variable (Catholic) by another (urbanization). Removal of the two role-instability variables, then, does not greatly affect the relative power of the other predictors.

In Table 29-C an answer is attempted to the question implicit in much of the discussion in the earlier part of this chapter—what are the predictors of consequences for a given level of behavior? For this purpose a subsample of the N3 respondents is used, consisting of those with a score of 1 to 3 on problematic intake. We are, then, assessing the relative and total power of the social differentiation variables in predicting tangible consequences of drinking among those who, as heavy drinkers, put themselves at some risk of the consequences. Interestingly, in spite of the restriction of range in this subsample, the over-all prediction of tangible consequences by the social differentiation variables is stronger within this subsample than in the total sample, accounting for 18 to 20% of the variance. The early entrants in the regression include ISP, work-role instability and two indices of "rural dry" environment (having been brought up in a low-population place and

living in a dry region). Omission of the role-instability variables brings into prominence Latin American or Caribbean
ethnicity and two alternative indicators of a dry background—
being neither Catholic nor liberal Protestant, which more or less
amounts to being conservative Protestant. The predictors of
consequences among those with heavy drinking behavior, then,
amount to being poor and being from a traditionally dry background.

The results of AID[5] analyses on the entire N3 sample are
shown in Figure 6. The predictors entering in the early stages
of the analysis are, by and large, the early entrants in the regressions; however, some illuminating specifications and differentiations emerge. Work-role instability is a notably stronger
predictor of drinking problems among those of lowest ISP
than in the rest of the sample, accounting for 12% of the unexplained variance among those of ISP 60–77, but for only
3% among those of ISP 11–59. As might have been expected
from the relations with age discussed in the early sections
of this chapter, treating age as an interval scale, as was done
in the regressions, masks some discontinuities in its relationship with drinking problems. On the other hand, allowing it
to appear in 5-year intervals without constraints in the AID
analysis does take maximum advantage of fortuitous combinations. The results on tangible consequences suggest that with
only 3 social differentiation variables the sample can be parti-
tioned into groups with very different rates of consequences:
a large group ($N = 698$) aged 25 and over having an ISP under
60 (high status) with a mean tangible consequences score of
1.06; an intermediate group ($N = 232$) with a mean score of
2.58; and a small high group ($N = 48$) of those with low status
(ISP 60+) and high work-role instability (essentially, out of
work within the last 3 years) with a mean score of 6.50. Similarly, on problematic intake, the mean score of the 654 persons
aged 30 or more and of an ethnicity other than Black or Latin
American Caribbean is 0.30, the mean score of a middle group
of 275 respondents is 0.70, and the mean score of the 42 persons
of Black or Latin American Caribbean ethnicity and with a
religion other than conservative Protestant is 1.60. For both

---

[5] This technique has been described in Chapter 3.

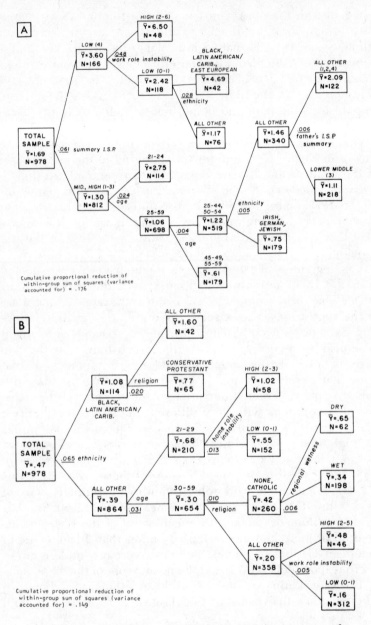

FIGURE 6.—*AID Analyses of Social-Differentiation Measures of Tangible Consequences* (A) *and Problematic Intake* (B)

analyses, the proportion of variance in the dependent variable accounted for by the tree as shown is 18%.

I. Summary

The leading correlates of problem drinking among men aged 21 to 59 are index of social position, residence in cities, rural to urban mobility, age, ethnoreligious group, home-role instability and work-role instability.

The youngest adult men (aged 21 to 24) have the highest rates on all 12 types of problems. The findings imply that the 20s may be an even more crucial time to apply remedial measures against problem drinking than are the 30s or 40s.

Those of lowest social position have much higher rates of drinking problems than do others, and they tend to get into trouble over drinking out of all proportion to the frequency with which they drink heavily. The rates of interpersonal problems from drinking (problems with the wife, friends and neighbors, relatives, the police and on the job) tend to be highest among those of lower status in the largest cities.

When regions of the country are classified (on the basis of historical and current temperance sentiments and drinking patterns), those living in the dryer areas have a lower rate of drinking problems. Those interviewed in the dryer areas also have a relatively higher prevalence of problems with interpersonal consequences, particularly in relation to the prevalence of heavy drinking behavior. The highest relative ratio of external consequences of drinking to heavy intake or binge drinking are found in the larger cities and rural areas of the dryer regions, which have larger proportions from old American and conservative Protestant stock. These patterns of problem-drinking behavior, as compared with the remainder of the country, appear similar in many respects to those found in Finland as compared with Denmark (28): low rates of per capita consumption coupled with high relative rates of social consequences in communities where there is a great deal of ambivalence about the respectability of drinking at all, and where guilt and explosive behavior are associated with drinking.

To sum up the interactions of independent variables in predicting problem drinking, Table 29 shows that the primary predictors of tangible consequences of drinking are those denoting or strongly correlated with low status: low ISP, Black or Latin American–Caribbean ancestry or work-role instability. The leading predictors of problematic intake (heavy intake or binge drinking) are also low-status variables. However, youth is a much stronger predictor of problematic intake than of tangible consequences, and home-role instability is also a somewhat stronger predictor of problematic intake. When the analysis of the correlates of tangible consequences is limited to those who are also high on problematic intake (Table 29-C), the best predictors are indicators of low status (ISP, work-role instability and Latin American–Caribbean ancestry) plus the indicators of dryness of the area (relatively dry region, size of place of upbringing and religious affiliation other than Catholic or liberal Protestant).

While the next chapter will show that additional sociopsychological or personality variables are of considerable importance as additional intervening variables in rates of problem drinking, it will be seen that the traditional demographic variables of age, socioeconomic status, urbanization, ethnic origin and religion, by themselves, predict problem drinking rather well. This attests to the heavily environmental character of the development of drinking problems.

Chapter 5

The Correlates of
Drinking Problems

A. *Childhood Predictors*

IN THE PRECEDING CHAPTER we confined our predictors to social-differentiation variables which tend to be relatively invariant and thus are commonly assumed to be logically prior to the dependent variable in Lazarsfeldian survey analyses (46, 52, 64). This assumption is open to some question; while changes on one of these variables in any given year may be unusual, change over a longer period of time is considerably more common. With dependent variables such as ours, whose very conceptualization involves a consistency over time and whose natural history is measured in terms of years rather than weeks, the assumption of priority for the social-differentiation variables is particularly questionable, especially when, as for urbanization, we found that change sometimes predicts problems better than any particular status on the variable.

A set of predictors with a fair certainty of preceding drinking problems, then, includes only a subset of the social-differentiation variables used in the preceding chapter. To this subset we can add a number of variables describing characteristics of the respondent's childhood, since consistent drinking problems are rare in the U.S.A. before the later teen-age years.

An analysis considering childhood predictors is of tactical importance in terms of the logical priority which can be assumed for these predictors over the criterion score. There are also some strategic benefits in such an analysis. Variables which give indications of childhood history bear on the question of the existence and strength of a "predisposing factor" which Jellinek (58) and others have postulated in the etiology of alcoholism. Some indication of the strength of such a putative factor should be gained from comparisons of the childhood histories of adults with and without drinking problems.

Furthermore, there is a relatively coherent and substantially based literature, drawing on longitudinal follow-ups of childhood samples, which has found an association of adult drinking problems with youthful aggressiveness, lack of control and impulsivity (62, 77, 80, 81, 110, 111), and with "low family social status; parental inadequacy, in particular antisocial behavior on the part of fathers; and serious antisocial behavior, as evidenced by records of juvenile court appearances and a clinic record of a variety of symptoms of antisocial behavior" (111, *p. 410*). In a previous study in the present series, Knupfer[1] found that adult drinking problems were associated with marital disruption and unhappiness, low socioeconomic status and drinking problems in the child's family, and with indicators of childhood stress and delinquency; and several of the same variables—parents' drinking practices and problems, and childhood delinquency—were also associated with adult heavy drinking (70, *p. 126*).

The list of childhood variables included in the N3 survey was designed to some extent with this literature in mind. They include (in addition to social-differentiation variables which are the respondent's "birthright") indicators of his parents' drinking and scores describing qualities and the history of his childhood: (*1*) childhood unhappiness, including both the respondent's over-all appraisal of his happiness and highly correlated items on troubles and lack of cohesion in the family; (*2*) childhood hardship, including the respondent's evaluation of hardships from poverty, prejudice and changes in neighborhood and school; (*3*) family disruption, combining parental separation and absence of a parent; and (*4*) youthful rashness, including playing hooky from school, getting sent to the principal for acting up and getting in fist fights as a youth.

The vertical dimension in Table 30 lists all the variables used in the analysis and shows those interrelations which were not included in Table 28. Care must be taken in interpreting these data. Several of the "birthright" variables (ethnicity, religion and region) are in fact defined in terms of the

---

[1] See Table 1 in KNUPFER, G. Ex-problem drinkers. Presented at the 4th Conference on Life History and Psychopathology, St. Louis, Missouri, November 1970. The work of Knupfer and her associates is now being compiled for publication by Walter B. Clark.

TABLE 30.—*Intercorrelations of Childhood Characteristics and Criterion Scores*[a]

	1	2	3	4	5	6	7	8
1. Father abstains		.42	−.63[b]	−.28	−.09	.00	−.04	−.09
2. Mother abstains			−.40	−.68[b]	−.06	.04	−.07	−.13
3. Father's max. quantity				.50	.21	.06	.11	.19
4. Mother's max. quantity					.15	.01	.11	.19
5. Youthful rashness						.13	.07	.22
6. Childhood hardship							.23	.40
7. Family disruption								.24
8. Childhood unhappiness								
Father's ISP low	−.02	.15	.04	−.17	.04	.18	.06	.06
Father born in U.S.	.07	.03	.01	.08	.06	.01	.03	.04
Size of place of upbringing	−.24	−.23	.16	.20	.11	−.04	.04	.09
Wet region	−.14	−.15	.08	.06	−.08	−.01	−.03	−.02
British	.02	.03	−.01	.03	−.01	−.08	−.08	−.06
Irish	.00	−.01	.00	.01	.02	−.04	−.04	−.04
German	−.03	−.07	.04	.02	−.05	−.09	−.03	.01
Italian	−.05	−.09	−.02	−.00	.05	−.04	−.00	−.02
Latin Amer.–Caribbean	−.01	−.06	.09	.09	.06	.13	.10	.09
Jewish	−.03	−.02	−.06	−.01	−.04	.01	−.05	.01
Black	.10	.11	−.12	−.07	.06	.34	.21	.09
Eastern European	−.08	−.07	.09	.06	−.03	.04	.00	.06
Catholic	−.14	−.14	.17	.08	.04	−.05	.03	−.03
Liberal Prot.	−.05	−.10	.01	.04	−.05	−.12	−.08	−.05
Conservative Prot.	.19	.24	−.17	−.16	−.02	.12	.01	−.03
Tangible consequences	−.02	−.07	.14	.08	.15	.20	.13	.21
Problematic intake	−.06	−.11	.21	.18	.20	.11	.14	.17

[a] Father's and mother's maximum quantities drunk on an occasion are coded in 9 steps ranging from abstainer to 20+ drinks. Youthful rashness, childhood hardships, family disruption and childhood unhappiness are described in Appendix C.

[b] Intercorrelation of a full-range variable and a dichotomization of the same variable.

respondent's adult status and are included here primarily because they seemed likely to be good approximations of status at birth. The questions about parents' drinking refer to lifetime patterns ("the most" the parent "has had to drink at any one time") and not necessarily to the time of the respondent's childhood. All of the questions are, of course, asked of the respondent as an adult and in the same questionnaire as the criterion variables so that response sets and selective adult memories of childhood are very real possibilities.

The intercorrelations of parents' drinking patterns are very high, and parents' abstinence in particular shows some relation with rural and dry-region residence, conservative Protestant religion and Black ethnicity (Table 30). On the other hand, parents' maximum quantities of drinking show a stronger relation than does abstinence with both the criterion scores.

Parents' maximum quantities also show a fairly strong relationship with three of the childhood-history variables, although not with childhood hardships. Childhood hardships and family disruption predictably show strong relations with low-status indicators: Black or Latin American–Caribbean ethnicity and low father's ISP. The childhood history variables are fairly highly intercorrelated and have relatively strong relations with the criterion variables, but relatively weak relations with the remaining childhood items.

Table 31 shows the results of regression analyses on the birthright and childhood-history variables. By omitting parents' drinking patterns, we can examine the predictive power of variables which not only precede the drinking problems but are relatively remote from them conceptually. To the extent that variations in drinking problems may be attributed to these relatively remote variables, public policies toward drinking problems which concentrate on drinking and proximate behaviors and attitudes may be limited in their effect.

Table 31-A shows that the birthright and childhood-history variables provide predictions of tangible consequences of roughly equal strength, each accounting for about 7% of the variance; the two sets together account for 10% of the variance. The strongest indicators among the "birthright" variables are those indicating low status (Black or Latin American–Caribbean ethnicity, and low father's ISP). Having a native-born father also enters the regression early, after partialling out the indicators of low status, although its raw relation with the criterion is negligible. Family disruptions appears to make the smallest contribution among the childhood-history variables, particularly when the effects of birthright variables are partialled out by forcing them into the regression first. Childhood unhappiness appears as the strongest childhood-history predictor.

Table 31-B reveals that birthright variables (10% of the variance) make a somewhat stronger prediction of problematic

TABLE 31.—*Multiple Regressions of Birthright and Childhood-History Variables on Criterion Scores*[a]

	Multiple Correlation Coefficient	Partial Correlation	Multiple Correlation Coefficient	Partial Correlation
A. TANGIBLE CONSEQUENCES				
	Birthright Alone		*Birthright after Forcing in Childhood History*	
			.27	
Latin Amer.–Caribbean	.16	.17	.30	.14
Black	.22	.12	.31	.08
Father's ISP low	.23	.09	.32	.08
Father born in U.S.	.24	.08	.32	.06
	Childhood History Alone		*Childhood History after Forcing in Birthright*	
			.26	
Childhood unhappiness	.21	.12	.31	.12
Childhood hardship	.25	.11	.33*	.06
Youthful rashness	.26	.10	.33*	.09
Family disruption	.27	.06	.33	.04
B. PROBLEMATIC INTAKE				
	Birthright Alone		*Birthright after Forcing in Childhood History*	
			.26	
Latin Amer.–Caribbean	.19	.21	.30	.19
Black	.26	.20	.34	.18
Conservative Prot. (neg.)	.29	−.13	.35	−.12
Father born in U.S.	.30	.09	.36	.07
	Childhood History Alone		*Childhood History after Forcing in Birthright*	
			.32	
Youthful rashness	.20	.16	.36	.14
Childhood unhappiness	.24	.10	.37	.10
Family disruption	.26	.09	.37	.05
Childhood hardship[b]	.26	.03	.37	−.03

[a] Variables listed in order of entry into the stepwise regression, except those asterisked (*). See descriptions of variables in Table 30. The two left-hand columns show the results of the first 4 steps of a stepwise regression on the set of variables named, including the partial correlations after the fourth step. The two right-hand columns show the results of the first four steps of a stepwise regression after another set of variables have been "forced" into the regression at step 0. The partial correlation is calculated as of the completion of the last step shown.

[b] Negative relation in at least one but not all partial correlations.

intake than do the childhood-history variables (7%); the combined predictive power reaches 13%. As we found in Chapter 4, indicators of wet background contribute prominently to the prediction of problematic intake but not of tangible consequences. Youthful rashness also appears to be a far better predictor of problematic intake than of tangible consequences, while childhood unhappiness loses all power in predicting problematic intake when the birthright variables are partialled out. Youthful rashness is our closest indicator to the "antisocial acts" of the Robins, Bates and O'Neal analysis (111); the partial correlations suggest that it is a better predictor of heavy drinking than of problems consequent to the drinking and that, while its predictive power on tangible consequences is not greatly affected by partialling out the birthright variables, its power is somewhat diminished when the childhood-history variables are taken into account.

In Table 32 we examine the predictive power of parent's drinking variables, both in their own right and when birthright and childhood-history variables are considered. Parental drinking patterns provide a somewhat better prediction of problematic intake (6% of the variance) than of tangible consequences (4%). In neither regression is the predictive power even near the strength of that from other childhood predictors. The primary predictor of both tangible consequences and problematic intake is a high maximum quantity of drinking by the father and the second strongest predictor is the father's abstinence. Both problematic intake and tangible consequences, then, have a curvilinear relationship with the father's drinking, so that both heavy drinking and, to a lesser extent, abstinence on the part of the father predict heavy intake and problems on the part of the son. Although the mother's drinking patterns have considerable raw correlations with the criteria—in fact, the mother's abstinence shows higher negative correlations than does the father's—mother's drinking patterns add essentially nothing to the predictive power of the father's patterns for either criterion, and what little is added for tangible consequences is in fact predicting in the opposite direction from the father's patterns.

These results are certainly suggestive, if not conclusive, about the relationships between parents' and children's drink-

TABLE 32.—*Multiple Regressions of Parents' Drinking and Other Childhood Variables on Criterion Scores*[a]

	Multiple Correlation Coefficient	Partial Correlation	Multiple Correlation Coefficient	Partial Correlation
A. TANGIBLE CONSEQUENCES				
			Parents' Drinking after Forcing Birthright and	
	Parents' Drinking Only		Childhood History	
			.33	
Father's max. quantity	.14	.15	.35	.10
Father abstains	.17	.09	.35	.07
Mother abstains (neg.)	.17	−.04	.35	−.06
Mother's max. quantity (neg.)	.17	−.01	.35	−.03
	All Childhood Variables			
Childhood unhappiness	.21	.15		
Latin Amer.–Carib.	.25	.15		
Black	.29	.14		
Father's max. quantity	.31	.11		
Youthful rashness	.31	.08		
Size of place of up- bringing (neg.)	.32	−.08		
B. PROBLEMATIC INTAKE				
			Parents' Drinking after Forcing Birthright and	
	Parents' Drinking Only		Childhood History	
			.37	
Father's max. quantity	.21	.17	.40	.14
Father abstains	.23	.09	.41	.08
Mother's max. quantity	.24	.06	.41	.03
Mother abstains (neg.)	.24	−.00	.41	−.02
	All Childhood Variables			
Father's max. quantity	.21	.19		
Black	.29	.21		
Latin Amer.–Carib.	.34	.17		
Youthful rashness	.36	.14		
Conservative Prot. (neg.)	.37	−.10		
Father abstains	.38	.09		

[a] Variables listed in order of entry into the stepwise regression. See footnote to Table 31.

ing. Since they do not match previous results with much looser
measures of children's drinking patterns (20, *pp.* 77–79; 44,
p. 16), further research is needed.[2] The present results would
suggest the importance of male-role modeling, and specifically of a moderate drinking style on the part of the father,
in the prevention of drinking problems in the son.

The right-hand columns of Table 32 show the residual power
of parents' drinking in the regressions after other childhood
variables are forced in: parents' drinking does raise the explained variance in problematic intake from 14 to 17% but
does not add much to the explanation of tangible consequences
by other childhood variables. The final partial correlations of
father's maximum quantity, however, retain some strength.

The initial steps of a regression in which all childhood variables, including parents' drinking, are allowed to enter without constraints on the stepwise procedure are also shown in
Table 32. Each of the three domains of predictors we have
discussed are represented relatively early in both regressions.
All the childhood variables together account for 12% of the
variance on tangible consequences, but 10% of this is accounted
for by just four: childhood unhappiness, the two low-status
ethnicities and father's maximum quantity of drinking. Similarly, 13 of the 17% total explanation of variance on problematic intake by childhood predictors can be accounted for by
father's maximum quantity, the two low-status ethnicities and
youthful rashness.

Figure 7 illustrates an AID analysis using the same variables.
Roughly the same proportion of the variance is explained by
this method as by the regressions, but some strong discrimina-
tions can be made on the basis of childhood predictors between
groups with high and low mean scores on the criteria. Thus,
combining the two groups with the highest means (combined
mean = 5.12, N = 93) on tangible consequences and comparing them with the group with the lowest mean (0.66, N = 329)
and the residual middle groups (1.73, N = 556) yields extreme
groups, one with about three times and the other with about
one-third of the risk of the middle groups.

This suggests that childhood indicators do allow differential predictions about the chances of problematic intake

[2] A partial replication of the results on a San Francisco sample can be
found in Chapter 8.

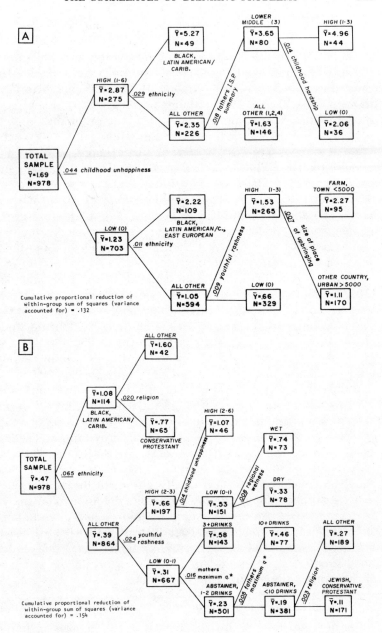

FIGURE 7.—AID Analyses of Childhood Predictors of Tangible Consequences (A) and Problematic Intake (B) (*"No answer" cases excluded)

and tangible consequences in adulthood, but these are not especially strong; not as strong, in fact, as those which could be made on the basis of social-differentiation variables alone (Chapter 4). Improved measures would no doubt enhance the predictions, but it seems unlikely that childhood factors by themselves will constitute either a necessary or sufficient condition for the development of adult drinking problems.

Many theories of alcoholism postulating genetic or childhood etiologies are cast in deterministic language, as if the genetic trait or childhood trauma will be both a necessary and sufficient explanation of institutionalization for alcoholism at, say, age 40. Yet the tests of these theories are usually in terms of statistical significance: Is there any association greater than chance which can be detected? Our evidence on childhood predictors suggests that there is a relationship, and there is at least one study which provides impressive evidence for a genetic influence greater than chance in adult alcoholism (101). But the strength of the relationships found here is not very great, and it seems unlikely that any conceivable refinement of concepts, measures and techniques will bring them closer to being deterministic relationships. The form of the tests, in fact, do not in any way follow the deterministic language common in hypotheses about "predisposing X factors," and the relations found should not be taken as undercutting or eliminating other "rival" etiologies. It may well be, for instance, that a genetic factor manifests itself in the form of a disposition to vomit after the second drink, providing a constitutional protection against drunkenness. Such a factor undoubtedly would show a statistically significant genetic influence on alcoholism, but it would hardly eliminate the necessity to consider other etiologies. Any genetic factor in alcoholism, in fact, seems likely to be secondary to cultural and environmental factors. A full longitudinal study may well establish what is already suggested by our cross-sectional data, that childhood predictors are secondary to adult history in the strength of their prediction of drinking problems.

B. Correlates of Drinking Problems

For the remainder of this chapter our attention turns to simple association since the question of priority between the characteristics of adults we are now about to consider and our dependent variables cannot be answered with our present cross-sectional data.[3] We shall continue to deal with our "predictors" in broad conceptual domains, assessing the relative strengths of contributions within each domain and the relations between the contributions of the different domains, but we shall now recombine some so that we are left with four broad domains of predictors: (1) Social-differentiation and childhood-history variables; (2) Personality variables; (3) Social-situation and habits variables; (4) Drinking-context variables, including parents' drinking patterns.

The boundaries between these categories are defined somewhat arbitrarily at points which seem to yield the greatest analytical clarity. As a result, the third category, the social-situation and habits variables, is rather a miscellany which seems to reflect more the respondent's history and interaction with his social situation than generalized dimensions of his personality.

Our procedure is to start our analysis from a base of the social-differentiation and childhood-history variables, whose relations with our criterion scores have already been explored in some detail. As we add the new domains and examine the regression equations formed on them, and their effects on the over-all regression equations when the new domain is added, we can gain some understanding of the relative power of variables in each domain in predicting drinking problems and heavy drinking, and of the extent to which each domain adds to the predictive power or merely provides an alternative set of predictors to the other domains.

As with childhood history, the personality, social-situation and drinking-context variables arise out of substantial work on the correlates of drinking problems and alcoholism. In general, the present variables are expanded and sharpened versions of the variables used in the N2 study (19); many are drawn from the work of Jessor and his associates (61) and Knupfer and her associates (70).[4]

Our modes of analysis, multivariate regressions and AID, explicitly assume the possibility of a complex multifactor etiol-

---

[3] Such limited longitudinal evidence on priority as we can yet muster can be found in Cahalan (19, *Chapter 6*).

[4] See Footnote 1 to this Chapter.

ogy of the dependent variables. If we were convinced that we were going to find a single necessary and sufficient cause, multivariate forms of analysis would be superfluous. But the likelihood of multifactor etiologies of drinking problems is well recognized and a number of such models have been proposed (e.g., 8; 19; 35, *p*. 49; 61; 69). The evidence so far can only be said to have established the plausibility (rather than the truth) of any of these models, and does not get us very far in differentiating between the various models in terms of degrees of plausibility. This remains true for the results of our present analysis and will continue to be true until (*a*) the forms of relation between variables in the models (interacting, specifying, potentiating, etc.) are made sufficiently explicit to allow for mathematical testing and the techniques for systematically testing all the possible forms are assembled; (*b*) areas where crucial tests would differentiate between the theories are identified; and (*c*) full longitudinal data on which to make the tests become available. For the moment, we are examining the various bumps in the blanket for clues to the general shape, rather than establishing the form and structure of what lies underneath.

C. Personality and Attitude Variables

We have collected here the variables which are primarily measures of intrinsic characteristics of the respondent—his personality, state of mind and general attitudes—rather than items concerned with his interactions with the social environment. For example, we have excluded the respondent's perception of the nonhelpfulness of others which, while reflecting something of his general state of mind, also reflects elements of a verifiable external social situation.

The nine variables included admittedly comprise a rather arbitrarily limited domain. More complete descriptions of these variables can be found in Appendix C. Some representative components are as follows:

Somatization: bothered by all sorts of pains and ailments, shortness of breath when not exercising (obviously these items may reflect physical realities and thus may, but should not automatically, be assumed to measure psychosomatic hypo-chondria).[5]

Affective anxiety: feels tense or nervous; depressed; is the worrying type.

Physical depression: cannot get going at times; hard time making up his mind.

Psychiatric symptoms: feels as if about to go to pieces; bothered by useless thoughts.

Intrapunitiveness or guilt: does things he regrets afterward; hard not to give up hope of amounting to something.

Alienation and paranoia: things are getting worse in spite of what people say; people often talk behind his back.

Impulsivity: often acts on the spur of the moment; does not let risk of getting hurt stop him from having a good time.

Tolerance of deviance ("it's not really bad"): getting into fights; having premarital sex; not paying back money owed, etc.

Sociability: likes to be with people; likes to belong to clubs; people think of him as very social.

The first six are included in the general area of "ego-resiliency," the first factor which has been found to emerge in factor analyses of the Minnesota Multiphasic Personality Inventory (12, *p. 111*), while impulsivity and tolerance of deviance fall into the general area of the second factor of "ego control" (12, *p. 115*). The first grouping is more relevant to traditional psychiatric descriptions of neurotic and psychotic disorders, while the second bears more relation to the themes of undercontrol and deviance in the delinquency literature, from which the childhood longitudinal studies cited earlier in this chapter primarily derive.

Table 33 shows the intercorrelations of these personality variables and their correlations with the other predictors introduced thus far and our two criteria. The first six variables are strongly intercorrelated and correlated a little less strongly with impulsivity. Correlations with and between the remaining two variables, tolerance of deviance and sociability, are systematically lower and in most cases negligible. All the variables except sociability show moderately strong correlations with the

---

[5] KNUPFER, G. The use of psychosomatic symptom lists in mental health surveys. Presented at the 1st annual meeting of the Society for Epidemiological Research, Washington, D.C., May 1968.

TABLE 33.—*Intercorrelations of Personality and Demographic, Childhood and Criterion Variables*[a]

	1	2	3	4	5	6	7	8	9
1. Somatization		.41	.46	.45	.36	.30	.20	.01	.03
2. Affective anxiety			.48	.53	.39	.38	.23	.11	−.07
3. Physical depression				.52	.47	.42	.30	−.01	−.10
4. Psychiatric symptoms					.53	.43	.32	.03	.00
5. Intrapunitiveness						.51	.39	−.01	.00
6. Alienation							.38	.11	−.06
7. Impulsivity								.12	.02
8. Tolerance of deviance									−.06
9. Sociability									
Father abstains	−.04	−.06	.00	−.04	.01	.02	.03	−.10	.00
Mother abstains	.04	−.07	.01	−.04	.00	.03	−.04	−.19	.03
Father's max. quantity	.04	.09	.02	.10	.03	.08	.10	.13	−.02
Mother's max. quantity	−.05	.08	.01	.08	.00	.00	.08	.24	−.02
Youthful rashness	.09	.10	.08	.15	.18	.18	.23	.16	−.02
Childhood hardship	.21	.19	.20	.23	.25	.32	.12	.07	.01
Family disruptions	.00	.07	.08	.11	.14	.14	.04	.01	−.05
Childhood unhappiness	.14	.28	.21	.32	.25	.30	.16	.14	−.07
Father's ISP low	.13	.06	.11	.09	.12	.13	.03	−.06	.04
Father born in U.S.	−.03	.03	.02	.04	.09	.08	.07	.01	−.06
Size of place of upbringing	−.05	.02	−.05	.01	−.04	−.03	−.03	.16	.03
Wet region	.03	.04	.06	.02	−.04	−.01	−.02	.13	.01
Age	.12	−.08	.00	−.08	−.02	−.07	−.16	−.18	−.03
Urbanization	−.04	−.02	−.01	.00	−.03	.00	.00	.14	.08
ISP low	.20	.07	.17	.14	.19	.29	.11	.00	.02
Home-role instability	.03	.05	.07	.12	.16	.09	.10	.20	.06
Work-role instability	.11	.13	.13	.18	.16	.22	.13	.14	−.03
British	.02	.04	−.01	.03	.02	−.02	.07	−.01	−.03
Irish	−.02	.02	−.05	−.03	−.02	−.08	.01	−.03	.01
German	−.07	−.10	−.05	−.10	−.07	−.11	−.06	−.05	−.03
Italian	.04	.02	.07	.02	.00	−.01	.02	−.02	.01
Latin Amer.–Carib.	.10	.05	.03	.14	.05	.07	.07	.06	−.02
Jewish	−.03	−.04	−.04	−.04	−.06	.02	−.04	.08	.03
Black	.01	.02	.08	.11	.19	.20	.01	.09	.13
East European	.00	−.03	.05	.02	.01	.01	−.02	.00	−.03
Catholic	−.02	−.03	.00	−.05	−.08	−.03	−.03	−.05	.03
Liberal Prot.	−.04	.00	−.06	−.05	−.08	−.12	−.05	−.02	.01
Conservative Prot.	.05	−.01	.05	.05	.11	.09	.05	−.09	−.01
Tangible consequences	.20	.24	.22	.27	.36	.30	.28	.15	.06
Problematic intake	.11	.15	.11	.18	.20	.20	.22	.22	.02

[a] Defined in Appendix C and Table 28 footnote.

criteria; tolerance is more strongly correlated with problematic intake than with tangible consequences, but the reverse is true of the remainder of the variables.

None of the correlations with the remainder of the variables, except the two childhood-history measures (hardship and unhappiness) which seem closest to covering the same domain as the first six personality variables, reach as high as .25, so that it seems likely that the personality variables will not merely reexplain the variance in the criteria already explained by the social differentiation variables. The two "ego-control" measures show modest associations with youth, as does somatization with higher age; and there is a general tendency for indicators of low status (low ISP, work-role instability and being Black) to show positive correlations with the psychiatrically relevant characteristics, as the long tradition of community studies of mental health would indeed lead us to expect.

As the correlations with the criteria in Table 33 would suggest, the regressions using the personality variables alone (regression I for both criteria in Table 34) provide a considerably better prediction of tangible consequences, with 20% of the variance explained, than of problematic intake (12%). In comparing these results with those in Table 29 using the social-differentiation predictors, we find that the personality variables appear to better predict tangible consequences than do the social-differentiation measures, but that the reverse is true for problematic intake. This pattern does provide some modest support for a two-stage model where social differentiations are the primary predictors of heavy drinking behavior per se—behavior which at least conceptually is necessary but not sufficient for drinking problems—while personality variables are the best predictors of tangible consequences of drinking emerging among those who have put themselves "at risk" by heavy drinking. This kind of model has been proposed by Knupfer (unpublished) and by Robins, Bates and O'Neal (111, p. 411).

Intrapunitiveness contributes the largest portion of the explanation of variance on tangible consequences, while tolerance and impulsivity show the highest partial correlations with problematic intake. On intrapunitiveness and impulsivity there would seem to exist the possibility of cross-contamination with the criterion, in the sense that they contain items describ-

TABLE 34.—*Multiple Regressions of Personality Variables on Criterion Scores*[a]

	Multiple Correlation Coefficient	Partial Correlation
I. *Personality Alone*	A. TANGIBLE CONSEQUENCES	
Intrapunitiveness	.36	.23
Tolerance of deviance	.39	.14
Impulsivity	.41	.11
Alienation	.42	.11
Sociability	.43	.08
	B. PROBLEMATIC INTAKE	
Impulsivity	.22	.11
Tolerance of deviance	.29	.20
Intrapunitiveness	.32	.08
Alienation	.33	.06
Psychiatric symptoms	.33	.05
II. *Personality without Intrapunitiveness, Impulsivity*		
	A. TANGIBLE CONSEQUENCES	
Alienation	.30	.19
Psychiatric symptoms	.34	.12
Tolerance of deviance	.36	.12
Sociability	.37	.09
Affective anxiety	.38	.07
	B. PROBLEMATIC INTAKE	
Tolerance of deviance	.22	.20
Alienation	.28	.12
Psychiatric symptoms	.30	.08
Sociability	.30	.04
Affective anxiety	.30	.03
III. *Personality after Forcing in Social Differentiation and Childhood History*		
	A. TANGIBLE CONSEQUENCES	
	.40	
Intrapunitiveness	.47	.23
Impulsivity	.49	.12
Tolerance of deviance	.50	.12
Sociability	.50	.07
	B. PROBLEMATIC INTAKE	
	.42	
Impulsivity	.44	.11
Tolerance of deviance	.45	.14
Intrapunitiveness	.46	.07
Somatization	.46	.05

[Continued on next page]

TABLE 34.—*continued*

	Multiple Correlation Coefficient	Partial Correlation
IV. *Social Differentiation and Childhood History after Forcing in Personality*		
A. TANGIBLE CONSEQUENCES		
	.44	
Work-role instability	.47	.14
Isp low	.48	.13
Latin Amer.–Caribbean	.49	.09
Childhood unhappiness	.49	.07
B. PROBLEMATIC INTAKE		
	.34	
Latin Amer.–Caribbean	.37	.14
Black	.39	.16
Catholic	.41	.13
Age (neg.)	.42	−.11

ᵃ Variables listed in order of entry into the regression. See footnote to Table 31. The personality variables are described in Appendix C.

ing behavior which the respondent could be using in reference to drinking behavior (intrapunitiveness—"I do many things which I regret afterwards"; impulsivity—"I often spend more money than I think I should"). The regressions were accordingly recalculated omitting these two variables (regression II). The over-all predictive power of the personality domain is somewhat reduced, but not drastically, for alienation and psychiatric symptoms more or less fill the breach in the regressions on both criterion scores. Consequently, any possible contamination in the sense that we have mentioned seems unlikely to alter drastically the relative positions of the predictor domains with respect to the criteria, so intrapunitiveness and impulsivity have been retained for the succeeding analyses.

A more substantive issue is the meaning of the patterns revealed in the regressions using the personality variables alone. Intrapunitiveness is a measure of the respondent's feelings about his behavior in everyday life and, specifically, his feeling that his behavior fails to conform to his ideals. We may expect his ideals to be related to and influenced by the norms of his significant others; in fact, his guilt is likely to be an internalization of the attempts of significant others to make him see the error of his ways. Analogously, our measures of tangible consequences tend, except at the rare extreme ends of the scores, to be measures of the significant others' negative reactions to the respondent's drinking behavior. The relation between intrapunitiveness and tangible consequences can be seen, then, as the relation between an internalized general disowning of one's own behavior and specific drinking-oriented criticisms and sanctions imposed on the behavior by the respondent's social environment. This kind of relationship is also suggested by discussions of the symptomatology of alcoholism, such as Jellinek's references to the social environment in connection with "guilt feelings about his drinking behavior" and "persistent remorse" (58, *pp. 678, 681*). This perspective would lead us to expect strong feelings of guilt to accompany other behavior which significant others are likely to find obnoxious, so that intrapunitiveness is a strong predictor of other behavioral deviances, including mental disorder (and indeed, in Table 33 there is a particularly high correlation with psychiatric symptoms).

There is, then, reason to suspect that intrapunitiveness, as we have measured it, is particularly likely to be a reflection rather than a prime mover of the respondent's tangible consequences of drinking. In a study now under way, we are attempting (albeit with retrospective data) to start disentangling the temporal priorities by asking additional items on guilt in childhood and when drinking is not involved.

The association of problematic intake with impulsivity, and the association of both with low social status and youth, suggest that part of what we are measuring is heavy drinking as part of a cultural complex of youthful devil-may-care "hellraising," particularly obtrusive in traditionally dry parts of the country, a theme to which we shall return later.

In spite of small raw correlations, sociability does make some contribution, particularly in the prediction of tangible consequences, suggesting that interactions with the other personality variables to some extent mask its relationship with the criterion. Nevertheless, dropping sociability along with all personality scores other than tolerance of deviance, impulsivity and intrapunitiveness would not greatly affect the ability of the domain to predict either criterion.

The contribution of the personality scores to the regressions remains fairly constant when we force the social-differentiation and the childhood-history variables into the regressions first (regression III, Table 34), although the partial correlation of tolerance is somewhat reduced, especially on problematic intake. The personality scores thus make a considerable addition, particularly on tangible consequences, to our accounting power on the basis of the social-differentiation and childhood-history variables alone, raising the proportion of the variance explained on tangible consequences from 16 to 26% and on problematic intake from 18 to 22%. Conversely, when the personality variables are forced in and the variables in the other domains allowed to enter freely (regression IV), the improvement in prediction from the addition of the social-differentiation variables is more marked in the regression on problematic intake (12 to 22%) than in that tangible consequences (20 to 26%). The only change from the regressions in Table 29 is the disappearance of home-role instability from the early steps of the regressions on both predictors, suggesting that this variable explains some of the same variance in our criteria as the personality variables.

D. Social-Situation and Habits Variables

As we have noted, this domain is a miscellany of the remaining predictors which do not specifically refer to drinking attitudes and environment. It includes several measures of the extent and quality of the respondent's relationships with his social environment, which are likely to include some specific effects of drinking as part of their general measurement of the extent of spoiling of relationships. The variables are listed below; fuller details can be found in Appendix C.

Nonhelpfulness of others: the potential sources of help in an emergency, co-workers, neighbors, wife, relatives, police, etc., that the respondent feels would not be helpful.

Home-role friction: a score combining dissatisfaction with marriage and the extent to which conditions round home are annoying or troublesome, with the latter doubly weighted for the unmarried.

Work friction: a score based on conditions troublesome at work, worry about work, and preference for a different occupation.

Lack of neighborhood roots: a score combining the number of moves in the last 10 years, never socializing with neighbors, and conditions troublesome round the neighborhood.

Social activity: a score combining items on frequent visiting and get-togethers.

Drug habits: a score combining the respondent's use of sedatives (excluding alcohol), stimulants and smoking.

Health problems: a score totaling the occurrence (within the last 3 years and before that) of a list of relatively severe medical conditions, particularly those considered likely to have some relation to drinking problems.

Tables 35 and 36 show, respectively, the intercorrelations of these variables (as well as of the drinking-context variables we shall consider in the next section) and their correlations with the other predictors and the criterion variables.

Drug habits and health problems show a fairly high intercorrelation, though the direction of causation implied is ambiguous. The relationships of nonhelpfulness with lack of neighborhood roots and with the role-friction variables is partly spurious, in view of the composition of the nonhelpfulness score. Home- and work-role frictions seem to be moderately strongly correlated; otherwise, the intercorrelations between variables in this residual domain are modest.

The correlations of the two role-friction variables and health problems are notably higher with tangible consequences than with problematic intake (Table 36). All three of the correlations with tangible consequences are likely to reflect the fact that tangible consequences are but a part of a larger sea of possible troubles. On the other predictors in this domain, the correlations with the two criteria are roughly equal and of modest strength.

Some of the correlation patterns between the predictors shown in Table 36 are worth noting. The relations of the adult situational variables with the social-differentiation variables are not very strong, except for the relatively strong relations of health problems to higher age, social activity and lack of neighborhood roots to youthfulness, nonhelpfulness to home- and work-role instabilities (again, partly implied by the content of the variables), social activity to home-role instability, and lack of neighborhood roots to work-role instability. These stronger relations, it will be noted, are all with adult social-differentiation rather than with birthright variables.

Several of the variables in Table 36 show high association with the six ego-resiliency personality variables: drug habits,

TABLE 35.—*Intercorrelation of Social-Situation and Drinking-Context Variables*[a]

	2	3	4	5	6	7	8	9	10
1. Nonhelpfulness of others	.02	.12	.06	.13	.11	.04	.12	.04	.14
2. Social activity		.07	.08	−.07	.00	−.03	.11	.11	.08
3. Lack of neighborhood roots			.08	.14	.12	−.05	.14	.13	.14
4. Drug habits				.11	.10	.21	.16	.10	.15
5. Home-role friction					.18	.08	.16	.08	.10
6. Work friction						.13	.00	.00	.07
7. Health problems							−.06	−.09	−.01
8. Heavy-drinking context								.36	.46
9. Others' attitudes to respondent's drinking									.36
10. Respondent's attitudes to drinking									

[a] Defined in Appendix C.

home- and work-role friction and health problems. The association of health problems with somatization is a reminder that somatic complaints are not necessarily psychosomatic. The correlations with drug habits are of special interest, since this provides some measure of possible alternative pharmacological recourses besides alcohol for those in an unhappy state of mind. The correlations of drug habits with somatization, affective anxiety, psychiatric symptoms, childhood unhappiness and youthful rashness are about as high as the correlations of either of our two criteria with these variables (Tables 30 and 33), suggesting that heavy drinking and problems with alcohol may be viewed as one among several overlapping alternative recourses or sequels of a depressed state of mind.

The relatively high associations of childhood unhappiness with lack of neighborhood roots and nonhelpfulness suggests a common strain among these three variables of withdrawal from close relations, since childhood unhappiness includes several items indicating the lack of affective bonds in the childhood family.

The first regression on each criterion in Table 37 shows the first steps of an analysis including all the predictor variables except those directly concerned with drinking contexts and attitudes. The combination of the social-situation and habits variables with the personality and adult social-differentiation variables completely freezes the childhood-attribute variables (birthright and childhood-history measures) out of the early stages of the regression on tangible consequences. The three

TABLE 36.—Correlations of Social-Situation and Drinking-Context Variables with Personality, Demographic and Childhood Variables and Criterion Scores[a]

	Nonhelpfulness of Others	Social Activity	Lack of Neighborhood roots	Drug Habits	Home-role Friction	Work Friction	Health Problems	Heavy-Drinking Context	Others' Attitudes to R's Drinking	R's Attitudes to Drinking
Somatization	.07	.01	.05	.20	.10	.18	.42	.04	−.02	.06
Affective anxiety	.14	.01	.09	.28	.23	.34	.34	.10	.04	.10
Physical depression	.09	.02	.04	.16	.17	.24	.30	.02	−.04	.07
Psychiatric symptoms	.17	.02	.12	.26	.23	.26	.29	.04	.00	.10
Intrapunitiveness	.13	−.01	.08	.22	.19	.28	.23	.00	−.07	.04
Alienation	.26	−.04	.13	.14	.22	.32	.17	.01	−.05	.09
Impulsivity	.11	.05	.12	.17	.14	.14	.06	.17	.04	.20
Tolerance of deviance	.21	.06	.13	.12	.09	.03	−.01	.21	.17	.29
Sociability	−.01	.18	−.02	−.04	−.06	−.07	.06	.11	.01	.09
Father abstains	−.09	−.02	−.04	−.06	−.10	−.07	.02	−.24	−.25	−.22
Mother abstains	−.08	−.07	−.13	−.08	−.11	−.07	.08	−.33	−.36	−.24
Father's max. quantity	.06	.06	.15	.14	.10	.07	−.01	.27	.43	.28
Mother's max. quantity	.11	.13	.14	.12	.07	.08	−.07	.28	.48	.27
Youthful rashness	.14	.04	.12	.18	.01	.11	.02	.12	.13	.17
Childhood hardship	.13	−.02	.12	.12	.12	.22	.15	−.03	−.09	.03
Family disruptions	.07	.02	.05	.08	.00	.09	−.02	.05	.05	.03
Childhood unhappiness	.23	.03	.18	.23	.16	.20	.08	.07	.02	.13

Father's ISP low	−.03	−.12	−.02	−.08	.04	.11	.07	−.08	−.17	−.05
Father born in U.S.	−.01	.09	.05	.08	−.08	−.02	−.02	−.06	.07	−.05
Size of place of upbringing	.11	.01	−.05	.05	.07	.04	−.07	.20	.11	.20
Wet region	.07	−.05	−.03	−.06	.08	−.01	−.05	.16	.05	.16
Age	−.14	−.21	−.34	−.08	−.05	−.10	.19	−.21	−.27	−.23
Urbanization	.18	.09	.03	−.02	.05	.04	−.03	.23	.05	.22
ISP low	.09	−.05	.02	.03	.01	.15	.17	−.11	−.13	−.01
Home-role instability	.22	.22	.04	.11	−.02	−.02	.07	.11	−.01	.09
Work-role instability	.17	.12	.22	.09	.11	.12	.08	.07	.04	.14
British	.01	.02	−.02	.04	−.01	−.04	.00	−.01	.05	−.02
Irish	−.02	.06	.02	.04	.00	−.04	.00	.06	.03	.01
German	−.06	.00	.03	−.03	−.03	−.04	−.06	.00	.07	−.01
Italian	−.01	−.02	−.08	−.01	.06	.02	−.02	.07	.02	.04
Latin Amer.–Carib.	.06	.01	.12	.03	.12	.07	.04	.06	.00	.09
Jewish	.00	.03	−.02	−.02	.01	.03	.02	−.04	−.01	.06
Black	.13	.02	.10	.02	.01	.11	.06	−.02	−.11	.03
East European	.04	.00	−.05	.00	−.01	.00	−.01	.01	−.02	.05
Catholic	.00	−.04	−.09	−.02	.05	.01	−.03	.21	.15	.16
Liberal Prot.	−.03	.01	.01	.04	−.01	−.06	−.08	.07	.06	.02
Conservative Prot.	−.08	.00	.04	−.05	−.06	.02	.08	−.26	−.21	−.19
Tangible consequences	.11	.11	.15	.21	.21	.13	.18	.27	.03	.24
Problematic intake	.13	.14	.13	.21	.14	.08	.02	.42	.20	.29

a Defined in Appendix C and Table 28 footnote.

TABLE 37.—*Multiple Regressions of Social Situation, Social-Differentiation and Childhood-History Variables on Criterion Scores*[a]

	Multiple Correlation Coefficient	Partial Correlation
I. Social Situation, Social Differentiation, Childhood History and Personality Entering Freely		
A. TANGIBLE CONSEQUENCES		
Intrapunitiveness	.36	.22
Work-role instability	.41	.14
Isp low	.44	.17
Home-role friction	.46	.13
Impulsivity	.47	.11
Drug habits	.48	.11
Tolerance of deviance	.49	.10
Social activity	.50	.10
B. PROBLEMATIC INTAKE		
Impulsivity	.22	.13
Tolerance of deviance	.29	.17
Latin Amer.–Caribbean	.34	.16
Black	.38	.18
Drug habits	.41	.15
Catholic	.43	.14
Social activity	.44	.12
Intrapunitiveness	.45	.09
II. Social Situation, Social Differentiation and Childhood History Entering Freely after Forcing in Personality		
A. TANGIBLE CONSEQUENCES		
	.44	
Work-role instability	.47	.13
Isp low	.48	.16
Home-role friction	.49	.12
Drug habits	.50	.10
Social activity	.51	.09
B. PROBLEMATIC INTAKE		
	.34	
Latin Amer.–Caribbean	.37	.15
Drug habits	.39	.15
Black	.42	.17
Catholic	.44	.14
Social activity	.45	.13
III. Personality Entering Freely after Forcing in the Other Variables		
A. TANGIBLE CONSEQUENCES		
	.47	
Intrapunitiveness	.51	.20
Impulsivity	.52	.11
Tolerance of deviance	.53	.10
Sociability	.53	.06
B. PROBLEMATIC INTAKE		
	.46	
Impulsivity	.47	.09
Tolerance of deviance	.48	.13
Intrapunitiveness	.49	.06
Somatization	.49	.04

[a] See footnote to Table 31.

domains of adult attributes are each represented in the early steps of this regression by their two or three strongest predictors: work-role instability and low ISP from the adult social-differentiation variables; intrapunitiveness, impulsivity and tolerance from the personality variables; and drug habits, home-role friction and social activity from the social-situation and habits variables. A comparison with Tables 29 and 34 shows that the addition of the social-situation and habits variables into the regression does not substantially affect the relative strengths or the partial correlations of the early entrants from the other domains. The final multiple correlation coefficient from the regression is .53, so that about 28% of the variance in tangible consequences is explained—a relatively modest increase from the 25% without the social-situation and habits variables.

In the regression on problematic intake, the birthright variables (Latin American and Black ethnicities and Catholic religion) maintain a strong early showing; the partial correlation of being Catholic is, in fact, increased after the personality and habits variables are partialled out. The three personality scores which entered first in the regression on the personality domain only (Table 34) enter here in the same order and with no great change in their partial correlations; it seems likely that their early entrance accounts for youthfulness dropping out of the early steps of the regression. Only drug habits and social activity from the social-situation and habits domain enter in the first eight steps. The addition of this domain brings the final multiple correlation to .49, improving the proportion of variance explained from 21 to 24%.

Regressions II and III in Table 37 show, respectively, the results of forcing all the nonpersonality variables into the regression and then allowing the personality variables to enter freely, and the opposite procedure of forcing all the personality variables in and then allowing the rest to enter freely. Even after we have added the social-situation and habits variables to what we may broadly call the social-factors variables, we find that the personality and social-factors variables are not sufficiently interrelated to affect substantially the partial correlations of each group's leading predictors. Nevertheless, the over-all improvement in predictive power from adding one set of predictors to the other is quite modest, except for the addition of the social-factors to personality variables in explaining problematic intake.

E. Drinking-Context Variables

We have saved for last in our present series of regression analyses the domain of measures of drinking context, including the indicators of parents' drinking already used in the childhood-predictors analysis (section A of this Chapter) and three measures of adult-drinking context:

Heavy-drinking context: a score combining the frequency of visiting bars or cocktail lounges, the proportion of close friends the respondent considers to "drink quite a bit," and the proportion of get-togethers with close friends at which alcohol is served.

Attitudes of others to respondent's drinking: how leniently the top limit considered appropriate for the respondent's drinking is set by the respondent's wife, parents and most important other persons.

Respondent's attitudes to drinking: a score composed from responses to nine items indicating acceptance of drunkenness, having good things to say about drinking, giving sociable reasons for drinking.

Obviously these variables are all conceptually close to the criterion variables. Table 35 shows that they have high inter-correlations with one another, but Table 36 reveals somewhat different degrees of association with the criteria: all three are quite strongly associated with problematic intake, especially heavy-drinking context; heavy-drinking context and respondent's attitudes, but not attitudes of others, are quite strongly associated with tangible consequences. All three show strong associations with parents' nonabstinence and maximum amount of drinking, with respondent's youthfulness, with tolerance of deviance and with being Catholic and nonconservative Protestant. Heavy-drinking context and respondent's attitudes also show relatively strong relations with impulsivity and with urbanization and wetness of region. By and large, the variables show notably low correlations with the first six personality variables; apparently immersion in a heavy-drinking context is more a function of youth and "wet" social context than of happiness or despair.

The first regression on each criterion in Table 38, which shows results using only the drinking-context variables, reveals that these variables predict problematic intake much more strongly than tangible consequences. Comparing the first regressions in Tables 37 and 38, all other predictors taken together account for essentially the same amount of variance in problematic intake (24%) as the drinking-context variables (22%), but the other variables predict tangible consequences notably better (28%) than does drinking context (13%). While a few drinking-context and attitudes variables thus provide a relatively strong prediction, particularly of heavy drinking, it is interesting to note that we can predict heavy drinking about as well from a knowledge of the respondent's social situation and background and personality dimensions.

On both criteria, father's maximum quantity makes about as strong a contribution to the prediction when drinking-context variables are included in the analysis as without them (Table 32), and father's abstinence has a stronger positive partial correlation in both regressions when the drinking-context variables are included. Father's abstinence is negatively associated with drinking-context variables (Table 36); thus, the association between father's abstinence and son's heavy drinking and drinking problems becomes stronger when the effects of the son's immersion in drinking context is partialled out, suggesting that heavy drinking and drinking problems are more likely to occur without involvement in a heavy-drinking context among those from dry backgrounds.

Although attitudes of others to the respondent's drinking had considerable raw correlation with problematic intake, the variable makes essentially no contribution to the prediction once heavy-drinking context and respondent's attitudes to drinking are partialled out. Thus, it seems that the lenient attitudes of others, at least as described by the respondent, play at most a secondary role in explaining heavy drinking. Such lenient attitudes, however, emerge with a fairly strong but negative contribution to the prediction of tangible consequences, once the other two drinking-context variables are partialled out. The leniency of others concerning the respondent's drinking seems likely to reduce rather than increase his problems with drinking—a result which makes sense when it is kept in mind that a large component of the tangible consequences score is the complaints and actions of the respondent's significant others in reaction to his drinking.

TABLE 38.—*Multiple Regressions of Drinking Context and Other Variables on Criterion Scores*[a]

	Multiple Correlation Coefficient	Partial Correlation
I. Drinking Context Only	**A. TANGIBLE CONSEQUENCES**	
Heavy-drinking context	.27	.21
R's attitudes to drinking	.30	.15
Others' attitudes to R's drinking (neg.)	.32	−.15
Father's maximum quantity	.33	.16
Father abstains	.36	.13
	B. PROBLEMATIC INTAKE	
Heavy-drinking context	.42	.34
R's attitudes to drinking	.44	.11
Father's maximum quantity	.45	.16
Father abstains	.47	.15
II. Forcing in All Other Predictors, Drinking Context Entering Freely		
	A. TANGIBLE CONSEQUENCES	
	.53	
Heavy-drinking context	.57	.21
R's attitudes to drinking	.58	.10
Others' attitudes to R's drinking (neg.)	.58	−.09
Father's maximum quantity	.58	.07
Father abstains	.58	.06
	B. PROBLEMATIC INTAKE	
	.49	
Heavy-drinking context	.58	.35
Father's maximum quantity	.58	.13
Father abstains	.59	.10
Mother abstains	.59	.05
III. Forcing in Drinking Context, All Other Predictors Entering Freely		
	A. TANGIBLE CONSEQUENCES	
	.36	
Intrapunitiveness	.49	.30
ISP low	.52	.19
Work-role instability	.54	.13
Home-role friction	.55	.12
Social activity	.55	.10
	B. PROBLEMATIC INTAKE	
	.47	
Intrapunitiveness	.51	.14
ISP low	.53	.12
Black	.54	.17
Latin Amer.–Caribbean	.55	.15
Drug habits	.56	.12

[Continued on next page]

TABLE 38.—continued

	Multiple Correlation Coefficients	Partial Correlation
IV. All Predictors Entering Freely	A. TANGIBLE CONSEQUENCES	
Intrapunitiveness	.36	.29
Heavy-drinking context	.45	.22
Isp low	.50	.20
Work-role instability	.52	.14
R's attitudes to drinking	.53	.11
Home-role friction	.53	.11
Health problems	.54	.10
Social activity	.55	.09
After all predictors enter	.583	
	B. PROBLEMATIC INTAKE	
Heavy-drinking context	.42	.41
Isp low	.47	.13
Intrapunitiveness	.50	.14
Latin Amer.–Caribbean	.51	.16
Black	.53	.15
Drug habits	.54	.12
Tolerance of deviance	.55	.12
Social activity	.56	.10
After all predictors enter	.594	

a See footnote to Table 31.

Perhaps the most important finding from these analyses is the strength of prediction shown by heavy-drinking context; for both tangible consequences and problematic intake it shows even a stronger prediction than do the respondent's own attitudes toward drinking. This reemphasis of the importance of contextual factors in understanding drinking behavior, also suggested by some results in previous studies in this series (70, pp. 123–125; 117), will be further explored in Chapters 7 and 8 and in future reports from this series.

When all other predictors are forced into the regression first and then the drinking-context variables are allowed to enter freely (regressions II, Table 38), the major effect on the partial correlations for the drinking-context variables is to reemphasize the dominance of heavy-drinking context and somewhat diminish the contributions from father's drinking. Thus the predictive power of father's drinking is partly the result of associations it shares with other predictors, while heavy-drinking context's relationship with the criterion is essentially irreducible by the partialling out of the contributions of our other predictors. The additional power of prediction contributed by the drinking-context variables is greater for the problematic intake regression (from 24 to 35%) than for the tangible consequences regression (28 to 34%).

When the opposite procedure, forcing the drinking-context variables in first and letting the remainder enter freely, is used (regressions III, Table 38) the effects on order of entry and partial correlations of the remainder variables in the tangible consequences regression is relatively minor: social activity appears to move up somewhat in the order of entry, compared to the first regression in Table 37. In the regression on problematic intake, however, the effects are quite marked: intrapunitiveness replaces impulsivity and tolerance as the earliest entrant, while low ISP joins the low-status ethnicities as a relatively strong entrant. This result suggests that heavy drinking outside of a heavy-drinking context, and with personal attitudes at variance with behavior, is particularly associated with respondents of low status and with generalized feelings of guilt. Again, we seem to have caught a glimpse from a different perspective of intrapunitiveness as an internalization of the disjunction between the respondent's behavior and his context of norms and others' behavior.

As would be expected from the results of the previous regressions, the additional contribution of the remaining variables to a prediction on the basis of only drinking-context variables is considerably greater for tangible consequences than for problematic intake.

In regression IV in Table 38 all predictors, including the drinking-context variables, are allowed to enter in a free stepwise procedure. The patterns in regression III on problematic intake, when the drinking-context variables were forced in, carry over into this regression, in which heavy-drinking context makes an early and very strong entry, and potentiates low ISP and intrapunitiveness as considerably stronger predictors than in regression I of Table 37. Respondent's attitudes and father's drinking patterns do not appear in the initial steps of this regression using all our predictors.

Both heavy-drinking context and respondent's attitudes appear relatively early in the regression on tangible consequences, but secondarily to intrapunitiveness and without affecting the order of entry of the other early entrants in the regression. The main effects of introducing the drinking-context variables are to drop drug habits, impulsivity and tolerance from the list of early entrants, add health problems, and—again—to potentiate intrapunitiveness (in the sense of raising its partial correlation at the end of the eighth step). Again, the result is to suggest the possibility of alternative styles of acquiring tangible consequences, one associated with immersion in a heavy-drinking context and the other with an intrapunitive estrangement from one's social matrix.

An earlier work (19) using the N2 sample employed regression techniques to predict a combined over-all problems-with-drinking score. The sample included both sexes and all ages over 21 and the set of predictors was drawn from much the same set of conceptual domains as in the present analysis. The variance accounted for in that analysis (19, *p. 106*) was 18%, while in our present analysis we have accounted for 34% of the variance on tangible consequences and 35% on problematic intake. It is perhaps worth recording the differences in the two studies and the probable effect of each difference on the results: (*a*) the restriction of the range of variation, limited to men aged 21–59 in the present study, may have slightly diminished the strength of the predictions; (*b*) the disaggregation of the over-all problems criterion, so that parts of the content of the over-all problems score on N2 appear as our two criteria in the present analysis, appears not to have had a substantial effect on the over-all power of predictions, though we would contend it has improved our understanding of the meaning of the results; (*c*) in both criterion measures, the number and spread of items were substantially greater on N3, improving the predictions; (*d*) many of the early entrants in the regressions on N3 have been made both more specific than the N2 "molar" variables and have been filled out with new items, also improving the predictions on N3.

The early entrants in the N2 regression included attitudes toward drinking, ISP, sex, alienation–maladjustment and impulsivity–noncompliance. Heavy-drinking context was not included in the N2 analysis, and it can be seen from Tables 36 and 38 that attitudes toward drinking would be a likely replacement for it if heavy-drinking context were omitted in the N3 analysis. Intrapunitiveness forms a portion of the general area, roughly including the dimensions of the six N3 "ego-strength" personality variables, used in combined form under the title "alienation and maladjustment" in the N2 analysis. N3 impulsivity and tolerance are subdivisions within the general area scored together as impulsivity–noncompliance on N2. Work-role instability and home-role friction were not measured as separate variables in N2. We considered it more important in the present analysis to improve the design than to undertake an exact replication, but it can be seen that there is at least a rough conformance in the results of the regression analyses on the two studies.

Figure 8 shows the results of AID analyses using the same full field of predictors as in regression IV in Table 38. Both AID analyses attain essentially the same explanation of variance as their counterpart regressions if allowed to run on beyond the steps shown in Figure 8. On tangible consequences, the AID differs from the regression in the predictors chosen in the early stages primarily by the absence of work-role instability and home-role friction. Both of these variables have upper score levels with relatively few cases but high mean values on the criterion, a pattern which weighs more heavily in the product-moment correlation statistics underlying the regression than in the dichotomizing procedure of AID. Looking at the results as early in the "tree" as after the first three splits, we find that three variables will yield subsamples very highly differentiated on the criterion: (1) a "high" group ($N = 41$), with high intrapunitiveness scores and highly positive attitudes to drinking, and a mean score of 8.10 on tangible consequences; (2) an "intermediate" group ($N = 331$) combining the two intermediate boxes, and a mean score of 2.45; (3) a "low" group ($N = 606$), with low intrapunitiveness scores and low involvement in heavy-drinking contexts, and a mean score of 0.84.

The AID analysis on problematic intake shows quite a divergence from the results in Table 38. Heavy-drinking context provides the first and strongest split, but alienation emerges where intrapunitiveness might have been expected and low ISP does not appear although other indicators of low status do. Again, looking at the results as of the third split, as few as

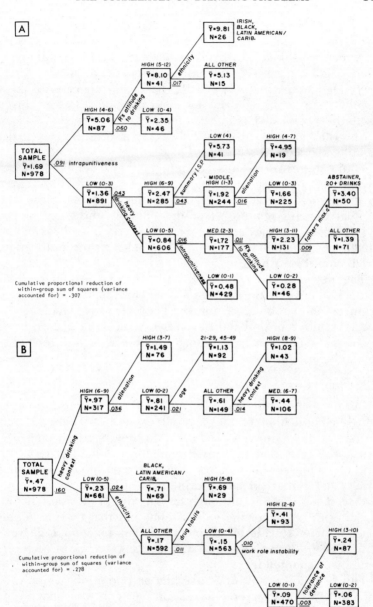

FIGURE 8.—*AID Analyses of All Predictors on Tangible Consequences*
(A) and Problematic Intake (B) (*"No answer" cases excluded)

three predictors will yield groups with very diverse means on the criterion: (1) a "high" group ($N = 76$), including high involvement in heavy-drinking contexts and high alienation scores, and a mean score of 1.49 on problematic intake; (2) an "intermediate" group ($N = 310$), with all others with high involvement in heavy-drinking contexts, plus those of Black or Latin American–Caribbean ethnicity, and a mean score of 0.79; (3) a "low" group ($N = 592$), composed of the rest of the sample, and a mean score of 0.17.

While these AID results conform to the general lay of the explanatory land we found in the regressions, the differences in details and in the particular variables representing a conceptual domain remind us of the possible influence of the algorithm of the particular technique used, as well as of the effects of chance variations, on the details of the multivariate prediction results.

The AID analyses confirm the picture of considerable differences between the strongest predictors of tangible consequences and problematic intake. They also give evidence of the very different probabilities of heavy drinking and drinking problems which can be predicted on the basis of a relatively few independent variables.

F. Summary

In this chapter, the essential analytical questions have been, which combination of these variables best predicts the criterion and how strong a prediction do they jointly make? The brief answer is that the best predictions of both criteria are made by a measure of feelings of guilt, a measure of immersion in a social context of heavy drinking, and measures of disadvantaged social status, although the mixture of these predictors is rather different for the two criteria; and that the prediction of both criteria made by all our predictors together is reasonably strong; as much as 34 to 35% of the variance in each criterion is accounted for.

This brief answer is, of course, the end point of the analyses reported in this chapter. The reason we took what may seem such an unconscionable time in getting there is our belief that this answer may obscure more than it reveals. If there is any surprise in the strong relationship of heavy-drinking context and our criteria, it is only because alcohol research has tended to neglect the obvious. And we have argued that the strong relationship between intrapunitiveness and tangible consequences also has an inherent but not very evocative logic: intrapunitiveness involves the internalized recognition of disjunction between behavior and ideals, while tangible consequences is largely the external notice of such disjunctions in the area of drinking behavior. The result of an analysis in which all predictors are treated as being in equal conceptual status, then, tends to be an emphasis on the more obvious relationships at the expense of some of the more conceptually interesting ones.

The implication for an eventual understanding of the etiology of alcohol problems is then that the process we have gone through in this chapter seems more likely to bear fruit than will the end point. The methods we have used to focus attention on the weaker but more interesting interrelations in the course of the series of regression analyses undertaken in the last two chapters have included (a) separating the predictors into ad-hoc conceptual domains in accordance with dimensions defined by the particular analysis, i.e., at one stage or another, according to priority in time, conceptual nearness to the criterion, relative probability of change over time and internal coherence; (b) restricting the field of predictors in regression analyses to those in particular conceptual domains; and (c) examining the contributions of a domain of predictors to the regression when the contributions of another domain are taken into prior account, by using the technique of "forcing" a set of predictors into the regression prior to allowing another set to regress freely on the residuum.

By these means we have been able to examine in detail the interrelationships of the various domains of predictors, in the course of arriving at the brief answer of how they all add up altogether. In the first series of analyses, we examined the predictive power of items which can be assumed to be characteristics of the respondent's childhood. These were divided conceptually into three domains—the respondent's "birthright" (the social-differentiation characteristics which were true of him at birth), aspects of his childhood history and his parents' drinking patterns. In general, our results matched those from longitudinal studies of childhood samples, in that childhood history did discriminate between adults with and without drinking problems. We also found that parents' drinking did predict adult drinking patterns and problems, but that a knowledge of the mother's patterns added very little to a knowledge of the father's in terms of predictive power, and that either heavy drinking or abstinence versus moderate drinking on the part of the father predicted tangible consequences on the part of the son. Including all childhood predictors together in a summary analysis, we found that each of the three, birthright social-differentiation variables, childhood-history variables and parental drinking patterns, made early contributions to the stepwise regression. The over-all predictions of tangible consequences and problematic intake which can be made on the basis of all the childhood predictors taken together is stronger for problematic intake (17%) than for consequences (12%); the power of the prediction of consequences is slightly less than that which can be made on the basis of all social-differentiation variables, including those defined for adult status (Chapter 4). The childhood predictors tend to be eclipsed from the earlier stages of regressions when adult personality and life-history variables are added to the list of predictors.

Turning from time-ordered prediction through childhood characteristics to prediction from patterns of association with no specified time order, we started from a base of birthright, adult social-differentiation variables and childhood-history variables and explored the predictions from within new domains as they were added, and the relations between these predictions. The variables in the domain of personality provided a considerably better prediction of tangible consequences than of problematic intake. As a result, more of the variance on consequences could be explained by the personality variables than by the total pool of social-differentiation variables, but the reverse was true for problematic intake. The strongest predictors of tangible consequences among the personality variables were indicators of depressed and guilty states of mind, while the strongest predictors of problematic intake were indicators of impulsivity and tolerance of deviant behavior other than drinking. This pattern provides some support for a two-stage model of the etiology of drinking problems, where social differentiations are the major factors of who puts themselves "at risk" of drinking problems by their heavy drinking behavior, but personality variations are the major determinants of those "at risk" who end up with drinking problems.

When adult social-situation, habit and history variables are added to the analysis, it emerges that the personality variables and the total pool of social-differentiation, situation and history variables each make independent contributions to the prediction of both our criteria, but that the personality variables make a somewhat more substantial contribution to the prediction of tangible consequences than to the prediction of problematic intake. Twenty-seven per cent of the variance on tangible consequences and 24% of the variance on problematic intake are explained by these over-all regressions, using all predictors which involve no reference to drinking attitudes and contexts.

As we have mentioned, the drinking-context variables assume strong positions in the stepwise regressions on each criterion. The association of heavy-drinking context with problematic intake is especially strong, and its addition to the regression substantially affects the list of early predictors from other domains, notably by partially eclipsing the contributions of impulsivity and tolerance and by potentiating the contribution of intrapunitiveness. Heavy-drinking context emerges as a stronger predictor of both criteria than the respondent's own attitudes to drinking, reemphasizing the importance of taking into account in future studies the social matrix of "heavy-drinking worlds" within which problem drinking emerges and is maintained.

G. Methodological Implications

In the last three chapters, our task has been to pull together an enormous profusion of variables having a variety of conceptual relationships with one another. As we shall describe, we believe that we found ourselves with a unique analytical situation which forced us to break some new ground in the elaboration and application of analytical techniques. At times, we are sure, we have fallen prey to many errors: losing sight of the forest in exploring some of the more tangled thickets; oversimplifying in the course of the data reduction and the analysis (partly to meet the exigencies of analytical techniques); and not taking fully into account the results of one analysis in the design of another. We hope that our failings will in the course of time be pointed out and that more elegant analytical solutions will be found to fit the problems we found before us.

Part of our predicament was the necessity of undertaking an explanatory analysis of a dependent variable—"alcoholism" or "problem drinking"—whose very nature and coherence were a matter of increasing dispute. The variety of our measures of drinking problems is a reflection of the extraordinarily variegated set of activities and conditions which have been conventionally classed under the single rubric of alcoholism. Our own writings have reflected a tendency to question the utility of such a polymorphous conglomeration, an "oddment of aggregation," as Seeley described it (128, p. 355), as is usual in the standard definitions of alcoholism. Usual approaches to explanatory analysis by epidemiologists or survey analysts, however, do not make much allowance for dissecting the set of phenomena to be explained; in fact, the existence of a coherent and well-defined (usually dichotomous) dependent variable is frequently taken for granted in discussions of epidemiological method.

Our response has been to spend a great deal of energy in Chapter 3 "taking apart" the general over-all problems score which we have tended to use (with whatever qualms) as our "placeholder" dependent variable in previous analyses (e.g., 19).[6] And in the subsequent explanatory analyses of Chapters 4 and 5, we have systematically resisted the convenience of settling on a single interval-scale dependent variable, using instead as appropriate either a typology, the whole series of problem-area scales or summary scores for particular subareas of the over-all problems arena.

The other part of our predicament involved the sheer numbers and variety of possible predictors we had made available to ourselves with a relatively lengthy interview schedule. The precedents are numerous, but not entirely satisfactory. The tendency has been either to forget the whole garment and con-

---

[6] See footnote 1 to this chapter.

centrate on elaborating a buttonhole, or to bundle everything up in an all-purpose hand-me-down shroud. What we have tried to do in Chapters 4 and 5 is to keep one analytical eye on the fascinating details within conceptual domains of our independent variables, and the other on the patterns of relationship by which the details fit together. Our analytical garment may not be a very good fit, but we hope that we at least got the sleeves where the arms are and the buttons into the buttonholes.

Unfortunately our analysis does not speak very much to the needs of the large and growing army of those concerned with alcohol policies and the treatment of alcoholics. Given the collapse of the theoretical underpinnings of the Jellinek estimation formula (105), their most urgent need is for certainty, particularly in the form of a single numerical estimate of "alcoholics" that can be used for planning and evaluation purposes; and, understandably, they are likely to have small patience with our desire to disaggregate and complexify, particularly if we show no inclination to end with a new single estimate. It is our contention, however, that a primary failing in research on alcohol problems has been a tendency to jump to broad conclusions on the basis of very limited evidence. The result has been a plethora of plausible etiological theories, each with some evidence to support it, some but not all of which can be true at the same time. It is our hope that the present analysis has contributed evidence in a form which will be useful to the task of sifting through the rival etiologies in the future.

Chapter 6

Correlates of Variability in Heavy and Problem Drinking

IN OUR ANALYSIS in the preceding two chapters, the complexities of analysis and requirements of the multivariate procedures often forced us back on summary problem scores. To carry out such analyses taking into account all the relevant dimensions of the dependent variables discussed in Chapters 2 and 3 would be beyond the scope of the present report and, to some extent, also of the capabilities of the available procedures and the sample size.

In the present chapter, we shall sketch roughly some of the more interesting territory of such analyses, by examining the correlates and interactions of "periodic" and "steady" heavy drinking, and by comparing the characteristics of those with current tangible consequences of drinking with those who used to have them but do not now.

A. Characteristics of Very Heavy and Steady Fairly Heavy Drinkers

Over the years, many specialists in the study of alcohol-related problems have felt it important to preserve a clear distinction between those who drink very heavily at intervals and those who drink fairly heavily on a regular basis. One question institutions for inebriates of the 19th century asked their inmates was whether their excess was "periodic" or "steady" (139, pp. 140–151). Pearl (103) distinguished between "heavy in amount, occasional as to frequency, and abstainers in the interval between heavy drinking bouts; heavy in amount, occasional as to frequency, and moderate drinkers in the intervals between heavy drinking; [and] heavy in amount, and steady as to frequency" (p. 73). In her paper comparing types of drinking patterns of men alcoholics, Jackson (54) remarks that "according to alcoholics themselves, several types of drinking patterns can be differentiated. . . . Alcoholics speak of 'periodical' and 'steady' drinkers" (pp. 269–270).

The practical implications for distinguishing between intermittent and steady heavy drinking are fairly obvious, from medical and social-control standpoints. On the one hand, the intermittent heavy drinker is often more likely to give public offense because of the contrast between his usually sober and occasionally drunken behavior, whereas the steady drinker may remain less conspicuous; the latter is recognized in the anecdote of the advertising executive whose business acquaintances hardly knew he drank until one day he showed up sober. On the other hand, the steady drinker rather than the sporadic heavy drinker may do more damage to his liver in the long run.

The distinction between steady and intermittent heavy drinking also fits into the medical dichotomy between "chronic" and "acute." Thus Jellinek (59), much of whose work may be seen as a codification into medicolegal language of the folklore of alcoholism, made a sharp distinction between the "spree" (or intermittent) drinker's "inability to stop once started" (which is the "loss of control" of his gamma alcoholic) and the "inability to abstain" of the inveterate drinker (or delta alcoholic) (pp. 37–38). The implication is that the two types of drinking are alternatives and do not appear in combination. Justice Marshall drew upon this distinction in *Powell v Texas* (153), remarking that, in order to fit legal tests for an uncontrollable compulsion, an alcoholic would have to have both patterns, inability to stop once started and inability to abstain. Thus important medical and social-control considerations are involved in the issue of whether intermittent and regular heavy drinking tend to be behavior patterns which are distinct or whether they tend to go together.

The present body of data permits a comparison of intermittent and steady heavy drinking only from the 978 interviews in the N3 sample because the N2 study did not gather data on the drinking of more than 5 drinks per occasion. In this analysis, "very heavy" drinking is defined as drinking 12 or more drinks per occasion at least once a month, or bingeing at least at the "high problems" level. "Steady fairly heavy drinking" is defined as drinking 5 or more per occasion at least once a week.

Table 39 shows the distribution of very heavy drinkers and steady fairly heavy drinkers. The grand total (top row) shows

TABLE 39.—*Interaction of Current Very Heavy and Steady Fairly Heavy Drinking with Demographic Characteristics, in Per Cent*[a]

	N	Very Heavy and Steady Fairly Heavy	Steady Fairly Heavy Only	Very Heavy Only	Neither
Total	978	7	13	4	76
Age					
21–24	130	15	19	10	56
25–29	117	10	18	3	69
30–34	122	5	12	4	80
35–39	124	9	15	3	73
40–44	133	5	15	3	77
45–49	114	4	10	4	83
50–54	123	3	9	2	86
55–59	115	4	5	3	88
Index of Social Position					
Upper	302	5	10	5	81
Upper middle	250	5	12	4	78
Lower middle	257	6	14	3	77
Lower	169	14	17	4	65
Family Status					
Wife & children at home	608	5	13	3	80
Wife, no children	229	7	12	5	76
No wife or children	141	16	16	7	61
Ethnic Groups					
British	196	6	8	7	79
Irish	100	8	5	6	81
German	187	3	12	3	82
Italian	47	4	23	0	72
Latin Amer.–Carib.	33	33	21	9	36
Jewish	25	4	0	4	92
Black	81	17	24	4	56
East European	73	4	16	1	78
All others	236	5	14	2	79
Religion					
Catholic	327	8	18	4	69
Jewish	25	4	0	4	92
Liberal Prot.	127	3	17	2	78
Conservative Prot.	380	6	8	4	82
No religion	64	14	16	5	66
Other	55	9	11	4	76
Region					
Wetter regions	570	7	16	3	74
Dryer regions	408	7	9	5	79
Urbanization					
Central cities of SMSAS	376	12	15	5	68
Other cities and towns (2500+)	335	4	13	3	79
Rural	276	4	9	3	84

[a] N3 data only. Very heavy = drinking 12 or more drinks per occasion at least once a month. Steady fairly heavy drinking = 5 or more drinks per occasion at least once a week.

that it is more common for very heavy drinking to occur in conjunction with steady fairly heavy drinking (7% of the total N3 sample of men aged 21 to 59) rather than separately (4% of the total sample). Three-fourths of the high-risk sample of men gave responses indicating that their patterns of drinking failed to reach either the very heavy or the steady fairly heavy criterion. Altogether, 11% of the aggregate at least matched the very heavy criterion and 20% the steady fairly heavy criterion.

The interaction between very heavy and steady fairly heavy drinking is further analyzed by various demographic variables in Table 39, with the following findings:

Age. Younger men (especially those aged 21 to 24) have the highest rates of both very heavy and steady fairly heavy drinking.

Social Position. Lowest-status men have much higher percentages of very heavy drinkers, particularly in combination with steady fairly heavy drinking.

Life Cycle. Those not living with wife or children have higher rates of both types of drinking, particularly in combination with each other. The results of Table 14 suggest that this result is not an artifact of age. Nevertheless, the direction of causation is thoroughly ambiguous.

Ethnic Groups. Those of Latin American–Caribbean and Black ethnicity show the highest rates of very heavy drinking. Germans, Italians and East Europeans show the lowest ratio of very heavy to steady fairly heavy drinking, which is congruent with past studies of frequencies of drinking in contrast to quantities per occasion (20, *p. 220*).

Religious Affiliation. The contrast between conservative Protestants and liberal Protestants in terms of the ratio of steady fairly heavy to very heavy drinkers is quite strong—very heavy drinking is in fact twice as common among the conservative as among the liberal Protestants, while steady fairly heavy drinking is more common among the liberal Protestants. It seems that the historical prohibitionist positions of the conservative Protestant churches are more associated with a restriction of the frequency of heavy drinking occasions among heavy drinkers than with a special limitation of the number of heavy drinkers.

The small primarily urban fraction of the population reporting no religion shows the highest rates of both styles of heavy
drinking. Patterns of Catholics reflect an averaging of the very
different patterns of the major constituent ethnicities.

Regions. The contrast between wetter and dryer regional
patterns resembles the related contrast between conservative
and liberal Protestants. The dry pattern can be seen as the result of social constraints operating to "enclave" drinking into
intermittent occasions, or as a reflection of a positive subcul-
tural tradition of "explosive" drinking like that associated
in the alcohol literature with Finland and with isolated occupational groups such as seamen, lumberjacks, miners and cowboys.

Urbanization. Both forms of heavy drinking, and particularly both forms together, are especially common in the central
cities of metropolitan areas.

In the profile analysis in Table 40 of the nondemographic
correlates of the different drinking patterns, the direction of
the percentages has been reversed to focus attention on the
contrasts between groups of drinking patterns of unequal sizes.
Because of the small sizes of the groups, the result should be
treated with caution; the sampling tolerances for comparisons
involving the smallest group are of the order of 20 percentage
points.

On almost all characteristics, there is a strong contrast between the two extreme groups—those with both very heavy
and steady fairly heavy drinking, and the residual group. The
most obvious exception to this generalization is on father's
abstinence, where the difference is quite small. The next smallest differences, on sociability, lack of neighborhood roots, work
friction and health problems, are all of the order of 10 percentage points. All the remaining comparisons show significant
differences between the extreme groups.

In general, although with a few exceptions, the two middle
drinking-pattern groups show prevalences between the two
extremes. The most notable exception is on tolerance of deviance, where the two middle drinking-pattern groups show
the highest proportions with a score above zero.

There is considerable variation within the general model,

TABLE 40.—*Profile Analysis of Current Very Heavy and Steady Fairly Heavy Drinkers, in Per Cent*[a]

	Very Heavy and Steady Fairly Heavy (N = 68)	Steady Fairly Heavy Only (127)	Very Heavy Only (38)	Neither (745)
Role History				
Home-role instability (2+)	35	20	26	14
Work-role instability (2+)	37	27	39	16
Childhood History				
Father's max. quantity				
8+ drinks	61	46	57	29
1–7 drinks	21	39	23	47
Abstainer	18	15	20	24
Youthful rashness (2+)	46	28	40	20
Childhood hardship (1+)	47	29	29	28
Family disruption (1+)	40	20	26	16
Childhood unhappiness (1+)	59	34	24	25
Personality				
Somatization (1+)	43	27	32	21
Affective anxiety (1+)	56	43	34	35
Physical depression (1+)	59	41	50	38
Psychiatric symptoms (1+)	63	38	53	37
Intrapunitiveness (2+)	60	43	37	32
Alienation (2+)	66	47	63	40
Impulsivity (2+)	68	46	47	35
Tolerance of deviance (1+)	69	78	84	54
Sociability (3+)	74	66	68	62
Social Situation				
Nonhelpfulness of others (1+)	43	40	50	30
Social activity (1+)	52	40	50	29
Lack of neighborhood roots (3+)	25	19	13	13
Drug habits (3+)	47	24	34	21
Home-role friction (3+)	37	23	29	17
Work friction (2+)	21	13	13	12
Health problems (1+)	52	36	43	43
Drinking Context				
Heavy-drinking context (5+)	90	82	66	35
Others' attitudes to R's drinking (1+)	60	76	68	38
R's attitudes to drinking (6+)	60	59	53	29
Current Drinking Problems[b]				
Psychological dependence	43	14	24	4
Loss of control	28	8	13	1
Symptomatic drinking	44	16	26	3
Belligerence	38	13	32	5
Wife	50	25	37	7
Relatives	43	12	21	4
Friends, neighbors	41	11	21	3
Job	34	8	13	3
Police	19	7	16	2
Health, injury	31	6	16	4
Financial	37	12	29	3

[a] N3 data only. Very heavy = 12 or more drinks per occasion at least once a month. Steady fairly heavy = 5 or more drinks per occasion at least once a month. Percentages are of respondents with the listed characteristic within each drinking-type category.

[b] High problems, optimal scales.

however, falling into several distinct patterns of comparison:

1. *Association Primarily with Very Heavy Drinking.* This pattern appears particularly on work-role instability, a high paternal maximum quantity, youthful rashness, psychiatric symptoms, alienation, social activity and drug habits. The pattern occurs on all current drinking problems and in a less marked form on many other variables; in general there seems to be a greater tendency for those with only very heavy drinking than for those with only steady fairly heavy drinking to resemble the category with both drinking patterns. The findings suggest a particular association of very heavy drinking with devil-may-care hell-raising, and a stronger association of very heavy drinking, even if only intermittent, than of steady heavy drinking with social and psychological consequences of drinking.

2. *Association Primarily with Steady Fairly Heavy Drinking.* This pattern is conspicuous by its rarity. The clearest example of it is on heavy-drinking context; but this might be regarded as artifactual since frequency of drinking situations is involved in both measures. The pattern shows up weakly on childhood unhappiness, affective anxiety, lack of neighborhood roots and respondents' attitudes to drinking. Those with only a steady fairly heavy drinking pattern are most likely to report the absence of constraints in the form of attitudes of others to their drinking; perhaps their drinking style poses the fewest threats to their significant others' equanimity.

3. *Association Primarily with the Combination of Both Patterns.* This pattern occurs on home-role instability, the childhood-history variables (other than youthful rashness and father's abstinence), impulsivity, and is to some degree characteristic of all the six personality scores generally indicating dysphoria except alienation, and of drug habits, home-role friction, work friction and health problems. The drinking problem scores also generally show no other group approaching the both-patterns group in prevalence. In general, then, indicators of potential psychological and adjustment problems are most strongly related to the joint occurrence of both heavy drinking patterns.

4. *Association Equally with all Three Combinations of Patterns.* Only attitudes to drinking show this pattern of a sharp distinction between the residual category and a relatively homogeneous grouping of all heavy drinking patterns.

The many differences between those who drink rather large amounts of alcohol and those who drink rather steadily but not so heavily are worthy of additional scrutiny in order to determine the environmental factors which encourage the development of one or other of these patterns, and to determine which group is the more likely to suffer adverse outcomes (either in health or interpersonal relations) over time. The first objective is covered in part in the next chapter; and the second will be studied in the next follow-up survey in this series, a few years hence.

B. Respondents with Current Problems and with Past Problems Only

It may be of interest to compare those who have "matured out" of drinking problems with those who still have them. Table 41 presents a summary comparison of men who have had tangible consequences of drinking (score of 3 or more within the last 3 years) with men who formerly had such problems, and in turn with those who have never had such problems. The comparison is limited to men aged 30 to 59, i.e., those who have reached a sufficient age to have both had the problems and matured out of them. To gain more stable results, the full N2–N3 sample is used, although this somewhat limits the available respondent-characteristic scores. Again, the results are reported as a profile analysis, percentaged by drinking-consequence groups across the other variables, to allow easy comparison of the groups.

The men with high current consequences are concentrated in the lowest socioeconomic group and the large central cities, while those who never had tangible consequences are concentrated in the highest socioeconomic status groups and outside the central cities. The results by ethnicity and religious affiliation show only small differences between men with current and those with only past consequences, except that Black

TABLE 41.—*Profile Analysis of Men Aged 30–59 with Current and Past High Tangible Consequences, in Per Cent*[a]

	Current (N = 145)	Past (174)	Neither Current Nor Past (891)	Totals (1210)
Index of Social Position				
Upper	20	22	35	32
Upper middle	14	28	24	23
Lower middle	25	25	25	25
Lower	41	25	16	20
Ethnic Groups				
British	21	25	21	21
Irish	12	16	11	12
German	10	14	22	19
Italian	3	3	5	5
Latin Amer.–Carib.	6	5	1	2
Jewish	0	1	4	3
Black	20	7	6	8
Eastern European	6	3	6	6
Religion				
Catholic	30	32	30	31
Jewish	0	1	4	3
Liberal Protestant	12	9	16	14
Conservative Protestant	46	47	42	43
No religion	9	6	4	5
Urbanization				
Central cities	48	37	25	30
Other cities and towns	27	31	40	37
Rural	26	32	35	33
Region: wetter	54	57	59	58
Home-Role Instability (2+)	18	17	10	12
Childhood History				
Father's max. quantity				
8+ drinks	36	39	25	28
1–7 drinks	39	44	48	46
Abstainer	24	18	27	26
Childhood hardship[b]	43	41	30	33
Family disruption[b]	21	18	13	14
Childhood unhappiness[b]	22	18	12	14

[Continued on next page]

TABLE 41.—continued

	Current (N = 145)	Past (174)	Neither Current Nor Past (891)	Totals (1210)
Personality				
Somatization (1+)	39	34	20	24
Affective anxiety (1+)	51	49	34	38
Alienation[b] (2+)	52	48	32	37
Impulsivity[b] (2+)	52	34	25	30
Tolerance of deviance[b] (1+)	63	57	50	53
Social Situation				
Nonhelpfulness of others (1+)	32	29	23	25
Social activity[b] (1+)	50	43	51	50
Lack of neighborhood roots (3+)	16	12	9	10
Drug habits[b] (4+)	27	23	12	15
Home-role friction (3+)	32	24	18	20
Work friction (2+)	13	16	10	11
Drinking Context				
Heavy-drinking context[b] (5+)	60	37	32	36
Others' attitudes to R's drinking (1+)	48	41	36	38
R's attitudes to drinking[b] (1+)	39	46	37	39

[a] N2–N3 data. High consequences score = 3 or more points on the N2–N3 tangible consequences score (Appendix B).

[b] Differs in details from the equivalent N3 score in Appendix C.

ethnicity shows a higher contribution to current consequences. There are essentially no differences by region according to consequences, and home-role instability differentiates only between having ever and having never had consequences.

Father's drinking at all and heavy drinking are both most prevalent among those with former but not current tangible consequences, suggesting that the father's drinking pattern is more influential in young adulthood than later. Only two other characteristics are most common among the former-consequences group: work friction and the respondent's own attitudes to drinking. Social activity is somewhat less common among this group than among either of the comparison groups.

Otherwise, two general patterns appear in the data: (1) *Current and former consequences both showing relatively high prevalences:* This pattern appears on the childhood-history items, including father's heavy drinking, on all personality variables except impulsivity, and on nonhelpfulness of others, lack of neighborhood roots and drug habits. This implies that these variables may be a better predictor of getting into problems with one's drinking than of whether the problems will continue or remit. (2) *Current consequences showing a higher prevalence*: In most instances of this pattern, and notably on tolerance of deviance, home-role friction and tolerant attitudes of others, the former-consequences group is in an intermediate position, while the current-consequences group more clearly predominates on impulsivity and on heavy-drinking context. These characteristics, and notably the latter two, thus show an association with concurrent tangible consequences of drinking even among men beyond their salad days.

The forthcoming follow-up study on the same respondents should provide additional clues as to whether certain characteristics (notably, lower social status, large-city residence, possession of certain sociopsychological traits, such as high anxiety and alienation and weak ego-controls, and certain environmental temptations to drink heavily) are as effective predictors of future changes in drinking problems as they are of drinking problems when measured on a retrospective basis.

Chapter 7

Neighborhood Characteristics
and Drinking Behavior

CONTEXTUAL VARIABLES are especially important
in alcohol studies since (as noted in Chapter 2) it is
very much an open question whether alcoholism
(or problem drinking) is to be viewed as a property of an individual, as diseases traditionally are, or as a property of a social group or situation. From an empirical standpoint, it has
been seen in this monograph that while individual personality variables explain a fair amount of the variance in problem
drinking, a large part is also explained by such environmental
or sociocultural variables as region, size and type of city, social
status and life cycle. And from an historical standpoint, liquor
control laws in the U.S. have evolved very much along local
option lines, with each area having the types of control over
sales and retail outlets (package stores, taverns, bars or none
of these) which developed from, and in turn served to reinforce, the peculiar ethnocultural and religious heritage from
the early settlers or latter-day pressure groups (117, *pp.* 82–83).
Such sociocultural considerations seem to play a powerful role
in present-day drinking behavior: there is still a close correlation between drinking behavior today and the Prohibition
sentiment of 40 years ago. Since drinking customs and laws
tend to have considerable continuity over time, we hypothesized that most adults develop a fairly strong awareness of
what are the norms for drinking behavior in their communities
and that thus we could expect that these norms, measured for
the respondent's neighborhood cluster, should have some effect on his own drinking behavior—by conforming to such
norms, moving to another locality or trying to conceal his drinking from the immediate community; or by becoming defiant
and alienated, or by suppressing his desire for drinking until
particular circumstances lead to what might be termed "explosive" drinking.

161

A. Defining Neighborhood Cluster Scores

In our analysis so far, we have been concerned primarily with associations between variables at the individual level even though some of the demographic variables used (e.g., city size, region, family income) are fundamentally properties of collectivities. In this we have followed the usual practice of survey research analysis, which by the nature of the random-sample methodology tends to treat respondents as essentially isolated individuals.

The result is that, except on a few demographic variables, our only measures of the social context of the individual and of the relation between him and his milieu are as interpreted to us by the respondent himself. This raises obvious issues of response invalidities because of selective perception and re-call. It also raises more substantive issues: can social norms, for example, be defined in a meaningful and useful way on the basis of the response of an isolated respondent?

The social context of individual behavior seems to us an inescapable issue in a discussion of drinking behavior and problems. Even if the problems are defined as properties of an individual, they are obviously formed in a matrix of customs and norms concerning drinking in the social milieu. Drinking is preeminently a social activity and, as we have seen in Chapter 5, the behavior and attitudes of associates are highly correlated with drinking problems.

It therefore seemed important to analyze such data as we could obtain on the social milieu in which our respondents lived and moved and did their drinking. In the present chapter, the data on context are for the respondents' "neighborhood"—a few blocks in the city, a square mile or two in the countryside—an area small enough to ensure considerable internal homogeneity, but not small enough to make face-to-face interaction between each of its residents a high probability.

These neighborhood data were available for the national studies by accident rather than forethought. The neighborhood unit in fact is the survey cluster, and the data are derived from the survey itself: the aggregation of the 20 to 50 persons interviewed at each sampling point in the National 1, 2, and 3 studies. As in almost all national surveys, the sample was clustered in units convenient for single interviewer assignments. As described in Appendix A, 100 clusters were assigned throughout the country, each approximately equal in size to a Census Primary Sampling Unit (PSU) or a subdivision, usually only a few blocks in congested urban areas. After enumeration of all households within the selected PSU, the research office assigned every Nth household for interviews. In the 1964–65 N1 survey in which the initial sample was selected, the sampling rate was planned for an average of about 30 interviews per cluster, with 100 sample points, thus yielding 2746 interviews. In order to supplement the subsample of men aged 21–59 interviewed in the N1 survey and reinterviewed in the 1967 N2 follow-up, N3 entailed drawing a new sample of households from the same neighborhoods, so that the total number of households covered in all 3 surveys was 3742, or an average of 37 for the 100 clusters. This size is large enough to permit classifying the respondent in terms of the cluster's characteristics. Thus, rather ironically, a sample-clustering design which utilized clusters too large for optimal efficiency from a sampling standpoint had the somewhat fortuitous advantage of providing a useful basis for classifying the characteristics of the respondent's neighborhood.

Cluster scores were computed on a number of items, either on the basis of the men aged 21 to 59 in the N2–N3 sample, or by averaging the results of the two sexes in the N1 or N1–N3 samples. Scores were computed for any cluster only when the base of relevant respondents was at least 10 (at least 5 in each sex for the sex-averaged scores). On this basis, scores of the variables used in the present analyses were computed for between 63 and 97 clusters. In most cases the cluster scores were originally percentages on dichotomies; for convenience in manipulation, they were standardized to a mean of 4.5 and a standard deviation of 2.0 and rounded to form integer scales ranging from 1 to 9.

The 97 clusters for which we were able to aggregate general measures of drinking behavior were classified according to a summary measure of "cluster dryness": *(1)* "Dry" clusters were identified as those with at least 50% of respondents reporting themselves as current abstainers (do not now drink as often as once a year). The estimate of abstainers was an average of the separate responses of men and women, in order to control for variations by sex, since a much larger proportion of women are abstainers. (2) "Wet" clusters were those in which at least one-third (sex-averaged) consumed at least occasionally five or more drinks per occasion (there was no overlap with the dry criterion). (3) "Medium" clusters were all those which did not meet the criteria for either dry or wet clusters.

As we noted in Chapter 4, the general boundaries of wetter and dryer regions are only roughly isometric for drinking behavior. For example, there are three downstate Illinois clusters with a majority of abstainers and several clusters (primarily urban) in the dryer regions in which a third or more of the respondents at least occasionally drink fairly heavily.

The distribution of wetness by region and urbanization of the 97 clusters is shown in Table 42. The relationship is regular and substantial: the proportion of wet clusters increases additively with wetness of region and with urbanization, while the converse is true of dry clusters. There are no dry clusters in wet-region cities and only one wet cluster in the rural parts of the dryer regions. Of the N2–N3 men aged 21 to 59, 50% of those living in dry clusters live in rural areas of the dryer regions, while 54% of those living in wet clusters live in urban areas of the wetter regions.

B. Region, Urbanization and Cluster Wetness as Correlates of Individual Drinking Patterns

The joint effects of cluster wetness, urbanization and region on individual drinking behavior are explored in Table 43. Individual behavior is measured for the present purposes by a trichotomous variable, with current abstinence at one extreme and "heaviest intake" at the other. This general measure of heavy drinking is roughly the same as the combination of either the intermittent very heavy or steady fairly heavy patterns of Chapter 6 (see Chapter 2, section F). The intermediate group of "moderate drinkers" constitutes those in neither of the extreme categories.

One special caution about Table 43 is the problem of numbers. The Ns shown are for individual respondents. One of the variables involved, however, is a cluster variable, meaning that results in many cells of the table are based on just a couple

TABLE 42.—*Cluster Dryness by Region and Urbanization*

| | Wetter Regions | | | Dryer Regions | | |
	Central Cities	Other Cities & Towns	Rural Areas	Central Cities	Other Cities & Towns	Rural Areas
Cluster dryness[a]						
Dry	0	1	5	1	1	12
Medium	8	10	10	5	6	6
Wet	12	12	1	4	2	1

[a] Defined by N1–N3 sample (sex-averaged). Three clusters with Ns too small are excluded. Dry = 50% or more abstainers. Wet = at least 34% or more high-maximum drinkers.

of neighborhoods, allowing much greater scope for random variation than the respondent Ns would imply. (There is also the caution that each respondent's own drinking patterns contribute about 1/35 of the variation, on the average, in the measure of cluster wetness.)

Abstainers are fairly uniformly uncommon in wet neighborhoods and fairly uniformly common in dry neighborhoods.

TABLE 43.—*Drinking and Heaviest Intake by Cluster Dryness, Region and Urbanization, in Per Cent*[a]

| | Wet Regions | | | Dry Regions | | |
	City	Town	Rural	City	Town	Rural
Dry Clusters	(N = 0)	(11)	(39)	(25)	(47)	(123)
Current abstainers	0	(3)[b]	36	40	45	44
Moderate drinkers	0	(7)[b]	46	48	51	45
Heaviest intake	0	(1)[b]	18	12	4	11
Medium Clusters	(N = 173)	(153)	(74)	(80)	(136)	(67)
Current abstainers	14	8	7	10	16	22
Moderate drinkers	61	69	78	64	78	73
Heaviest intake	24	23	15	26	6	4
Wet Clusters	(N = 335)	(106)	(17)	(79)	(89)	(0)
Current abstainers	5	8	6	10	8	0
Moderate drinkers	65	76	82	51	64	0
Heaviest intake	30	15	12	39	28	0

[a] Heaviest intake = minimal-severity heavy intake or binge (Appendix B). City = cities of 50,000+; town = towns and small cities; rural = rural areas of under 2500.
[b] Not percentaged because of small N.

There is no particular tendency for region or urbanization to add to the effects of wet or dry neighborhood status.

In practical terms, these results may well mean that the cluster-wetness measure is a further geographical specification within the dry regions; we might expect Baltimore and sub-urban Virginia, for instance, to produce wet clusters within the dry region. The results may also reflect other neighborhood-specific patterns, however—for example, social-status patterns.

In the medium clusters the results on abstinence are more interesting, though they should be regarded as tentative. Abstinence seems to be associated with ruralness in the dry regions, but slightly with urbanization in the wet regions. There does not seem to be any dramatic over-all difference in comparing the regions. This may be seen as reflecting a greater dissensus on drinking, at least measured behaviorally, in the city than in the country. A fairly regular finding throughout the table is that the proportion of moderate drinkers is lowest in the big cities, no matter how wet the neighborhood.

Results by heaviest intake are provocative. In the cities and towns of the dry regions, and in the cities of the wet regions, the proportion with heaviest intake varies directly with the wetness of the neighborhood, and may be seen, then, in terms of status, culture, common fate and such variables which "hold together" the inhabitants of a neighborhood. Heaviest intake in these areas is part of a "culture of wetness."

The results are reversed in the other areas—in the rural parts of both regional groups and perhaps in the towns of wet regions heaviest intake appears to be more prevalent in the dryer neighborhoods, so that presumably it is a phenomenon at odds with the dominant culture. The pattern is perhaps a little reminiscent of Clinard's findings on rural criminals—that they are more at odds with their milieu, do a lot of traveling, etc. (32).

C. Association of Cluster and Individual Scores

In the sociological literature, the relation between variables defined for individuals and those defined for neighborhoods has been discussed primarily as a methodological problem, with emphasis on the advisability and methodology of estimating associations at the individual level from those at the neighborhood level (25, *pp. 205–212*). Our concern is rather with the substance of the associations: What are the relative strengths of relations at the individual and at the neighborhood level? Does the individual or neighborhood form of a predictor have a higher association with a given individual outcome? Do the correlations suggest that a variable is more predictable when treated as property of an individual or of a neighborhood?

The intercorrelations of nine representative variables defined at both the individual and neighborhood levels are shown in Table 44. The cluster scores of variables 5, 6 and 7 were defined on the total population, the remainder on men aged 21–59. The variables at each level were dichotomized to put them into an equivalent metric. The variables included in the table can be viewed as falling into four general domains of meaning:

1. *General Attitudes and Norms.* (*a*) Nonhelpfulness of others (scored from responses on the helpfulness of various potential resources "if you were in trouble"—people at work, neighbors, wife, relatives and police). At the cluster level, this variable presumably measures a lack of social cohesiveness; at the individual level, it indicates some alienation from potential sources of help. (*b*) Tolerance of deviance (scored from responses expressing sentiments about flouting various kinds of nondrinking conventional norms—e.g., on sex relations and marriage, work ethic). At the cluster level, this variable presumably gives some indication of the general degree of tolerance of unconventional behavior.

2. *Attitudes and Norms on Drinking.* (*a*) Lenient limits on drinking (scored on the respondent's estimates of the most his significant others think he should drink on an occasion). At the individual level, associations between this variable and both the respondent's own maximum drinking quantity and his estimates of others' heavy drinking (Table 44, I-7 and I-8) may well be influenced by response artifacts. At the cluster level, this variable would seem to provide a fairly good indication of the general level of informal constraints on drinking in the community, i.e., of the extent to which people, whatever their attitudes on drinking, actually attempt to place limits on the drinking of those around them. (*b*) Positive attitudes to drinking (scored from, e.g., the respondent's assent to social reasons for drinking, acceptance of others' heavy drinking). Presumably this is the counterpart for drinking attitudes of the tolerance of deviance score of other areas of behavior. (*c*) "Nothing good" about drinking (derived from volunteered answers to an open-ended question and is the best indication of traditional temperance sentiment). Its direction of meaning obviously tends to be opposite to that of positive attitudes to

drinking, but not necessarily since there is room for opinions between intolerance of drinking at all and approval of heavy drinking.

3. *Drinking Behavior.* (*a*) Abstinence. Not currently drinking. (*b*) High-maximum drinking. At least occasionally having five or more drinks on an occasion. At the individual level, it is obviously impossible to be both an abstainer and a high-maximum drinker. The combination is theoretically possible for clusters, but did not in fact occur. These two variables at the cluster level are the basis for the cluster-dryness summary used above. (*c*) Heavy drinking by others (based on the respondent's reports of the maximum his significant others ever drank on an occasion, and of having relatives and friends with drinking problems). At the individual level, this is an indication of the respondent's perception of being surrounded by heavy drinkers. At the cluster level, it is an alternative to high-maximum drinkers as an indicator of the prevalence of heavy drinking in the neighborhood.

4. *Tangible Consequences* (determined by a high score on current tangible consequences). At the individual level, this is an indicator of possible social problems viewed as seated in the individual. At the cluster level, the variable may be interpreted as indicating the extent of social problems with drinking in the community.

In Table 44, the upper left triangle contains the correlations between variables defined at the cluster level, the lower right triangle shows the correlations between variables defined at the individual level, and the upper right square shows the between-level correlations of the variables. The bold-face correlations on the diagonal within the square are of the same variable at the individual and the cluster level, and are somewhat inflated by the fact that the individual respondent contributes slightly to the total variance in the cluster score.

Correlations within each domain of meaning are fairly substantial at both the individual and the cluster levels. Over-all, these tend to be higher at the cluster than at the individual level, as the methodological discussions would lead us to expect, but there are considerable variations in the comparison between levels. The correlations are much higher at the cluster levels on the two general attitude variables, on the correlations of lenient limits with both positive and negative attitudes to drinking and on the correlations of abstinence with high-maximum drinking (in spite of the mutual exclusivity at the individual level). On the other hand, the correlations are as high or higher at the individual level on positive attitudes with "nothing good" (i.e., there is more consistency of drinking attitudes

TABLE 44.—*Intercorrelations of Nine Dichotomized Cluster and Individual Variables*

Cluster Scores	C-2	C-3	C-4	C-5	C-6	C-7	C-8	C-9	I-1	I-2	I-3	I-4	I-5	I-6	I-7	I-8	I-9
C-1. Nonhelpfulness of others	.47	.15	.36	−.09	−.24	.43	.15	.18	.27	.17	.07	.14	−.12	−.18	.15	.07	.09
C-2. Tolerance of deviance		.19	.22	−.07	−.18	.27	.25	.20	.18	.26	.12	.14	−.10	−.15	.13	.06	.10
C-3. Lenient limits on drinking			.53	−.48	−.59	.60	.46	−.15	.05	.10	.29	.19	−.23	−.25	.18	.17	−.05
C-4. Positive attitudes to drinking				−.33	−.45	.50	.34	−.05	.11	.13	.20	.27	−.22	−.25	.20	.15	.01
C-5. "Nothing good" about drinking					.54	−.45	−.13	.42	.05	−.04	−.20	−.17	.26	.24	−.14	−.11	.13
C-6. Abstinence						−.69	−.20	.11	−.03	−.09	−.20	−.19	.24	.33	−.19	−.13	.01
C-7. High maximum drinking							.33	−.04	.08	.13	.23	.20	−.22	−.32	.26	.17	.04
C-8. Heavy drinking by others								.07	.05	.09	.20	.13	−.14	−.17	.16	.21	.08
C-9. Tangible consequences									.08	.07	−.08	−.03	.10	.04	.00	.00	.24
Individual Scores																	
I-1. Nonhelpfulness of others										.18	.01	.01	−.02	−.08	−.08	.10	.08
I-2. Tolerance of deviance											.16	.14	−.09	−.13	.19	.17	.11
I-3. Lenient limits on R's drinking												.29	−.25	−.30	.43	.41	.08
I-4. Positive attitudes to drinking													−.42	−.30	.33	.26	.13
I-5. "Nothing good" about drinking														.37	−.31	−.22	−.05
I-6. Abstinence															−.51	−.22	−.13
I-7. High maximum drinker																.31	.25
I-8. Heavy drinking by others																	.15
I-9. Tangible consequences																	

at the individual than at the collective level) and on heavy drinking by others with the two respondent's behavior measures (although this may be the result of response artifacts).

The correlations between individual and cluster scores within each domain are definitely lower than both the analogous individual–individual and cluster–cluster correlations, i.e., both neighborhood and individuals' characteristics show more coherence within themselves than between each other. Even if we can assign a definite characterization to a neighborhood, this implies that there is a sufficient assortment of individuals within the neighborhood that its characteristics yield only a modest prediction of individual characteristics.

Over-all, the cluster–individual correlations tend to be reflexive, both within and between domains of meaning—that is, the correlation of cluster variable A and individual variable B tends to be about the same as the correlations of individual variable A and cluster variable B. There are a few exceptions: the cluster score on nonhelpfulness is more strongly negatively related to individual abstinence and "nothing good" about drinking, and the cluster score on high-maximum drinking is more strongly negatively related to individual abstinence than the reflexive correlation. These patterns may reflect the relatively strong predictive power of urban neighborhood for the individual's drinking at all.

Looking at the correlations with individual tangible consequences as indicators of the gross power of other variables in predicting consequences of the individual's drinking, we find no strong relationships: the two strongest are the artifactual correlations with cluster tangible consequences and with individual high-maximum drinking. The general attitudes and norms variables show a modest association, both as defined for the cluster and the individual. Positive attitudes and drinking-behavior variables at the individual level (describing both the individual and his close associates) are associated with tangible consequences, as Chapter 5 would have led us to expect, but the only cluster-level variable in these areas with a strong association with individual tangible consequences is the indicator of temperance sentiment. This poses the hypothesis that tangible consequences are particularly associated with heavy drinking in what may be a supportive close environment but in a generally hostile community.

If we examine the relations with individual high-maximum drinking as an indicator of relatively heavy-drinking behavior, the findings form a strong contrast with those on individual tangible consequences. With the exception of the individual nonhelpfulness score and the cluster tangible consequences, all variables shown are more highly correlated with individual high-maximum drinking than with individual tangible consequences. Individual relatively heavy drinking seems, therefore, to be more predictable both from cluster and individual variables like those used in the table than are tangible *consequences* of drinking to the individual.

Generally speaking, the same patterns hold when a comparison is made between high-maximum drinking and tangible consequences defined at the cluster level. Again, a relatively high level of heavy drinking in the neighborhood is more predictable with the type of variables used, whether for the cluster or the individual, than a relatively high level of socially disruptive consequences of drinking. By far the strongest correlate of cluster tangible consequences is cluster temperance sentiment, whereas cluster temperance sentiment is strongly associated with a low proportion of heavy drinkers in the cluster.

All in all, the associations found in Table 44 suggest that it is the interaction of general community temperance sentiment with individual relatively heavy drinking, within an immediate personal context of other relatively heavy drinkers, that provides the most likely circumstance for acquiring tangible consequences of a given behavior. We will shortly explore this hypothesis in a more direct fashion. In its general form, it bears some resemblance to an earlier study (96) of the relation of context and individual characteristics to a very different dependent variable, academic failure: "there is more to the process of failure than can be explained by either individual attitudes or contextual atmosphere alone. The *relation* of the individual to his milieu is an essential ingredient as well" (*pp. 292–293*).

D. *Interaction of Abstaining Environment and Explosive Drinking*

In general, the correlations with tangible consequences found in Table 44 fit into the patterns of relations in the current problems typology by urbanization and region discussed in Chapter 4. From these relations, and the earlier discussions of U.S. regional and Finnish versus Danish patterns, we may propound the hypothesis that while steady relatively heavy drinking, and its eventual long-term medical complications, are associated primarily with wet areas, it is in the dry areas with a strong abstinence tradition that explosive drinking patterns, social disruptions associated with drinking and acute alcohol poisonings (119) predominate.

Before proceeding to test further aspects of this hypothesis, it is worth discussing in some detail its several possible statistical meanings. In descending order of stringency, the hypothesis can be interpreted to mean (1) that there is a larger proportion of intermittent explosive drinkers in the total population of abstaining milieus than elsewhere; (2) that there is a larger proportion of intermittent explosive drinkers among the population of drinkers in abstaining milieus than elsewhere; and (3) that the "mix" of heavy drinkers is different in abstaining milieus than it is elsewhere, i.e., the ratio of intermittent explosive to steady heavy drinkers is higher in abstaining milieus.

The practical implications of these versions of the hypothesis are somewhat different. If the first version is true, it suggests that there is something in the abstaining milieus which is positively associated with binge drinking. It lends plausibility to the "inoculation" theorists (e.g., 27, 35), for it suggests that the absolute number of explosive drinkers might decline if moderate drinking were tolerated, especially in one's formative years.

If only the second version of the hypothesis is true, the result can be viewed as fitting a "reaction" model—a prohibitory environment effectively discourages proscribed behavior, but a greater proportion of the behavior that does occur will be extreme, perpetrated either by those whose need to drink heavily is very great or by those in defiance of social constraints. However, whether the extreme behavior can be regarded as "produced" by the abstaining milieu is open to serious question: it is perhaps more plausible to focus instead on a middle mass of people to whom drinking is just not a very important issue, so that they are easily swayed by contextual constraints— they are abstainers in dry areas, occasional drinkers in wet areas. If there is such a group of "fair-weather drinkers" shifting back and forth across the boundary of abstinence according to context, the fact that there is a higher proportion of extreme behavior among drinkers in a dry environment would seem to be not so much an argument that the dry environment produces extreme behavior as that the dry environment strips off the protective cocoon of light and moderate drinkers. In any case, if the absolute number of intermittent explosive drinkers is smaller in dry areas (i.e., if hypothesis 1 is not sustained) the results must be regarded as tending against the "inoculation" theory.

If only the third hypothesis is true, we might surmise that living in a dry region "causes" heavy drinkers to bunch their drinking. We can think of a number of practical reasons why this could be so (e.g., forcing people to buy a bottle at a time or only on weekends). Or the reasons could be of somewhat grander theoretical status (e.g., aspects of the culture).

We have pursued these logical possibilities in some detail because there is a great temptation to expand on the assertion that there is an association between an abstaining milieu and the occurrence of extreme behavior, often based on findings like hypothesis 3 above, and to use the findings to make assertions about cause and effect.

In the following sections, we present some summary evaluations of the correlates of living in a dry area. A fuller test in the same samples of formally analogous theses concerning the effects of religious background is undertaken in a dissertation by Seifert (129).

E. Cluster and Intermittent Very Heavy Drinking

Table 45 pursues the hypothesis that those who do drink within a highly abstinent environment will tend more than those in other environments to go on binges or to drink very heavily at sporadic intervals rather than steadily, reacting to the unfavorable drinking climate by occasional release of pent-up compulsions or response to temptations to drink heavily. Data from the N3 sample are used since only this portion included the questions appropriate for classifying very heavy drinking. In the table very heavy is compared with steady

TABLE 45.—*Current Very Heavy and Steady Heavy Drinkers by Cluster Dryness and Region and Urbanization, in Per Cent*[a]

	CLUSTER DRYNESS			REGION AND URBANIZATION					
				Wet Regions			Dry Regions		
	Wet	Medium	Dry	City	Town	Rural	City	Town	Rural
% of Total Sample	(N = 444)	(405)	(129)	(355)	(145)	(70)	(139)	(174)	(95)
Very heavy	15	7	8	13	6	4	20	9	5
Steady fairly heavy	29	19	8	27	16	14	24	15	9
% of Drinkers	(N = 414)	(347)	(64)	(320)	(131)	(58)	(121)	(142)	(53)
Very heavy	16	8	16	15	7	5	22	11	9
Steady fairly heavy	27	22	16	30	18	17	26	18	17

[a] N3 data only. Dry = 50% or more (sex-averaged) abstainers; Wet = 34% or more (sex-averaged) high-maximum drinkers. City = cities of 50,000+. Town = towns and small cities. Rural = rural areas of under 2500. Very heavy and steady heavy drinking are not mutually exclusive.

fairly heavy drinking, defined as in Chapter 6, for clusters of varying wetness and for urbanization within wet and dry regions.

The results of the cluster scores in Table 45 suggest that the first hypothesis is not supported, but that the third is: the ratio of very heavy to steady heavy drinkers is higher in dry neighborhoods, but the actual proportion of very heavy drinkers is higher in wet neighborhoods. The results for the second hypothesis are equivocal: the proportion of very heavy drinkers among drinkers in dry neighborhoods does slightly exceed the average proportion elsewhere (wet and medium), but in fact the distribution is bimodal—the lowest ratio of very heavy drinkers to all drinkers is in clusters which are neither wet nor dry.

The results by region and urbanization offer some further illumination and specification. At least in terms of current patterns, very heavy drinking is commoner in the cities than in the rural areas of both wet and dry regions. But it is commonest in the cities and towns of the dry rather than the wet regions. For urban but not rural populations, then, these results would be in accord with the first hypothesis.

It is worth noting that the ratio of very heavy to steady heavy drinkers is consistently higher in the dryer region and more rural groups than in the wetter and more citified. The third hypothesis is systematically supported.

There are a number of possible alternative explanations for why binge drinking is most common in urban areas of dry regions (e.g., ethnic mix, historical peculiarities). One suggestion from Finnish research (1) is that highly disruptive drinking styles are an accompaniment of rapid urbanization. In the subsistence economy of the country, there is little cash and when some is accumulated, it is traditionally blown on occasional communal sprees. When these mores are transplanted to the cash economy of the city, the patterns persist, but now there is enough money to do it often. Another equally plausible possibility is that the urban areas of dry territories serve as oases in the desert, to which the dedicated heavy drinker tends to migrate at least temporarily, and in which a frontier drink-it-up atmosphere evolves to respond to the needs of both the more permanent and the week-end spree immigrants.

F. Social Consequences and Type of Heavy Drinking

The next hypothesis to test is whether the social consequences of heavy drinking (in terms of having drinking-related problems with one's wife, friends or neighbors, on the job or with the police) are more severe in dry neighborhoods than in wet. This would be expected in view of our finding (Chapter 4) that a given level of intake in the drier regions of the country is associated with a higher level of consequences (including the above social consequences) than is true in the wetter regions.

Two points to establish, as a preliminary to the cluster analysis, are whether the more explosive type of current very heavy drinking (which is more prevalent in relation to steady fairly heavy drinking in dryer areas) is more highly associated with social consequences than is the steady fairly heavy drinking which is more common in the wetter areas; and whether the association between current very heavy drinking and social consequences still applies regardless of the definition of cutting points for social consequences. Table 46 shows an orderly progression in the magnitude of the proportion of persons having social consequences (regardless of whether the cutting point is set at a "moderate" or at a "severe" level), with those with both very heavy and steady fairly heavy drinking patterns having the highest social consequences rates, and those with neither very heavy nor steady fairly heavy patterns having a negligible rate of social consequences.

Table 46 also shows that the level of social consequences appears to distinguish between the four drinking groups more sharply at the severe level than at the moderate level. Very heavy drinking, then, seems to be specially associated with relatively severe social consequences.

The relationships between intake and social consequences, holding cluster and regional wetness or dryness constant, are shown in Table 47. In order to include the larger numbers of the combined N2–N3 sample, both the definitions of social consequences and of intake differ somewhat from those used in the N3 sample reported in Table 46. The heaviest-intake category, as discussed earlier (Table 43), is roughly equivalent to the combination of current very heavy and current

Table 46.—*Current Social Consequences of Drinking by Type of Heavy Drinking, in Per Cent*[a]

	N	Severe Consequences	Moderate to Severe Consequences
Very heavy and steady fairly heavy	68	29	57
Very heavy only	38	18	34
Steady fairly heavy only	127	4	16
Neither	745	1	4

[a] N3 data only. Severe social consequences = a score of 5 or more, moderate to severe = a score of 3 or more, on the combination of problems with wife, friends and neighbors, on the job or with police (Appendix B).

steady fairly heavy drinking; it is not possible to distinguish between these two categories in the N2–N3 combined data. However, the cutting points for both the social consequences and intake measures in the combined N2–N3 sample fulfill the basic objective of setting the intake measure relatively low to provide sufficient numbers so that it can function as a kind of control for equal behavior: given approximately equal drinking behavior, what are the chances of social consequences in different milieus?

In Table 47-A we again view for comparative purposes the steady progression of intake from dry to wet environments. Whether the cutting-point is at the moderate or severe level, however, we find bimodality in social consequences: higher in wet and dry than in medium-wetness neighborhoods, higher in the city and country than in towns. In fact, if we dichotomize the measures at dry versus wet region, dry versus wet and medium neighborhoods, and rural versus urban, we find the proportion of social consequences higher in each instance on the "dryer" side, in dry-region cities.

Social consequences are the net result of an interaction between the respondent's behavior and his environment. In wet milieus, the excess of consequences undoubtedly reflects an excess of behavior; in dry milieus, the excess may be largely a function of community censure, but may also relate to peculiarly obnoxious styles of drinking.

In Table 47-B the intake control is applied—e.g., of those with a heaviest intake, what proportions have at least moderate

TABLE 47.—*Interaction of Intake and Social Consequences, by Cluster Dryness and Region and Urbanization*[a]

| | CLUSTER DRYNESS | | | REGION AND URBANIZATION | | | | | |
| | | | | Wet Regions | | | Dry Regions | | |
	Wet	Medium	Dry	City	Town	Rural	City	Town	Rural
A. % of the total sample with:	(N = 626)	(683)	(245)	(508)	(271)	(130)	(184)	(278)	(190)
Heaviest intake[b]	26	17	11	27	18	15	27	12	9
Severe social consequences	5	2	5	4	2	3	7	3	5
Moderate or severe social consequences	10	6	12	10	6	9	14	8	9
B. % of those with heaviest intake who have:	(N = 160)	(118)	(26)	(137)	(50)	(20)	(49)	(33)	(17)
Severe social consequences	13	8	27	12	8	5	20	6	29
Moderate or severe social consequences	28	19	62	26	14	40	38	24	41

[a] N2–N3 data and problem scores. Social consequences severities defined analogously to Table 46. Seven respondents from clusters unclassified on cluster dryness are excluded from the cluster dryness tabulations.
[b] Minimal-severity heavy intake or binge (Appendix B).

and at least severe consequences? In general, we again find bimodality, but with a much higher proportion in abstaining environments than elsewhere. Except for the small-N wet–rural group, the choice of severe, or of moderate or severe, social consequences does not appear to make much difference.

Even when current intake is set at a relatively modest level, many people apprently end up with social consequences out of all proportion to at least their current drinking: 37% of the 60 with "severe" social consequences and 45% of the 85 with "moderate" social consequences do not qualify on the current intake criterion. These anomalous cases do not seem to be particularly concentrated in wet or dry milieus. Some may stem from denial or underreporting of intake, and some respondents may experience maximum social consequences from a minimum of drinking—through an environment inhospitable to drinking, or their inability to hold their liquor. Further, the suffering of social consequences without current heavy intake may illustrate (1) the "reverse halo" effect found in the time orderings (Chapter 3), where consequences may persist long after causes; (2) Mulford's failure to show universal heavy drinking in his Cedar Rapids "identified alcoholics" samples (95, p. 21); and (3) the consistent finding of a minority of institutionalized alcoholics who do not drink very much (114).

Our follow-up studies may shed additional light on the circumstances in which a given amount of intake may, or may not, be followed by social consequences. For the moment, the evidence indicates that while the general tenor of community permissiveness about drinking has considerable bearing on whether or not the heavy drinker suffers social consequences, this appears in many instances to be contingent upon individual circumstances. In other words, some heavy drinkers appear to be more competent in organizing their lives and interpersonal relationships so as to avoid all but a minimum of consequences from their drinking.

G. Interaction of Neighborhood and Individual High Intake

In general we have found that heavy drinkers in dry neighborhoods, in comparison to heavy drinkers in wet neighborhoods, have a higher rate of tangible consequences of drinking and are more likely to do their heavy drinking only intermittently. There are two major possible lines of interpretation of these findings:

1. The findings reflect special characteristics of individuals who choose to drink heavily in spite of social disapproval. This interpretation, of course, fits with traditional psychological theories of deviance, which tend to stress immanent psychological defects as explanations of the occurrence and continuation of deviant acts in the face of social pressures. For this interpretation to carry weight, we should find that heavy drinkers in dry communities differ systematically on relevant dimensions from both heavy drinkers elsewhere and other respondents in the dry communities.

2. The findings are simply a result of community pressures against drinking, which act both to diminish the frequency of drinking occasions and to increase the probability of tangible consequences of drinking. This interpretation resembles functionalist labeling interpretations of deviance in sociology: individual deviance is a result of social processes external to the individual expelling him from "normality," and these processes of labeling are part of the community's "boundary-maintaining" public reassertions of the limits of the acceptable. If this interpretation is to provide a full explanation, the individual characteristics we find among heavy drinkers should not vary substantially between those in wet and in dry communities.

Of course, the two lines of explanation can be and are often combined. Thus labeling theory describes an internalization of the deviant label as the process of "deviant socialization" and often contemplates a metastasis of the deviant status into a "master status" that transforms the deviant person's whole identity. Conversely, recent theories usually accord an important role to questions of "social etiology." Prior to thrashing out the intricacies of the interactive processes which may be involved, however, it would seem necessary to establish whether evidence for both lines of interpretation can be found in our data.

The plausibility of the explanation in terms of social constraints has already been fairly well established by the results of Table 44: a community attitude that there is "nothing good" about drinking was found to have a very high correlation with the community level of tangible consequences of drinking, and to show a higher correlation with individual consequences than with any other community variable (except for the partly artifactual relationship with community level of tangible consequences). To explore the plausibility of interpretations in terms of individual characteristics, we show in the following three tables profile analyses of three general categories of drinking behavior—abstaining, moderate drinking and the heaviest-intake group—separately for each of the three characterizations of neighborhoods in terms of cluster wetness. The crucial group in these comparisons, the heaviest-intake respondents living in dry clusters, is also unfortunately the smallest; our results cannot therefore be regarded as conclusive.

Table 48 shows the results of such a profile analysis of the social-differentiation variables. Heaviest-intake respondents in dry neighborhoods indeed seem to be the group with the highest proportion in the lowest socioeconomic status. There is room for doubt about whether this result represents a characteristic peculiar to them, however: people in dry neighborhoods in general are more likely to be of low status, whatever their drinking habits, while heavy drinkers also tend to be disproportionately concentrated in the lowest status no matter where they live, so that the result for the dry-area heaviest-intake category can be seen merely as the culmination of these two trends.

Cluster wetness clearly makes no difference for any class of drinker in terms of age distribution, although, as we would expect, age is heavily related to individual drinking patterns. On ethnicity, the major variations by cluster wetness within drinking groups are a concentration of British ethnicity among heavy drinkers in dry clusters and of Blacks among abstainers in wet clusters; both of these results, however, would disappear with a shift of as few as four cases. On religious affiliation, the patterns of Catholicism and conservative Protestantism provide each other's obverse: Catholicism increases and conservative Protestantism decreases regularly with both individual drinking and cluster wetness. Liberal Protestantism appears to be identified particularly with conformity: liberal Protestants are a disproportionate part of the abstainers in dry

TABLE 48.—*Interaction of Neighborhood and Individual Drinking Characteristics by Social-Differentiation Variables, in Per Cent*[a]

Respondent's Drinking Cluster Wetness:	Abstainer			Moderate Drinker			Heaviest Intake			Totals
	Dry (N=102)	Medium (87)	Wet (43)	Dry (116)	Medium (476)	Wet (408)	Dry (27)	Medium (120)	Wet (175)	(1561)
Index of Social Position										
Upper	15	28	33	15	34	38	22	21	27	30
Upper middle	27	23	23	24	28	26	15	32	19	26
Lower middle	30	29	28	36	27	22	26	28	24	26
Lower	28	21	16	25	11	14	37	19	30	18
Age										
21–29	13	12	7	16	23	21	33	33	35	23
30–39	21	20	26	31	24	27	26	28	29	26
40–49	28	26	33	25	30	28	19	24	21	27
50–59	38	43	35	29	23	24	22	14	15	24
Ethnic Groups										
British	26	23	21	31	25	16	33	13	15	21
Irish	12	12	12	14	11	13	15	9	9	12
German	21	17	14	17	23	21	7	22	12	20
Italian	0	2	2	1	5	6	0	9	6	5
Latin Amer.–Carib.	0	2	9	0	1	3	0	4	11	3
Jewish	0	3	0	0	3	5	0	1	1	3
Black	5	7	16	6	3	6	15	7	22	8
Eastern European	1	5	5	0	7	7	0	10	6	6
Religion										
Catholic	0	20	33	1	29	41	4	54	46	31
Jewish	0	3	0	0	3	5	0	1	1	3
Liberal Prot.	13	9	2	7	15	19	7	11	14	14
Conservative Prot.	82	61	56	88	42	25	74	24	24	42
No religion	2	2	2	1	6	6	7	8	7	5
Home-Role Instability (2+)	11	9	9	11	11	16	22	18	29	15

[a] N2–N3 sample. See definitions in footnotes to Tables 45 and 47. Seven respondents unclassified on cluster dryness are tabulated only in the Totals column.

areas and of the heaviest-intake category in wet areas. Cluster wetness does not appear to affect the general relationship between heavy drinking and home-role instability.

On father's maximum quantity of drinking (Table 49), cluster wetness affects the association with the respondent's drinking pattern only for abstaining and moderate-drinking respondents: these respondents from dry localities are more likely to have an abstaining father and less likely to have a heavy-drinking father than abstainers and moderate drinkers from wetter localities. That the extent of intergenerational linkage of drinking patterns fails to be affected by general community context for respondents who are heavy drinkers perhaps can be seen as suggesting that the genesis of heavy drinking is relatively impervious to community pressures. In general, partly as a result of this pattern, the association of father's with son's drinking patterns is far stronger in dry than in wet clusters.

The three single-item indicators of childhood history available from the N2–N3 sample do not show any differences by cluster wetness among heaviest-intake respondents, although heavy drinking itself shows some association with each of the items. This result suggests that any special personal peculiarities which may be attributed to heavy drinkers who live in dry neighborhoods are not likely to have been foreordained from childhood.

The results by the available personality scores, which are crucial to any theory of special personal maladjustment underlying heavy drinking in dry environments, are rather mixed. Cluster wetness appears to have no influence on affective anxiety at any level of individual drinking. Heaviest-intake respondents living in dry clusters appear to have lower rates of tolerance of deviance than other heavy drinkers and lower rates of alienation than any other category. The tolerance finding fits into a general pattern: tolerance of deviance varies directly with both cluster wetness and individual drinking pattern. The alienation finding is, however, anomalous, both in terms of the empirical patterns and of theory. Some new twist in theory, perhaps of cosmopolitan interests and attachments among rural and small-town heavy drinkers, is needed if this result holds up in future studies with larger Ns. On the

TABLE 49.—*Interaction of Neighborhood and Individual Drinking Characteristics by Personality, Social and Drinking-Context Variables, in Per Cent*

Respondent's Drinking: Cluster Wetness:	Abstainer			Moderate Drinker			Heaviest Intake			Totals
	Dry (N=102)	Medium (87)	Wet (43)	Dry (116)	Medium (476)	Wet (408)	Dry (27)	Medium (120)	Wet (175)	(1561)
Childhood History										
Father's max. quantity										
8+ drinks	12	23	26	23	28	31	46	52	47	31
1–7 drinks	29	41	46	43	52	54	38	35	36	46
Abstainer	60	36	28	35	20	15	17	13	17	23
Childhood hardship[a]	24	31	37	29	34	35	43	35	45	35
Family disruption[a]	7	19	21	11	14	11	22	19	23	14
Childhood unhappiness[a]	9	18	9	11	11	15	19	18	26	15
Personality										
Somatization (1+)	27	16	26	29	24	17	44	32	28	24
Affective anxiety (1+)	34	38	48	36	37	36	52	41	47	39
Alienation[a] (1+)	42	45	44	44	34	34	33	52	52	40
Impulsivity[a] (2+)	28	23	23	37	28	24	59	44	45	31
Tolerance of deviance (1+)	31	31	40	47	54	60	52	73	78	56
Social Situation										
Nonhelpfulness of others[a] (1+)	11	28	16	23	27	26	30	35	41	27
Social activity[a] (1+)	53	41	44	56	50	54	48	65	61	53
Lack of neighborhood roots (3+)	6	10	14	10	13	10	15	16	18	12
Drug habits[a] (4+)	13	11	14	11	17	17	18	17	21	16
Home-role friction (3+)	13	14	21	21	18	17	22	24	27	19
Work friction (2+)	8	13	9	15	12	10	11	17	14	12
Drinking Context										
Heavy-drinking context[a] (5+)	0	3	14	16	32	47	59	69	77	39
Others' attitudes to R's drinking (1+)	5	10	12	16	45	48	52	65	67	42
R's attitudes to drinking[a] (1+)	20	24	28	51	44	32	52	39	35	37

[a] N2–N3 sample. See footnote to Table 48. Differs in details from the equivalent N3 score in Appendix C.

other hand, the dry-cluster heavy drinkers do show the highest prevalence of somatization and of impulsivity. The somatization pattern conforms to the pattern we would expect if heavy drinking in dry areas were a particular result of individual maladjustment—that is, a solitary deviation from a relatively flat pattern of the other eight groups. Theoretical grounds for explaining why this pattern should appear particularly on somatization, and not, say, on affective anxiety, however, are not immediately obvious. The impulsivity pattern shows a greater regularity across the nine groups: impulsivity seems to be higher everywhere among drinkers, and particularly among heavy drinkers, than among abstainers, but also to be consistently higher at all levels of drinking in dry clusters. The association of impulsivity with dry neighborhoods is an interesting reversal of the general trend of results that would seem worth following up in further research.

Heavy drinkers in dry neighborhoods are somewhat less likely than other heavy drinkers to see others as nonhelpful, although in this they reflect a general tendency among residents of dry neighborhoods. Interestingly, the categories showing the greatest discrepancy between individual and collective behavior (abstainers living in medium or wet areas and heavy drinkers living in dry areas) show lower rates of social activity than any other groups; their out-of-step drinking behavior seems to be associated with a more general isolation from the community. The other situational and habits variables show essentially no differences by cluster wetness on comparisons at a given level of individual intake.

Like tolerance of deviance, but even more dramatically, both drinking context and the tolerant attitudes of others toward the respondent's drinking show a regular and cumulative relation with both cluster wetness and individual drinking. Heavy drinkers in dry areas thus appear to show less attachment to a drinking subculture than do heavy drinkers in wet areas, at least as this is measured by frequency of contact with other heavy drinkers and of visiting taverns. The drinking behavior itself may be more "enclaved" in dry communities, but it does not appear to form a larger portion of the lives of heavy drinkers there than elsewhere. On the other hand, heavy drinkers in dry areas appear to be more attached to their drinking behavior than heavy drinkers elsewhere, at least as this is measured by the expression of positive attitudes toward drinking. This result does not carry any heavy theoretical implications, however; it would perhaps be more of a surprise if those who engaged in a socially devalued behavior did not show positive individual attitudes toward the behavior.

It has already been shown that heavy intake carries a stronger probability of tangible consequences in dry than in wet areas. Table 50 shows that this result is primarily attributable to differences in the specific consequences of wife and job problems, suggesting that the special constraints of a dry locale are more likely to be felt in the heavy-drinking person's major roles of family and work responsibility than through the impersonal processes of police action. Dry-area heavy drinkers also show higher rates of binge drinking, symptomatic behavior and indications of loss of control over drinking. These findings would seem to suggest a greater "preoccupation with alcohol," as some scales dealing with these areas have been called, among heavy drinkers in dry communities. But again, this pre-

TABLE 50.—*Interaction of Neighborhood and Individual Drinking Characteristics, by High Problems, in Per Cent*[a]

Respondent's Drinking: Cluster Wetness:	Moderate Drinker			Heaviest Intake			
	Dry (N = 116)	Medium (476)	Wet (408)	Dry (27)	Medium (210)	Wet (175)	Total (1561)
Heavy intake	0	0	0	11	32	26	6
Binge	0	0	0	30	11	16	3
Psychological dependence	3	3	2	19	8	14	5
Symptomatic drinking	6	4	5	48	28	31	9
Loss of control	3	3	3	37	12	20	6
Belligerence	6	6	5	30	12	28	8
Wife	16	8	7	44	30	28	12
Friends, neighbors	9	2	4	22	13	18	6
Job	7	3	3	30	7	17	5
Police	5	1	2	7	8	10	3
Health, injuries	4	4	6	22	11	14	6
Financial	8	3	2	15	8	14	4

[a] N2–N3 sample. Abstainers are excluded. The zero prevalences on Heavy intake and Binge for moderate drinkers is a result of the automatic inclusion of these patterns in the Heaviest intake category.

occupation can be socially conditioned: someone has to be trying to watch for a respondent to respond positively to a symptomatic behavior item such as "I sneak drinks when no one is looking." Contrary to an hypothesis of a special association of drinking and violence in dry areas, the rates of belligerent behavior while drinking do not vary by cluster wetness.

Although the small number in the most crucial category suggests caution about any conclusions, it seems that theories of maladjustment of heavy drinkers in dry areas, whether it is seen as immanent or as a result of social interaction, have received at best limited support from this analysis. At least at the levels of heavy drinking and tangible consequences which can be dealt with in a general-population sample, it remains plausible that the specially strong association of tangible consequences with heavy drinking in dry areas is more a matter of the strong local reactions to heavy drinking behavior than of strong inherent maladjustments of the heavy drinker.

H. Cross-Pressures in Interaction of Neighborhood and Respondent Behavior and Attitudes in Drinking Problems

In our analyses so far, the primary measure of the interaction of neighborhood and individual characteristics has been a summary measure of actual drinking behavior by the respondent and in the community. The effects of interactions for a broader range of variables on social consequences of drinking and the ratio of social consequences to heavy intake are shown in Table 51. For each characteristic examined, the sample is divided into four groups according to whether the individual possesses the characteristic and according to whether the sample cluster in which he lives has a high or low proportion with the characteristic ("True of Cluster" means a high proportion with the characteristic). The table thus allows us to examine the effects of cross-pressures in the interaction of neighborhood and respondent characteristics on drinking problems.

At the cluster level, a number of the characteristics examined —wife's abstinence, father's abstinence, respondent's abstinence, respondent's favorable attitude, and "nothing good" about drinking—may be regarded as highly interrelated indicators of the general level of acceptance of drinking in the

TABLE 51.—*Interaction of Neighborhood and Respondent Behavior and Attitudes, in Per Cent*[a]

Behavioral Items	Not True of Respondent or Cluster	True of Respondent Only	True of Cluster Only	True of Both Cluster and Respondent
Wife an abstainer	(N = 605)	(118)	(221)	(252)
Heaviest intake	7	4	5	4
High social conseq.	8	5	12	10
Drinks served more than half the time when with close friends	(N = 468)	(104)	(395)	(479)
Heaviest intake	1	13	2	12
High social conseq.	7	19	8	12
Father a lifelong abstainer	(N = 626)	(66)	(375)	(224)
Heaviest intake	7	5	5	5
High social conseq.	8	5	12	9
Weekly drinking[b]	(N = 378)	(214)	(319)	(643)
Heaviest intake	0	7	0	11
High social conseq.	4	17	5	12
Current abstainers[b][c]	(N = 877)	(95)	(377)	(205)
Heaviest intake	8	0	5	1
High social conseq.	9	4	14	4
Bar-going at least occasionally	(N = 522)	(194)	(302)	(322)
Heaviest intake	3	9	3	11
High social conseq.	5	12	5	18
Close friends drink quite a bit	(N = 534)	(171)	(391)	(350)
Heaviest intake	2	5	3	14
High social conseq.	6	15	7	15
Significant others drink rather heavily	(N = 371)	(217)	(317)	(431)
Heaviest intake	2	7	4	9
High social conseq.	6	13	6	14
Close relatives or friends with drinking problem[b]	(N = 389)	(358)	(291)	(516)
Heaviest intake	7	8	5	4
High social conseq.	8	11	8	10

[Continued on next page]

TABLE 51.—*continued*

Attitude Items	Not True of Respondent or Cluster	True of Respondent Only	True of Cluster Only	True of Both Cluster and Respondent
Significant others seen as approving of R's heavy drinking	(N = 464)	(182)	(295)	(225)
Heaviest intake	2	7	3	11
High social conseq.	11	16	6	8
Respondent favorable attitude toward drinking	(N = 390)	(236)	(252)	(458)
Heaviest intake	3	7	5	8
High social conseq.	8	15	7	10
Nothing good to be said about drinking[b]	(N = 779)	(178)	(347)	(250)
Heaviest intake	7	2	6	4
High social conseq.	7	6	16	9
Others (wife, friends, neighbors, co-workers, police) would not be helpful in emergency	(N = 623)	(127)	(344)	(242)
Heaviest intake	5	3	7	8
High social conseq.	7	12	9	16
Tolerant of deviance	(N = 589)	(199)	(269)	(242)
Heaviest intake	3	7	7	9
High social conseq.	8	12	8	13

[a] Table to be read as follows: of the 605 respondents whose wives were not abstainers, and for whom the total respondents for that cluster showed a below-average rate of abstaining wives, 7% had high intake scores and 8% had high social-consequences scores. Total Ns vary for each item according to the number of clusters which could be scored and the number of applicable individuals.

[b] Cluster score computed (sex-averaged) on total N1–N3 samples. (All others shown are computed on men aged 21–59 only.)

[c] Abstinence is defined by current pattern, intake and social consequences by the last 3 years.

respondent's community (see the relatively high cluster-level intercorrelations for some of these characteristics in Table 44). As our previous analysis might suggest, both the prevalence of social consequences for the respondent and the ratio of social consequences to heaviest intake are positively related to the cluster's dryness on these characteristics. At the individual

level, however, these characteristics hold different implications—some are indications of the respondent's dryness, while
some indicate the dryness of his immediate circle of relatives.
We might expect that dry relatives would contribute to an especially severe ratio of consequences to intake for respondents
in dry milieux. In fact, however, for all these characteristics,
the dryness of the respondent-level characteristic does not have
much effect on the ratio of social consequences to intake, and
is regularly negatively related to the absolute level of social
consequences. Wife's and father's abstinence thus seem to
function in this analysis simply as indirect indicators of the
dryness of the related respondent. Consistently, the highest
prevalence of social consequences occurs for the wet individ-
ual-level and dry cluster-level pattern.

A somewhat different consistent pattern occurs for characteristics indicating regular drinking and immersion in a regular-
drinking milieu—drinks served with friends, weekly drinking,
close friends drinking quite a bit, significant others drinking
heavily, and significant others approving the respondent's
drinking. Again, the highest prevalence of social consequences
tends to occur in the dry-milieu–wet-respondent category, although for the two items indicating others' heavy drinking the
prevalence is matched by the wet–wet category. But the ratio
of consequences to intake is fairly even except for the wet–wet
category: respondents with a personal regular-drinking milieu
living in a regular-drinking cluster appear to be especially likely to drink heavily without social consequences.

Two other drinking-related characteristics show special patterns. The general lack of variation for close relatives or friends
having a drinking problem probably reflects that "drinking
problem" in this item appears to be sufficiently differentially
interpreted by differently situated respondents that this item
shows little variation between wet and dry milieus (20, *Table
A-75*). The tendency of high social consequences to be associated with both individual and cluster-level bar-going, and to
show no great variation on the ratio of consequences to intake,
also partially reflects that bar-going is not especially a "wet
area" phenomenon, so that a greater proportion of the drinking in dry areas than in wet areas may be done in bars (117,
Table 5).

The two indicators of general attitudes and norms show somewhat disparate patterns. For the nonhelpfulness of others, the prevalence of social consequences appears to be related to lack of cohesiveness in the cluster as well as more strongly to individual alienation. The ratio of consequences to intake, however, is primarily related to individual alienation, and is especially high in cohesive clusters. For tolerance of deviance, social consequences are higher in the presence of tolerance at the individual level, but are not higher with its absence at the cluster level, as we might have expected. Intolerant individuals in tolerant clusters appear to have an especially low ratio of social consequences to heavy intake.

In general, the results in Table 51 reemphasize the interactive roles of wet behavior and dry context in producing the social problems associated with drinking. This general relationship shows somewhat different patterns according to the characteristics compared, and is particularly strong for items measuring "dry" rather than "wet" characteristics. The relationship appears to be relatively specific to drinking characteristics associated with general "wetness" and "dryness," and does not straightforwardly extend to more general attitudinal characteristics such as tolerance of deviance.

I. Summary

This chapter has analyzed the association between respondents' drinking behavior and attitudes toward drinking and neighborhood and regional patterns, as measured by aggregating the data for the sampling areas within which respondents live. These aggregate data give us an independent measure of the social context in which the individual respondent acts.

In general, it was found that heavy drinking was more likely to result in tangible consequences (particularly wife and job problems) in dry contexts than in wet. Heavy drinking in dry contexts also tended to have its own style: although infrequent very heavy drinking was not more generally common in dry than in wet areas, it did form a proportionately greater part of all heavy drinking in dry areas. Heavy drinking was also more associated with indications of symptomatic drinking and loss of control in dry areas than in wet.

The consistent association of high rates of tangible consequences of drinking with heavy drinking in dry environments suggested two lines of further exploration. One was that such heavy drinkers had personality characteristics that made them specially consequence-prone. A comparison of the profiles of this group with other drinkers and with others in the dry environment yielded a number of provocative results, though with small Ns, but no consistent picture of specially damaged personalities emerged. The other line of explanation was that tangible consequences of drinking were not to be viewed simply as behavioral characteristics of the individual respondent but rather as properties of the interaction between the respondent's behavior and the reactions of those in his environment. In fact, the general level of disapproval of drinking in a cluster, as measured by responses that there is "nothing good" about drinking, provides a strong prediction of the general level of tangible consequences in the cluster, and a weaker prediction, which nevertheless is second only to the predictions of measures of individual drinking behavior, of tangible consequences at the individual level. The combination of individual heavy drinking behavior and general community disapproval thus yields quite a strong prediction of individual tangible consequences of drinking, and the results suggest that special personality characteristics may not greatly improve this prediction.

Binge drinking was most common in the urban areas of the dryer regions. It has not yet been established whether this is attributable to social pressures, to ethnic, religious and socioeconomic factors, or possibly to the immigration of drinkers to the more permissive urban areas. The findings do illustrate, however, that not only the rates but also the forms in which alcohol problems may manifest themselves will vary considerably as the result of sociocultural pressures.

Chapter 8

The San Francisco Survey

A. Scope and Implications

THROUGHOUT this program of studies of drinking practices and problems, there have been closely parallel surveys conducted in the San Francisco bay area and nationally, with the San Francisco area studies usually preceding the national surveys by 2 or 3 years. Thus the early descriptive studies of drinking practices in the San Francisco area (67, 68) were followed by the first national survey of drinking (20), and the first San Francisco survey conducted on drinking problems (30, 66) was followed by the first national survey on drinking problems among adults of both sexes and all ages (19). This has permitted the application of research methods pilot-tested in San Francisco community surveys on a national scale, and has provided certain comparisons between findings in the more intensive community surveys and those in the more quantitative national studies.

The San Francisco area was initially selected partly because of its reputation as a hard-drinking town, based on past cirrhosis rates and gross-consumption statistics. A recent comparison of drinking and problem-drinking rates in San Francisco with approximately equivalent subsamples of "middle Americans" in comparable large cities throughout the country shows that the rates are no higher in San Francisco than in other central cities, and evidence has been adduced which indicates that the elimination of artifacts would raise cirrhosis rates in other central cities to match San Francisco's (122). The same analysis showed, however, that San Francisco does have unique characteristics compared to most other U.S. cities, e.g., more frequent light drinking, more drinking of wine and less of beer. But an even more important reason to use the San Francisco studies to complement our national studies is the greater opportunity, in a community survey, to explore in greater detail the association between local environmental characteristics and drinking behavior. Accordingly this chapter presents a selection of results from the San Francisco survey of 1967–68 which serves to supplement those reported above from the combined N2–N3 surveys. More detailed findings of the San Francisco survey will be published separately.

Both the San Francisco and the N2–N3 surveys were probability samples of men aged 21 to 59, conducted for the purpose of intensive study among those at higher risk of drinking problems. The national study covered all racial groups, while the San Francisco study was confined to the White population to control for variance occasioned by San Francisco's unusual racial mix; and the San Francisco interview was more intensive (averaging about 2 to 2½ hours) than the national survey interview (approximately 1 to 1½ hours). The basic design and content of both surveys, however, were sufficiently similar to permit using the studies to complement each other. Details on the sampling and interviewing procedures are presented in Appendix A.[1]

In this chapter we will concentrate on analyses of the San Francisco data which provide further illumination of issues raised earlier in this monograph. These include some different methods of approaching the ecology of drinking problems, some data bearing on the relation of ethnicity to drinking problems, a further consideration of childhood and adult attributes and their contribution to drinking problems, and some results on time-ordering drinking experiences by a different survey procedure than in the national study.

B. The Ecology of Drinking Problems

In examining the correlates of drinking problems in San Francisco, the central city of a wet-area metropolitan region, we are, of course, drastically restricting the range of variability which was available in the national data. As has been shown in a previous study (70), abstainers in this environment are both relatively rare and not particularly militant; only 8% of our sample had not taken a drink in the last year.

The San Francisco ecological unit is larger than the neighborhood cluster in the national studies and thus likely to con-

---

[1] The field work for the San Francisco survey was carried out by West Coast Community Surveys, Selma Monsky, field director.

tain more internal variation. Since the sample was not substantially clustered by area, its respondents are distributed more or less in proportion to the total population sampled throughout the city. To get numbers sufficient for analysis, then, the respondents were aggregated into areas with greater populations than the few city blocks of the national sample clusters.

Our basic geographical units are the 127 San Francisco census tracts (as of 1960) and aggregations of these tracts. Although the census tracts were originally defined with considerable attention to their internal homogeneity, they often include quite disparate populations and do not always conform to present-day neighborhood designations. The Haight-Ashbury district, for instance, has approximate boundaries that cut through the middle of most of the tracts in its area of the city.

Several analytical frameworks are available in examining ecological variations in drinking problems (25, *pp. 169–170*). For the present, we are using a description of the distribution of drinking problems in terms of the traditional districts of the city, and an analysis of relations and interactions of drinking problems with general census-derived characteristics of the tract in which the respondent resides.

For the descriptive study, San Francisco was divided into 13 "traditional districts" along census-tract boundaries, adapting a classification made originally by the city's Planning Department (149). The exact denotation of a "traditional district" is rather fuzzy. In many cases, a district name identifies an area with the same general kind of housing built at approximately the same period. On the other hand, a "second growth" of new apartment buildings and subdivisions may result in a district changing its character or becoming heterogeneous. Some districts are considerably better defined and characterized than others; "North Beach" carries associations of its character and history, but "West of Twin Peaks" smacks more of cartographic convenience.

Figure 9 shows the districts as we have defined them outlined on a census-tract map. The Downtown area includes the Tenderloin and South-of-Market Skid-Row area, districts with a variegated population of Skid-Row alcoholics, old peo-

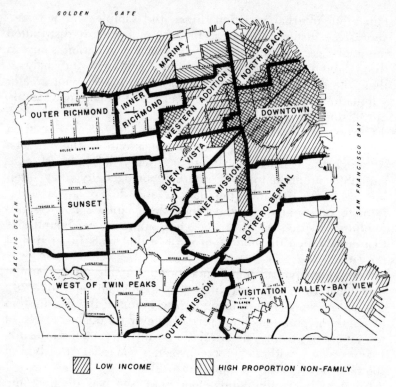

LOW INCOME   HIGH PROPORTION NON-FAMILY

FIGURE 9.—*Traditional Districts of San Francisco and Tracts of Low Median Income and Low Familiation*

ple, rooming-houses and cheap residence hotels. The Mission districts and the areas to the east are predominantly working-class. The wealthiest areas of the city are in the West of Twin Peaks area and in some of the tracts immediately bordering on the Presidio. North Beach is variegated and includes China-town and some small upper-middle class areas on the hilltops. The Marina district is now at least partly characterized by "swinging singles" apartments. There is a large but not pre-dominant Spanish-speaking population, Central American as well as Mexican, in the Inner Mission. The Black population is concentrated in the Western Addition, in Hunter's Point (part of the Bay View area) and in Ocean View, an enclave in the southeast part of West of Twin Peaks.

Table 52 shows the proportion with a "high" problem score (as defined in Appendix B) in the 13 districts. There is considerable variation from one district to another in the prevalence of any given problem, e.g., from 7 to 25% for high social consequences. On measures of both drinking behavior and general social consequences of drinking, more respondents living in the Downtown area than in any other had high problems. Core-city areas like the Downtown district, of course, are associated with the highest rates of many kinds of disabilities and problems, for example, mental illness (43), suicide (5) and notably cirrhosis of the liver (102). The Downtown district's predominance in social consequences was, however, concentrated in job and police problems. Problems with wife are rare because there are few married couples in the area; and other interpersonal problems are relatively less common, perhaps because many social ties have long been broken for those living there. Yet the district does not predominate at all in indications of psychological involvement with alcohol: 4 others show roughly equal prevalences of psychological dependence, and loss of control is more prevalent in the 2 districts immediately to the south of the Downtown district.

Although data, such as shown in Table 52, are of descriptive value, and also of some value in planning the distribution of services for those with drinking problems, they are not of any great significance in a discussion of possible social etiologies. There are too many possible correlates to the patterns found. As Clausen and Kohn (31) noted in a discussion of an analogous analytical situation, "the areas in which highest rates of hospitalization for schizophrenia occur are characterized by high population mobility, by low socioeconomic status, by high proportions of foreign-born population, and by a high incidence of social and health problems. The imputation of etiological significance to any of these variables stems, for the most part, not from the ecological findings themselves, but from general theoretical formulations or from hunches derived from clinical study or life-history materials" (p. 141).

As a start on disentangling the ecological conditions and determinants of individual drinking problems, statistics were computed for the San Francisco census tracts from the 1960 census data. Previous analyses of related data have shown

TABLE 52.—*Current High Problems by District, in Per Cent*[a]

	N	Heavy Intake	Binge	Psychol. Depend.	Loss of Control	Symptom. Drinking	Wife	Inter-personal	Job	Police	Acci-dents	Social Conse-quences
Total	786	13	7	12	3	10	7	10	7	4	3	14
Downtown	79	24	11	17	6	23	3	14	15	11	5	25
North Beach, etc.	67	16	6	19	6	13	5	18	5	5	3	16
Marina	30	10	10	17	7	7	0	10	7	3	3	10
Western Addition	50	16	4	18	2	8	8	6	10	4	4	16
Inner Richmond	30	17	3	3	7	23	7	3	10	10	3	20
Buena Vista	73	6	6	14	3	7	4	12	8	1	6	16
Inner Mission	103	12	13	14	4	14	9	16	8	4	3	18
Potrero-Bernal	68	15	13	9	7	7	7	9	9	2	2	12
Visitacion Valley—												
Bay View	33	15	0	0	0	3	18	3	3	3	0	12
Outer Mission	35	6	6	6	0	3	3	9	6	3	6	11
West of Twin Peaks	60	7	7	10	0	8	10	5	2	2	2	7
Sunset	116	11	5	6	0	6	5	10	6	3	3	10
Outer Richmond	42	5	2	17	0	7	10	5	2	0	0	7

[a] San Francisco, 1967. High problems are defined in Appendix B.

quite high intercorrelations between many of the census-tract variables; and two previous analyses of Bay Area data, on the basis of totally different premises, arrived at the conclusion that the variables can be adequately summarized by three dimensions: what Tryon (141, 142, 143) termed the F (family life), A (assimilation) and S (socioeconomic independence) dimensions; and what Shevky and Bell (130) termed urbanization, segregation and social rank.

For the present analysis, three variables were chosen which related both to the dimensions found in this previous research and seemed of potential significance to the etiology of drinking problems. Our measure of social status is the median income (of family and unrelated individuals), the closest equivalent in the census data to the "family income" variable in our interview data. The measure of "segregation" is the proportion of the tract's population which is non-White or of Spanish surname. It should be noted that Shevky and Bell's use of the label "segregated" to denote neighborhoods with a large minority population is somewhat to reverse the realities of segregation: as of 1960, more than one-quarter of San Francisco tracts were at least 90% White non-Spanish surname, but only 3 tracts in Chinatown were less than 20% White non-Spanish surname. For the third dimension, we use low "familiation," the proportion of the tract population not members of nuclear families (combining the census categories of "unrelated individuals" and "other relatives of head of household"). Each dimension is used here in dichotomous form, so that about one quarter of our sample is in the category which we would predict to be associated with drinking problems—that is, the areas with low status, low familiation and high minority population.

Table 53 shows that, in a sample of White men aged 21 to 59, there is a consistent association between drinking problems of any variety and living in a tract of low familiation or low social status. Living in a tract with a high minority population, however, shows little or no association with drinking problems, other than a modest association with heavy intake.

Figure 9, on which the areas of low familiation and low social status are shown by cross-hatching, demonstrates that there is a heavy correlation between these two variables, and

TABLE 53.—*Current High Problems by Tract Characteristics, in Per Cent*[a]

| | Minority Population | | Median Income | | Familiation | |
	Low (N = 634)	High (152)	High (603)	Low[b] (183)	High (603)	Low (183)
Heavy intake	11	17	10	21	10	20
Binge	7	10	7	10	7	8
Psychological dependence	11	15	9	21	10	19
Loss of control	3	5	2	6	2	7
Symptomatic drinking	10	11	8	18	8	18
Wife	6	8	7	6	7	6
Interpersonal	10	10	9	14	9	14
Job	7	9	6	13	6	12
Police	4	3	2	9	3	7
Accidents	4	1	3	5	3	5
Social consequences	14	15	12	22	12	22

[a] San Francisco, 1967.
[b] Low = less than $4500 in 1960.

for that matter a definite clustering in certain traditional districts of the city, again raising the question (31) of whether we are not explaining the same variance over and over again under different guises. Table 54 provides at least a partial answer, by showing the interaction of tract familiation and tract social status. It is only the residents of tracts with both low familiation and low status who show elevated rates of over-all social consequences. On the other hand, on heavy intake, low familiation and low social status seem to be additive in their effects. Loss of control, binge drinking and police problems appear to be relatively specific to tracts of low social status—to revert again to rough traditional district terms, they affect primarily the South of Market and Inner Mission inhabitants, rather than the "swinging singles" in the Marina. The former districts are the main locus of regular police sweeps by the police department's "drunk detail."

The relatively strong association between living in a low-income tract and drinking problems (Table 53) is in fact generally stronger than any association with the individual's own family income (Table 55, first two columns). The right-hand columns of Table 55, which show drinking problems by the interaction of individual family and tract income scores, confirm that family income is generally secondary to tract income

TABLE 54.—*Current High Problems by Tract Median Income and Familiation, in Per Cent*[a]

Tract Median Income:[b] Tract Familiation:	Low		High	
	Low (N = 134)	High (49)	Low (49)	High (554)
Heavy intake	22	16	12	10
Binge	8	14	8	7
Psychological dependence	22	18	10	9
Loss of control	8	2	4	2
Symptomatic drinking	21	10	8	8
Wife	6	6	4	7
Interpersonal	15	10	12	9
Job	15	8	2	6
Police	8	10	2	2
Accidents	5	4	4	3
Social consequences	25	14	14	12

a San Francisco, 1967.
b Low = less than $4500 in 1960.

in its relation to problems other than wife and interpersonal. It is notable, however, that the most straightforward measure of drinking behavior (heavy intake) is most prevalent among high-income persons living in low-income tracts.

Heavy drinkers thus seem to be particularly concentrated

TABLE 55.—*Current High Problems by Tract and Individual Incomes, in Per Cent*[a]

			TRACT INCOME			
			High		Low	
Individual Family Income:	High (N = 448)	Low (316)	High (392)	Low (191)	High (56)	Low (125)
Heavy intake	11	14	9	12	27	18
Binge	7	9	6	8	9	10
Psychological dependence	9	16	8	12	21	21
Loss of control	2	5	2	4	7	6
Symptomatic drinking	10	12	8	8	18	18
Wife	7	6	7	6	9	5
Interpersonal	9	13	7	13	16	13
Job	6	9	6	6	11	14
Police	3	5	2	3	7	10
Accidents	2	4	2	4	4	6
Social consequences	12	18	11	15	21	22

a Low tract median income = less than $4500 in 1960; low individual family income = less than $7500 in 1967.

among those who choose to live in neighborhoods whose inhabitants are generally poorer than themselves. This could be explained by a "downward drift" hypothesis, that relatively heavy drinkers seek out the anonymity of a poor central-city neighborhood, or alternatively by a hypothesis that relatively heavy drinking absorbs income which could otherwise be spent on better housing.

The result in general confirms the findings of Faris and Dunham (43) on alcoholic psychosis in Chicago in the 1930s: "the alcoholic psychoses come from communities with the lowest monthly rentals as compared to any of the principal psychoses. . . . The bulk of the cases are in fact concentrated more heavily at the center of the city than in the schizophrenic series." However, the highest rate among those of relatively high-status ethnicity (i.e., Whites) was in those living in a lower ethnic-status neighborhood—the Black apartment-house areas (43, *pp. 114–115, 117*).

C. Ethnicity and Drinking Problems

Ethnic differences in rates of drinking problems have long been recognized and well documented. There is no shortage of hypotheses about the differences; but there has been a distinct shortage of studies which allow us to choose among competing explanations.

As a modest effort in this direction, the San Francisco 1967 respondents were asked not only their ethnicity[2] but also what proportion of their friends were of various ethnic backgrounds, including those which have served as benchmarks in discussions of cultural differences in drinking styles and problems, the Irish, Italian, Jewish, Scandinavian and British. With these questions we can try to assess whether ethnic differences in drinking problems are likely to be due to characteristics fixed before adult life or whether they seem related to associations and characteristics of adulthood.

Table 56, which shows the proportions with current high drinking problems in the major White ethnic groups in San Francisco, in most ways agrees with other studies: the ethnic groups with the highest prevalences of social consequences

[2] Defined primarily by their closest ancestry; see Footnote to Table 56.

TABLE 56.—*Current High Problems by Ethnicity, in Per Cent*[a]

	Irish (N = 109)	Jewish (61)	Italian (73)	Scandi-navian (50)	British (144)	German (88)	Other West. Europe (61)	Central & East. Europe (38)	Latin Amer. (96)	Other (60)
Heavy intake	16	2	12	12	12	10	8	18	18	12
Binge	10	0	6	10	8	5	5	11	10	8
Psychol. dependence	16	7	10	20	13	10	13	16	4	15
Loss of control	6	0	1	4	4	0	7	5	2	2
Symptomatic drinking	14	2	12	22	13	11	10	8	5	3
Wife	11	0	6	6	4	9	8	5	6	7
Interpersonal	17	2	16	18	8	6	10	5	12	5
Job	14	3	4	16	5	5	8	5	6	7
Police	7	0	3	8	3	5	3	3	4	0
Accidents	6	0	3	6	3	3	7	3	2	0
Social consequences	25	0	12	24	14	10	13	8	16	10

[a] San Francisco, 1967. Ethnicity is defined by responses to "What country or countries did most of your ancestors come from?" and "Which one do you feel closest to?" if more than one country of ancestry; except for Jewish ethnicity, which was based on respondent's religion, or at least one parent Jewish and neither Christian if respondent had no religion. Irish includes Northern Ireland, British includes Scotch-Irish, German includes Austrian, Latin American includes Spanish.

of drinking are the Irish and Scandinavians; the ethnic group with the lowest rate is the Jews. The rates of drinking problems among those of Latin American ethnicity are not very different from the San Francisco average, a finding which contrasts strongly with the national sample (Chapter 4). A possible explanation is the chance effects of clustering in national samples for a highly geographically specific population. A more substantive explanation would be the differences in composition of the samples; nationally, this ethnic category is composed primarily of those of Puerto Rican and Mexican ancestry, while in San Francisco the mix is primarily of Central Americans and Mexicans. A high rate of drinking problems in urban Mexico has been reported, but a generally low rate in urban Central America (121). Conversely, those of Italian ethnicity in San Francisco do not show a markedly lower rate of social consequences of drinking than the general population. There have been recent intimations in the literature that even in Italy rates of alcoholism may not be as low as had been traditionally assumed (37, p. 102).

In spite of equivocalities among some of the other ethnic groups, the table does support classical descriptions of the Irish and Scandinavians as having a generally high rate of drinking problems and of Jews as having a generally low rate.

If we regard the ratio of those with social consequences to heavy-intake drinkers as a rough indicator of differential vulnerability to social consequences of drinking, it can be seen that the Irish and Scandinavians appear to have a substantially higher vulnerability to consequences than those of other ethnicities—Italian, British, German, Central and Eastern European and Latin American—who have a roughly equal proportion with heavy intake.

The findings by ethnicity and ethnic friendship patterns are shown in Table 57. This table uses, in addition to the social-consequences score, measures of steady fairly heavy and of very heavy drinking analogous to those used for the N3 sample in Chapter 6. Patterns of friendship appear to make no difference in terms of cultural protections against drinking problems: thus Jews have low rates of heavy drinking and social consequences no matter what their patterns of friendship, while having Jewish friends does not appear to make any dif-

TABLE 57.—*Ethnicity and Friendships and Drinking Behavior, in Per Cent*[a]

Respondent's Ethnic Group	Ethnic Group of Friends	N	Steady Fairly Heavy Drinkers	Very Heavy	Current High Social Consequences
Irish	Half or more Irish	58	28	16	22
	Less than half	49	33	12	29
Non-Irish	Half or more Irish	94	32	17	23
	Less than half	563	20	10	11
Jewish	Half or more Jewish	35	11	0	0
	Less than half	25	12	0	0
Non-Jewish	Half or more Jewish	53	26	8	21
	Less than half	656	23	12	15
Italian	Half or more Italian	46	33	13	15
	Less than half	25	24	8	8
Non-Italian	Half or more Italian	97	26	9	16
	Less than half	598	21	11	14
Scandinavian	Half or more Scandinavian	14	29	29	29
	Less than half	36	14	8	22
Non-Scandinavian	Half or more Scandinavian	36	25	17	22
	Less than half	677	23	11	13
British	Half or more British	61	18	13	15
	Less than half	76	32	12	13
Non-British	Half or more British	75	20	7	20
	Less than half	548	22	12	14

[a] San Francisco, 1967. Steady Fairly Heavy Drinkers = at least 4 drinks on an occasion at least once a week. Very Heavy = at least 12 drinks on an occasion at least once a month, or binge drinking within the last year. Ethnicity defined in Table 56 footnote.

ference among non-Jews. But friendship patterns do appear to be important in terms of cultural vulnerabilities to drinking problems. Friendship patterns do not appear to make much difference among those of Irish ancestry, but having Irish friends is in general at least as good a predictor of heavy drinking patterns and problems as being Irish. Roughly the same patterns show up, though with rather unreliable Ns, in the Scandinavian comparisons: having Scandinavian friends is at least as important as or more important than being Scandinavian in predicting drinking problems.

These patterns suggest the possibility, at least in large American cities, of a relationship between ethnicity and drinking problems rather different from the hypotheses conventionally advanced in the literature. Problem drinkers may be seen as developing and existing in a subculture of heavy drinkers traditionally associated, for whatever reason, with particular segments of the urban population—particular ethnic groups, particular occupations. Those "born into" these segments of the population gain an automatic entrée to the heavy-drinking subculture; but it is also possible to gravitate into them from other beginnings, picking up patterns of association along the way (e.g., friends from heavy-drinking ethnicities) appropriate to that subculture. The plausibility of this reasoning will be further explored in future publications based on the San Francisco studies.

D. Childhood Influences

As noted in Chapter 5, attributes associated with a respondent's early upbringing should occupy a particularly strategic place in a discussion of the determinants of drinking problems. Accordingly, the San Francisco survey included several items concerning attributes of the respondent's parents or his childhood as he recollected it. The findings on the three variables with relatively strong correlations with drinking problems are shown in Table 58.

As noted in Appendix C, the childhood-unhappiness–lack-of-family-cohesion variable consisted of such items as not always living with both parents as a child, having an unhappy childhood, unhappiness of parents' marriage and tension and dissension in the household; the youthful hell-raising variable consisted of three items on the individual's early behavior (sent to principal for acting up in school, played hooky, got into fist fights); and trouble from father's drinking consisted of a single item.

It will be seen that both childhood-unhappiness–lack-of-family cohesion and youthful hell-raising (particularly the latter) have quite strong relations with drinking problems, with trouble from father's drinking also being significant to problem drinking. These findings are consistent with those of N3 (Table 30) in which three analogous variables showed high

TABLE 58.—*Correlations of Childhood Influences and Current Problems*[a]

	Childhood Unhappiness– Lack of Family Cohesion	Youthful Hell- Raising	Trouble from Father's Drinking
	r	r	r
Heavy intake	.08	.21	.09
Binge	.05	.21	.12
Psychological dependence	.10	.17	.09
Loss of control	.09	.19	.15
Symptomatic drinking	.18	.20	.11
Wife	.07	.15	.12
Interpersonal	.08	.19	.11
Job	.09	.22	.15
Police	.09	.15	.14
Accidents	.11	.12	.08
Financial	.09	.16	.16
Social consequences[b]	.13	.27	.19

[a] San Francisco, 1967. The full range of each score is used (Appendix B). None of the following additional variables have substantial correlations with any of the types of drinking problems: Trouble from mother's drinking when respondent was young; Number of siblings in family; Size of city in which respondent was reared; Father's educational level; and whether Family was on welfare or short of money when respondent was young.

[b] The combination of wife, interpersonal, job and police problems.

correlations with the criterion variables.

Somewhat surprisingly, there seems to be no strong relation between the trouble the mother's drinking made for the respondent's family and the respondent's own drinking problems, even though the intercorrelation of mother's and father's drinking troubles is .23. This finding is more striking than the findings on parents' drinking patterns in N3, where mother's maximum quantity of drinking did show a correlation with respondent's problematic intake, even though this disappeared when father's maximum quantity was partialled out (Table 32). The convergent results from the two samples do at least suggest the possibility that role modeling, with the son intentionally or otherwise following in his father's footsteps, may be a more important factor in the relation between childhood attributes and adult male behavior than Freudian-oriented explanations of strong maternal influence.

In a multiple regression of a number of early experiences on the current social consequences score (Table 59), youthful

TABLE 59.—*Multiple Regressions of Childhood Influences on Full Social Consequences*[a]

	Raw Correlation r	Multiple Correlation Coefficient R	Partial Correlation
Youthful hell-raising	.27	.27	.24
Trouble from father's drinking	.19	.31	.15
Family on welfare when growing up	.03	.32	.07
Size of place of upbringing	−.02	.32	−.04
Childhood unhappiness–lack of family cohesion	.13	.32	.03
Number of siblings	.02	.32	.02
Trouble from mother's drinking	−.07	.32	.02
Father's education level	−.02	.32	−.01

[a] San Francisco, 1967. The predictors are listed in the order of entry into the stepwise regression. Raw correlation = the initial correlation of each predictor with the criterion. Partial correlation = the partial correlation after the last step of the regression has been completed.

hell-raising and trouble from father's drinking showed up first and second in influence, as might be expected; but childhood unhappiness was so highly correlated to the other leading variables that it added almost nothing to the prediction of social consequences. This does differ from the N3 results where a somewhat differently composed childhood-unhappiness score provided the strongest prediction of any childhood variable.

It could be argued that the youthful hell-raising items refer primarily to high-school age and later, which other variables are likely to precede. This leaves us with the interim hypothesis that father's drinking problems and family disruption predict youthful hell-raising, which in turn predicts adult consequences of drinking. We shall explore this idea further.

E. Personality Variables

Fourteen personality scores or scales were included in the 1967–68 San Francisco study, each consisting of 2 to 7 items. These variables, described in detail in Appendix C, were aggregated into the present scales on the basis of factor analyses of larger pools of items, the conceptual relevance of the items, and the effectiveness of similar items in related studies, particularly the 1964 San Francisco and 1969 N3 studies. The coverage is oriented to the dimensions of personality considered likely to be related to drinking problems. A number of these variables are thus similar to those dealt with in Chapter 5.

Table 60 shows the associations between these 14 personality scales and indices of current drinking problems, including a summary social-consequences score. Only 1 of 168 correlations between drinking problems and personality scales is as high as .30 and only some of the personality dimensions show any substantial correlation with drinking problems in this population. Three of the 6 scales most highly correlated with various aspects of problem drinking are related to what has been called the "ego-control" factor or Factor II of the Minnesota Multiphasic Personality Inventory (MMPI) (12, *p. 115*): hotheadedness–belligerence, impetuosity, and daring, relevant to the general area of impulsive lack of restraint and rashness, which can be seen as one of the dimensions of personality traditionally associated more with the male than the female role, and with youth rather than age. The other 3 dimensions lie in the area of psychiatric concern, the "ego-resiliency" factor (Factor I of the MMPI) (12, *p. 111*)—indicators of relatively strong psychiatric symptoms or a generally tense or nervous state, here categorized as psychiatric symptoms, guilt and tension.

Other variables show a substantial relationship only with a limited number of types of drinking problems: somatic complaints correlated as high as .19 only with psychological dependence; and moralism, although negatively correlated with all problems, had a relatively high negative correlation particularly with job problems and social consequences. It must be kept in mind that certain variables which might predict problem drinking within the general population (both sexes, all ages) will be less effective within a population of restricted range such as this one. This is particularly likely to be true in the present sample of such masculinity–femininity measures as "macho" and "passive physical pleasures" (e.g., dozing by the fire), whose raw predictive value might well be higher in a sample including women or older persons. Further, the variable of "interpersonal isolation" may be a better predictor of drinking problems for elderly men than younger men, or for residents of rural areas or smaller towns than for this urban San Francisco sample.

TABLE 60.—Correlations of Personality Variables and Current Problems[a]

	Heavy Intake	Binge	Psychol. Depend.	Loss of Control	Symptom. Drink.	Wife	Inter-personal	Job	Police	Accidents	Financial	Social Conse-quences
Psychiatric symptoms	.10	.18	.32	.16	.18	.14	.22	.18	.15	.08	.17	.27
Guilt	.16	.26	.24	.16	.25	.13	.20	.21	.12	.11	.20	.26
Tension	.09	.08	.21	.18	.11	.12	.18	.09	.06	.05	.24	.19
Happiness	−.07	−.11	−.16	−.11	−.08	.01	−.09	−.11	−.05	.00	−.11	−.09
Somatic complaints	.11	.09	.19	.11	.07	.05	.17	.01	.02	.11	.13	.13
Interpersonal isolation	.00	.01	−.05	−.05	−.05	−.05	−.08	−.03	.01	−.03	−.08	−.07
Distrust	.07	.09	.12	.02	.04	.01	.10	.07	.01	−.03	.01	.08
Moralism	−.03	−.09	−.15	−.12	−.11	−.04	−.12	−.16	−.12	−.12	−.10	−.18
Hotheadedness	.13	.16	.19	.17	.17	.17	.17	.15	.09	.09	.14	.23
Impetuosity	.15	.18	.20	.14	.23	.09	.19	.15	.15	.10	.20	.22
Daring	.10	.14	.12	.12	.14	.11	.15	.14	.14	.17	.07	.22
Macho	.00	.03	.00	−.03	.01	.09	.02	−.03	−.01	.02	−.02	.03
Assertiveness	.02	−.05	.04	−.03	.02	.03	.07	−.03	.07	.01	.01	.05
Passive physical pleasures	.01	−.01	.03	.00	.03	.00	.05	.05	.04	.01	.07	.05

[a] San Francisco, 1967. The full range of each current problem score is used (Appendix B). The personality variables are defined in Appendix C.

Even when taking the effects of the ill-matched distributions into account, it is apparent that the association between any dimension of personality and any measure of drinking problems is not very strong. Only a few of the personality dimensions show any substantial relation with drinking problems. At least in a sample of men, many dimensions defining aspects of traditional masculinity attitudes do not distinguish between those with and those without drinking problems. Thus neither macho, composed of items favoring sportsmindedness and toughness over bookishness, nor passive physical pleasures, showing a liking for passive sensations, nor assertiveness show any substantial relation with drinking problems. Nor does interpersonal isolation (roughly, the obverse of gregariousness) or distrust, two scales heavily associated with old age in other studies, show any discriminating power on drinking problems in a sample confined to men under 60. The findings on interpersonal isolation, in particular, are worth comment. In several studies we have consistently failed to find a relationship of even medium strength between drinking problems and scales in the area of gregariousness or extent of social contacts. This is somewhat surprising, in view of our finding of a strong relationship between drinking problems and the respondent's performance in nuclear family roles, and the frequent mention in the alcoholism literature of gregariousness as a salient issue in the process of acquiring drinking problems. One possible explanation is that there are two contradictory facets to the literature, one stressing the old theme of the lure of evil companions, the seduction of barroom bonhomie, as a route to acquiring drinking problems; discussions of drinking problems in the business world in particular tend to mention such factors as relevant to acquiring drinking problems (113). On the other hand, there are also intimations in the literature of the alcoholic's loneliness, of the substitution of pharmacological for personal relationships and a pattern of "solitary drinking" in at least half of samples of identified alcoholics (54; 56, pp. 48–50). Perhaps our findings indicate that both these sets of perceptions are erroneous when applied to a general population. Or, perhaps our finding of a lack of association reflects that both hypotheses are correct, but only in part, so that we need to distinguish between subgroups. This would tend to be supported by the positive partial correlation between sociability and drinking problems which showed up in the N3 regressions when measures including alienation were partialled out (Table 34).

One further aspect of the negative findings in Table 60 is worth mention. Some of the scales measure essentially opposite ends of a common conceptual area. Thus happiness can be viewed as a measure of positive mental health, psychiatric symptoms and tension as measures of negative mental health. Similarly, moralism represents the opposite end of a dimension of adherence to norms of constraint and conventionality from hotheadedness and impetuosity (in fact, the correlations between these measures, though negative, are not very high: happiness with psychiatric symptoms $-.22$, with tension $-.16$; moralism with hotheadedness $-.09$, with impetuosity $-.28$).

It is apparent from Table 60 that the relations between the measures positively predicting drinking problems have a higher absolute-value correlation than the negatively predicting measures. Thus the correlations of hotheadedness ($.23$) and impetuosity ($.22$) with social consequences are higher in absolute value than the correlation of moralism ($-.18$); and the correlations of psychiatric symptoms ($.27$) and tension ($.19$) with social consequences are higher in absolute value than the correlation of happiness ($-.09$). Consequently, it may be speculated that personality dimensions are more likely to act as positive precipitators of (or accompaniments to) drinking problems than they are to act as protections against drinking problems: being happy or conventional is less of a protection than being miserable or unconstrained is a prediction.

F. Childhood and Adult Psychological States as Predictors of Drinking Problems

Two of the childhood variables that we found most highly associated with drinking problems can be regarded as rough analogues of the two general conceptual areas in the adult personality scores that were also relatively strongly associated with drinking problems. This raises the possibility of examining the relative effectiveness of childhood and adult personality attributes in "predicting" adult drinking problems. If we know the respondent's childhood history, how much predictive value is added by examining his current psychological state? Conversely, if we know his current psychological state, does knowledge of his childhood improve our predictive power? Answers to such questions will contribute to the assessment of whether adult drinking problems are more a response to adult situations or a legacy of childhood attributes.

In these comparisons, the adult personality variables have an automatic advantage since there is only one possible temporal sequence for the childhood variables and adult drinking problems, whereas both sequences are possible for the adult variables (in fact, a few items, notably in the impetuosity and guilt scales, could well be used by the respondent to describe drinking experiences). For purposes of these comparisons, a summary adult-rashness score was constructed, based on how many high scores the respondent had on the scales of hotheadedness–belligerence, impetuosity and daring. Adult dysphoria was constructed analogously from psychiatric symptoms, tension and guilt.[3] The dependent variable used is the full current social-consequences score. Table 61-A shows that the four independent variables of the analysis are fairly highly correlated, particularly the pairs within the one time period or covering the same content area.

In the stepwise regression using all four predictors (Table 61-B), about 12% of the total variance on the dependent variable is accounted for; but two scales (one from adulthood, one from youth) account for nearly all the variance explained. The final partial correlations after all four predictors have been entered confirm that adult dysphoria and youthful hell-raising are of primary importance in an over-all prediction of drinking problems.

In the regression using only the two childhood predictors (Table 61-C), about 8% of the total variance on the criterion is accounted for, primarily by youthful hell-raising. Comparison of the partial correlations of the adult variables with the criterion (after the childhood predictors have been partialled out, with the original raw correlations reveals that a knowl-

---

[3] Adult rashness and adult dysphoria each ranged from 0 to 3. The upper half of the dichotomizations used in their construction were as follows: hotheadedness–belligerence, 1–3; impetuosity, 4–7; daring, 2–3; psychiatric symptoms, 1–5; tension, 3–6; and guilt, 1–2.

TABLE 61.—*Multiple Regressions of Childhood and Adult Psychological States on Current Social Consequences*[a]

A. *Raw Correlations*

	Youthful Hell-raising	Adult Dysphoria	Adult Rashness	Social Consequences
Childhood disjunctions	.22	.24	.21	.13
Youthful hell-raising		.21	.40	.27
Adult dysphoria			.37	.23
Adult rashness				.27

B. *Total Stepwise Regression on Social Consequences*

	Multiple Correlation Coefficients	Partial Correlation[b]
Adult rashness	.27	.13
Youthful hell-raising	.33	.17
Adult dysphoria	.35	.13
Childhood disjunctions	.35	.03

C. *Childhood Predictors Only*

Youthful hell-raising	.27	.25
Childhood disjunctions	.28	.07
Adult dysphoria		.17
Adult rashness		.18

D. *Adult Predictors Only*

Adult rashness	.27	.21
Adult dysphoria	.31	.14
Childhood disjunctions		.05
Youthful hell-raising		.18

[a] San Francisco, 1967.
[b] Partial correlations after the completion of the indicated regression steps—i.e., 4 for part *B*, 2 for parts *C* and *D*.

edge of childhood attributes particularly affects our need to know about adult rashness.

It may plausibly be argued that there is in fact a logical priority between the two childhood variables; that youthful hell-raising primarily reflects behavior around or after high-school age, while childhood disjunctions refers primarily to earlier conditions. Childhood disjunctions provides the poorest prediction of any of the four variables; even so, it does explain a little of the same variance as each of the other three.

If we turn the analytical question round and ask how well do the adult variables by themselves predict (Table 61-D), we find the prediction a little better (10% of the variance) than for the childhood variables alone. The adult variables do partly mediate the relations between childhood attributes and adult drinking problems; but, at least in summary form, they do not totally intervene: there remains some partial correlation between each of the childhood attributes and the criterion when the adult personality scores are partialled out.

In terms of the Lazarsfeldian analytical categories (46), then, we may say that adult personality attributes partly interpret the relation between childhood attributes and adult drinking problems, or alternatively, that childhood attributes partly explain the relation between adult attributes and adult drinking problems; but each of the four variables we have been considering make some contribution, in a broadly additive fashion, to the prediction of drinking problems. In spite of the automatic advantages we noted for the adult variables, the childhood variables provided nearly as good a prediction, so that we must conclude that the considerable predictive power of childhood variables found in previous studies has been further confirmed.

G. Temporal Order of Drinking Experiences and Problems

Chapter 3 presented various approaches to establishing temporal sequences among various types of drinking experiences and problems, as reflected in retrospective data obtained in the N2 and N3 surveys, particularly the latter. Tables 9 and 10 showed that there were preliminary indications that problems with police and binge drinking tend to happen prior to having drinking-related problems with the wife, friends or neighbors, but the latter apparently tend to linger on after problems with police and drinking appear to have ceased.

Such issues of temporal sequence are of high importance in ultimately establishing typical models of the ways in which various types of drinking problems may lead to other types. Additional retrospective data on temporal sequences of problems were also gathered in the San Francisco survey; and these data were technically superior to the national retrospective data in that the temporal order was traced more precisely.

While the N3 survey distinguished a temporal sequence only when one problem occurred within the last 3 years and the other occurred only prior to that time, the San Francisco survey involved efforts to get the respondent to identify the calendar year during which a problem first occurred and the year in which it had occurred most recently. The San Francisco questions thus not only pinpointed the time of a problem more precisely, but also (since it dealt in single years instead of only the two time spans of last 3 years versus earlier) generated a much larger (and therefore more statistically reliable) number of comparisons of temporal sequence between pairs of problems than was available from the N3 data.

Table 62 and Figure 10 show the relative temporal order of the earliest occurrences of seven drinking experiences or problems. Here it will be noted (especially in Figure 10) that

TABLE 62.—*Order of Precedence of Drinking Experiences and Problems, in Per Cent*[a]

1. *Percentage reporting the vertical item as preceding the horizontal item*

	1	2	3	4	5	6	7
1. Period Resp. drank most	–	28	37	37	6	10	30
2. Drunken–driving arrest	71	–	54	50	12	29	56
3. Other drinking arrest	63	45	–	41	12	16	40
4. Police warning	63	50	59	–	11	19	39
5. Severest job problem	94	88	88	88	–	66	84
6. Trouble with wife	89	70	84	81	34	–	76
7. Trouble with friends, relatives	70	44	60	61	16	24	–

2. *Numbers of persons who had both of the compared experiences, where time sequence could be established (occurred in different years)*

	1	2	3	4	5	6	7
1. Period Resp. drank most	–	28	62	65	301	105	184
2. Drunken-driving arrest	28	–	11	10	41	17	25
3. Other drinking arrest	62	11	–	22	83	38	60
4. Police warning	65	10	22	–	78	32	54
5. Severest job problem	301	41	83	78	–	100	197
6. Trouble with wife	105	17	38	32	100	–	88
7. Trouble with friends, relatives	184	25	60	54	197	88	–

[a] San Francisco, 1967.

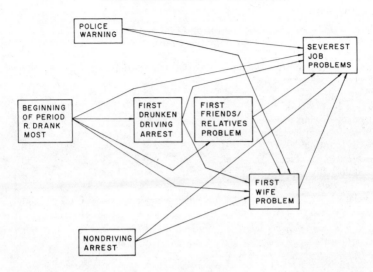

FIGURE 10.—*Time Ordering of Earliest Occurrences of Problems*
(At least 65% in the direction of the arrow)

the first drunken-driving and other drink-related arrests tended to precede the first problem with the wife because of drinking; and, in turn, problems with wife, friends or relatives tended to precede troubles on the job. This is approximately congruent with the N3 data on temporal sequence (see Table 9 and Figure 3).

The temporal order of the latest occurrences of the same seven experiences is presented in Table 63 and Figure 11. Here again (as in the N3 data shown in Table 10 and Figure 4) problems with the police tended to taper off before problems with friends, relatives or wife over one's drinking; why this might be is yet to be determined. Misogynists might contend that wives tend to hold the club of earlier indiscretions over men's heads long after the offensive behavior has ended; and those sympathetic with the wife's role may infer that it is most understandable if the wife retains a lingering fear that continued heavy drinking may lead to more arrests. Only a more detailed longitudinal study can sort out the more qualitative influences underlying these temporal orders of specific drinking problems. In any case, the present evidence certainly

TABLE 63.—*Order of Succession of Drinking Experiences and Problems in Per Cent*[a]

1. Percentage reporting the horizontal item as occurring later than the vertical item

	1	2	3	4	5	6	7
1. Period Resp. drank most	–	48	51	49	11	18	34
2. Drunken-driving arrest	52	–	55	44	9	39	32
3. Other drinking arrest	48	44	–	52	12	20	32
4. Police warning	51	55	48	–	9	16	17
5. Severest job problem	89	90	88	91	–	80	77
6. Trouble with wife	82	61	80	84	20	–	57
7. Trouble with friends, relatives	66	68	68	83	23	43	–

2. Numbers of persons who had both of the compared experiences, where time sequence could be established (occurred in different years)

	1	2	3	4	5	6	7
1. Period Resp. drank most	–	31	66	65	291	100	181
2. Drunken-driving arrest	31	–	9	9	42	18	25
3. Other drinking arrest	66	9	–	21	82	40	59
4. Police warning	65	9	21	–	76	31	53
5. Severest job problem	291	42	82	76	–	90	162
6. Trouble with wife	100	18	40	31	90	–	75
7. Trouble with friends, relatives	181	25	59	53	162	75	–

[a] San Francisco, 1967.

indicates that it is unrealistic to expect a clear-cut order of behavior (or "symptoms" in the Jellinek phaseology) which holds true for even a plurality of problem drinkers; but the findings thus far lend encouragement to establishing that certain types of problems (such as with police) are more likely to happen earlier in life than others (such as problems with the wife, friends or neighbors, or on the job).

H. Summary

This chapter has presented a few of the findings of the San Francisco 1967–68 survey which were considered most relevant to the findings of the national survey. (Details of the San Francisco survey will be presented in separate publications.) All of the findings of the San Francisco study thus far exam-

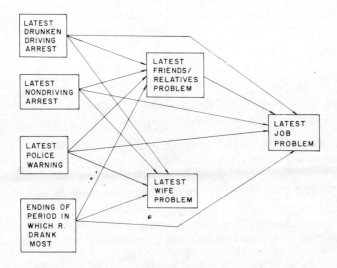

FIGURE 11.—*Time Ordering of Latest Occurrences of Problems*
(At least 65% in the direction of the arrow)

ined are quite consistent with those of the national survey. The principal findings were as follows:

1. The highest rates of problem drinking were found in census tracts with the highest proportions of low-income families combined with higher proportions of individuals who were not living with a family. Statistically, these would appear to be the areas where higher rates of general delinquency interact with higher rates of incidence of problems in general and with higher rates of motivations for heavy drinking to bring about higher rates of problem drinking. An additional factor in the higher rates of problem drinking may be a greater tendency for the police, and other protective agencies, to exercise constraints in such areas although this likelihood has yet to be examined in full detail.

2. San Francisco, like most cosmopolitan cities, has a number of ethnic groups of sufficient size that any resident could choose his friends from his own ethnic group or from among others. The survey findings indicate that the ethnic groups to which one's friends belong are just about as important as one's own ethnic origins in determining one's drinking behavior, particularly if one associates with members of groups with higher rates of problem drinking, such as the Irish and Scandinavians.

3. Both the San Francisco and national surveys underscore the high importance of early environment and family stability in the individual's subsequent susceptibility to drinking problems.

4. Personality scales in the San Francisco survey which differed somewhat from those in the national survey yielded findings that were congruent with the national findings. As discussed earlier in this chapter, the two factors of ego-resiliency and ego-control are significantly correlated with drinking problems despite the differences in the population of this cosmopolitan city and the national population.

5. The results of an analysis of the temporal order of various drinking experiences and problems were consistent with those from the national survey, particularly the findings that drinking-related problems with the police tend to occur earlier and to taper off earlier than problems with the wife, friends or relatives.

Chapter 9

Summary and Implications

THIS MONOGRAPH has presented the detailed findings from national surveys conducted in 1967 and 1969, totaling 1561 interviews with men aged 21 to 59, the section of the general population with the highest rates of problems associated with drinking. The findings from these national surveys have been supplemented by a more qualitative survey also conducted with men aged 21 to 59, in San Francisco in 1967–68. These surveys represent the current status of a longitudinal program of research which began in 1959 and will end in the mid-1970s. The perspective in all these studies is to describe the behavior, experiences and attitudes related to drinking of representative cross-sections of the noninstitutionalized population. The primary focus of these latest studies is to determine the rates and correlates of various problems associated with drinking to establish a baseline against which to measure change in drinking behavior over a period of time. Unless otherwise specified, the specific findings cited in this summary are from the two national surveys rather than the San Francisco study.

A. Rates and Correlates of Problems

Table 64 shows that among men aged 21 to 59 those classified as having some signs of 1 of 13 types of actual or potential drinking problems within the last 3 years ranged from 6% for police problems to 24% exhibiting at least some psychological dependence on alcohol. At least three-quarters of those who had any one problem of "high" severity also had at least one other problem. Despite this, a detailed study of the interactions between the problem measures in Chapter 3 found less overlap between specific problems than studies in clinic populations might lead one to expect. The problem measures have moderately high intercorrelations in the total population of men aged 21 to 59, but much of the strength of each pairwise correlation is attributable to the large "null" group who

221

TABLE 64.—*Current Prevalence and Uniqueness of Problems*[a]

	% Minimal Severity	% High	N with High Problem	% High on Additional Problems
Heavy intake	24	13	127	76
Binge	8	6	59	88
Psychological dependence	24	9	87	85
Loss of control	14	5	44	95
Symptomatic drinking	14	8	80	95
Belligerence	9[b]	9	92	82
Wife	21	14	132	79
Relatives	12	8	80	90
Friends, neighbors	9	7	72	99
Job	10	6	58	98
Police	6	4	42	79
Health, injury	16	7	68	76
Financial	15	7	72	97

[a] N3 optimal scales; $N = 978$. Current prevalences from Table 1, N with high problems from Table 4. The rows are cumulative rather than mutually exclusive: % Minimal Severity includes % High.

[b] No separate minimal severity level differentiated.

have no problems at all. Our results suggest that those with at least 1 drinking problem in the general population are in fact a rather diverse and diffuse "target" population.

At least as we have defined them, then, drinking problems are fairly common among American men aged 21 to 59 and especially so among the 21–24-year olds. Earlier tables in Chapter 3 showed that this youngest group had relatively high rates on every one of our 13 measures of actual or potential drinking problems and Table 65 shows that it is particularly in the area of tangible consequences of drinking that the youngest group stands out, so that the ratio of tangible consequences of drinking to heavy drinking behavior with no consequences is much higher in this age group than in any other.

This result is at odds with the picture, derived from clinical and institutionalized samples of "alcoholics," that drinking problems are a middle-aged phenomenon. Our results present a challenge for research, which we hope shortly to undertake, into the form and process of relationships between those with drinking problems in the general population and the institutionalized "alcoholics" who, in a sense, have been extruded

TABLE 65.—*Current Over-all Problems and Consequences by Age, in Per Cent*

Age	N	Over-all Problem Score 7+[a]	Intake or Binge: No Tangible Consequences[b]	High Tangible Consequences 3+[b]
21–24	147	40	16	31
25–29	204	22	18	13
30–34	186	20	13	14
35–39	216	21	14	12
40–44	226	17	13	12
45–49	201	17	9	12
50–54	199	17	8	13
55–59	182	11	7	9
Totals	1561	20	12	14

[a] Data from Table 8.   [b] Data from Table 14.

from that population. It also presents a challenge for policy-making, suggesting that as planning gets underway for educational and preventive programs concerned with drinking problems in the general population, it would be most unwise to assume that the target population is simply the institutional population writ large.

In Chapter 4 a number of social differentiations were examined for patterns of interrelations with drinking problems. Youthfulness, low socioeconomic status, an unstable marital and home life history and a disadvantaged ethnicity (Latin-American–Caribbean or Black) were all associated with high rates of problematic drinking behavior and tangible consequences of drinking. Having an unstable work history was particularly associated with problematic drinking patterns. Broadly speaking, it might be said that variables associated with being poor or disadvantaged, or both, were the strongest social-differentiation predictors of tangible consequences among men aged 21 to 59, while disadvantage, urbanization and youthfulness all figure prominently in the multivariate prediction of problematic intake. If we confine the analysis to those who are heavy drinkers, disadvantage figures prominently among the predictors (low socioeconomic status, work-role instability), but so does living in a relatively dry environment, that is, having been brought up in rural areas and living in regions (the South, Southwest, Plains and Mountain states) which have had the strongest historical temperance commitment.

B. Accounting for Variation in Drinking Problems

One line of analysis we pursued in some detail (Chapter 5) was following up the findings of three substantial longitudinal studies of adult drinking problems in samples first studied in childhood, assessing the extent and nature of the predictions which could be made on the basis of childhood characteristics. Our results conformed to and extended the results of the previous studies: each of three major domains of variables (the social-differentiation variables which would be ascribed at birth, measures of childhood history, and indicators of the parents' drinking patterns) made separate contributions to the prediction of adult drinking problems. Childhood unhappiness, disadvantaged ethnicity and father's heavy drinking provided the best prediction of adult tangible consequences of drinking, while father's heavy drinking, disadvantaged ethnicity and youthful acting-out behavior provided the best prediction of adult problematic intake. About 12% of the variance in tangible consequences, and 17% of that in problematic intake, was accounted for in a regression analysis using items which could be measured of a respondent in childhood—a respectable but not overwhelming prediction.

Dimensions of personality indicating a lack of ego-resiliency (intrapunitiveness, alienation, affective anxiety) and indicators suggesting a lack of ego-control (impulsivity and tolerance of deviance) showed some association with heavy drinking and drinking problems, with a lack of ego-resiliency more strongly associated with tangible consequences and a lack of ego-control showing a higher correlation with problematic intake. Over-all, personality variables predicted tangible consequences more strongly than problematic intake; their contribution to the regression equation on tangible consequences was separate from and approximately equal to the contribution made by social differentiation and life-history variables. Neither arena of predictive variables should, then, be neglected in future studies of the etiology of drinking problems.

The strongest prediction of problematic intake, and a strong prediction of tangible consequences, was made by a score indicating the respondent's immersion in a context of heavy drinking, i.e., frequenting bars, having heavy-drinking friends and drinking regularly in the course of socializing. Although the direction of causation implied by this association is certainly moot, it does at least suggest that future studies would do well to study the broad phenomenon of the world (or worlds) of heavy drinkers as an important factor in the nurturance of drinking problems.

C. Role of Neighborhood Characteristics

Since environmental considerations are found to be highly important in determining rates of drinking problems, it is most desirable to obtain some measure of environmental influences which is relatively independent of the individual respondent's own perceptions and verbal report, so as to ensure against spuriously high correlations between environmental influences and respondents' behavior from having the same individuals report both. Fortunately, as described in Chapter 7, the two combined national surveys had sufficient numbers of interviews in each primary sampling unit (or cluster) to permit assessing drinking behavior and attitudes against the norms for the immediate neighborhood. The chief relationships were as follows:

Respondents living in abstaining neighborhoods are less likely to be heavy drinkers, whether in the steady or the very heavy drinking styles; but very heavy drinking formed a greater portion of all heavy drinking in dry neighborhoods. Indications of symptomatic drinking and loss of control of drinking were also more commonly associated with heavy drinking in these neighborhoods. However, comparisons on personality characteristics of heavy drinkers in dry and in wet neighborhoods showed mixed results: there did not appear to be any consistent tendency for heavy drinkers in dry neighborhoods to be especially maladjusted.

The proportion of heavy drinkers suffering tangible consequences of their drinking (particularly wife and job problems) was markedly higher in dry than in wet neighborhoods. This suggests that tangible-consequences scores should be viewed as being a property of the interactions between the individual's behavior and the reactions of others. This view was supported by the finding that community sentiment that there was "nothing good" about drinking was strongly associated with the community's level of tangible consequences of drinking, and second only to measures of individual intake as a predictor of individual tangible consequences of drinking. Thus the distribution of tangible consequences in the total population according to the wetness of the milieu takes on a U-shape, with tangible consequences being more common in the wettest and dryest milieus than in between. Our analysis suggests that the drinking behavior itself plays a larger role in producing the tangible consequences in a wet milieu, while the social reactions to even quite modest behavior play a larger role in a dry milieu.

D. Temporal Sequence and Change in Drinking Behavior

Establishing the patterns of temporal sequence and change in drinking behavior and problems is all-important to a fuller understanding of the dynamics of behavior regarding drinking within the American culture, as well as to decisions on the points in the chain of problem-drinking behavior at which remedial or preventive action might be most effective. These surveys, being conducted at one point of time, cannot provide conclusive answers on issues of the temporal order of drinking problems. Sufficient questions were asked on a retrospective basis, however, about past changes in drinking behavior to provide helpful clues to some issues of temporal sequence on which to concentrate in the forthcoming follow-up surveys.

Chapter 3 poses some methodological questions about the techniques to use in measuring change and analyzes retrospective data in the form of cross-lagged correlations and paired comparisons of the orders in which problems were first developed and remitted. The preliminary findings are that certain types of problems (such as symptomatic drinking, belligerence and problems with police) tend to occur earlier in time than others (particularly drink-related problems with wife, friends and relatives). Utilizing somewhat different methods, these findings were independently borne out in most respects by the San Francisco survey.

E. San Francisco Findings

The community survey of San Francisco permitted analysis of certain ecological correlates of problem drinking which could not be measured as effectively in the national surveys (Chapter 8). The highest rates of problem drinking occurred in census tracts with the highest proportions of low-income families coupled with high proportions of persons not living in families. It was also found that early environmental influences (including family instability) are highly important in the individual's subsequent susceptibility to drinking problems and that friends belonging to different ethnic groups appear to be about as important as the respondent's ethnic origins in determining drinking behavior, especially if the individual associates with groups with relatively high rates of problem drinking.

F. Implications for Research and Action Programs

Not all of the following recommendations stem directly from the findings of these surveys on problem drinking among American men; but they provide at least some basis for our making certain recommendations based on our experience in conducting a number of such surveys.

In the first place, more longitudinal studies are needed to pin down the crucial issues of how drinking problems develop and how they diminish over time. Some of the answers will be provided in the longitudinal follow-up studies of this same sample (currently under way) and some will be contributed by current prospective studies (following a cohort of men from elementary-school age onward) being conducted by Lee Robins of Washington University.[1] Since our studies (as well as others) reveal the high prevalence of drinking problems among young adults, more are needed of the type being conducted by Richard Jessor of the University of Colorado among high-school and college students[2] and the follow-up study of the college students initially interviewed by Straus and Bacon

[1] Under grant No. MH-09247 from the National Institute on Alcohol Abuse and Alcoholism, National Institute of Mental Health.

[2] Under grant No. MH-16613 from the National Institute on Alcohol Abuse and Alcoholism, National Institute of Mental Health.

two decades ago (136), being conducted at the Rutgers Center of Alcohol Studies.[3]

It is more than likely that even such follow-up studies will not be sufficient to pin down the ebb and flow of drinking problems in minute detail. For that purpose, there should be more day-to-day panel studies of drinking behavior on a time-sampling basis, somewhat along the lines of the Finnish study of Ekholm[4] and the Italian study of some years ago by Lolli and associates (78). Because such studies are manifestly expensive on a per-individual basis (although not in terms of useful information per dollar expended), they should be done on a small-scale basis, singling out special types of drinkers (e.g., those of different problems, environments, personalities) for intensive study.

The findings thus far point to the importance of obtaining detailed information on environmental influences, particularly those which impinge upon a person at the critical periods (usually early in life) when perceptions and values in relation to alcohol are being formed. The importance of certain personality variables in problem drinking also have been established, particularly dysphoria or ego-resiliency and impulsivity or ego-control; especially when these interact with those environmental influences permissive of heavy drinking as a means of coping with problems.

To pursue arguments about the primacy of environmental versus personality variables in the etiology of drinking problems strikes us as rather pointless, since the findings clearly show that both environment and personality factors in combination are important. A more fruitful approach might well be to determine whether environmental and personality attributes which are associated with problem drinking tend to be long-lived or ephemeral, in order to establish the extent to which longer-term characteristics are more likely to result in deep-seated drinking problems. Obviously, finding these answers will require more longitudinal investigations, prefer-

---

[3] Under grant No. MH-20065 from the National Institute on Alcohol Abuse and Alcoholism, National Institute of Mental Health.

[4] EKHOLM, A. A study of the drinking rhythm of Finnish males. Presented at the 28th International Congress on Alcohol and Alcoholism, Washington, D.C., September 1968.

ably covering a wide range of coping behavior in addition to drinking.

Research among various relevant populations, treatment of problem drinkers, evaluation of alternative modes of treatment effectiveness and preventive programs of a public-health variety should all be more closely coordinated than at present. For example, those who are studying young people's behavior should utilize methods which are congruent with methods applied in studies of adults; those studying institutionalized populations should use methods which will make it possible to relate the findings to those for the noninstitutionalized population. (As it is, we still do not know whether the general stubbornness of drinking problems among institutionalized persons is primarily attributable to the special personality characteristics of the institutionalized, the ineffectiveness of the treatment they receive or the reinforcements which the institutionalized individual gets primarily from evading the realities of outside existence.)

We understand only poorly the processes behind relatively "nonaddictive" (but actually quite stubborn) processes of habituation to excessive use of tobacco and alcohol. We seem unable to find some socially reasonable (and effective) middle course of how to bring about moderation instead of falling into either the extreme of prohibition or punishment on the one hand, or the denial of the potential dangers of habituation on the other. Unless we learn more about the process of habituation and dehabituation concerning excessive consumption of alcohol, tobacco and calories, we certainly cannot hope to cope with the increased problems with the more addictive drugs—nor even to cope with our hardy perennial, the problem drinker in America.

Appendix A

Sampling and Field Procedures

1. The National 2 and 3 Surveys

As summarized in Chapter 1, the national sample reported in this monograph is the total of 2 national samples which were combined to yield a large enough sample for detailed analysis of the high-risk group of men aged 21 to 59. The National 2 survey conducted in 1967, was a follow-up of respondents who had been interviewed initially on their drinking habits in 1964–65 in the National 1 survey; 583 men aged 21 to 59 were obtained from this source. The National 3 survey was conducted in 1969 for the specific purpose of supplementing the previous sample; the combined 583 N2 and 978 N3 respondents yielded a total of 1561.

A. Data Collection. The National 2 and 3 surveys were carried out with comparable standards: only nonabstainer interviewers were utilized, since it was determined in other surveys that interviews conducted by total abstainers tend to yield a higher-than-average rate of abstainers (91, *pp. 710–711*).[1] For the same reason, only men interviewers were utilized, except for a small number of respondents who refused to be interviewed by one or more assigned male interviewers but who were finally interviewed by women.

All interviewers were trained and supervised by either members of the Social Research Group home office staff or by one of about 20 regional supervisors. The training consisted of written instructions, personal briefings and practice interviews; completed interviews were reviewed and reinterviewing required when any important data about drinking habits or problems were not obtained on the initial interview.

---

[1] A later study by Mulford suggests that the relationships found in the original study were an effect of ecology: "Interviewers living, as they do, in the same general locale as their respondents are likely to share many habits and attitudes, including those relating to alcohol" (89, *pp. 635–636*).

Supervisors verified interviews by personal visits or telephone callbacks in all possible instances, with reinterviews
whenever there was any reason to question the validity of
the initial interview.

B. *The National 2 Sample*. The National 2 sample was obtained in a 1967 follow-up of a subsample of the respondents
initially interviewed in the National 1 survey conducted between October 1964 and March 1965. In the original study
each person 21 years of age or older living within households
within the United States (exclusive of Alaska and Hawaii) was
given a known non-zero chance of selection. The sampling
operation followed established principles for probability
sampling: the selection of 100 primary sampling units distributed in proportion to the household population, the prelisting
of all households within each primary sampling unit, the selection of every Nth household on a random basis by central office
personnel, and the selection of an adult within the household
by use of a table of random numbers. The 2746 completed interviews constituted 90% of the eligible respondents in the occupied selected households, after setting aside those ineligible
because of senility or severe illness.

The 1967 N2 follow-up was designed to measure the correlates of problem drinking; consequently abstainers and very
infrequent drinkers were subsampled at a lesser rate than
those who had reported themselves in N1 as usually drinking
at least once a month. Abstainers (those who drank less than
once a year) were included in the follow-up sample at full
strength only if they had said they used to drink at least once a
year, or if the abstainer were a man; but because the proportion of women who had never drunk was rather large, only one-
fifth of the women abstainers were selected for reinterview. Of
the very infrequent drinkers in N1 (those who drank less than
once a month but at least once a year), all of the men and one-
half of the women were selected for the N2 survey. Among the
light drinkers (typically, those drinking about once or twice a
week but as many as five drinks only "once in a while"), half
the men and half the women were selected. All persons above
the "light" drinking category were eligible for National 2. This
subsampling process yielded 1810 persons eligible for reinterview; of these, 1359 were interviewed and the findings on

the drinking habits and problems were reported separately for men and women in a 1970 publication (19).

The completion rates of assigned interviews are shown in Table 66. Many special procedures were utilized to achieve the completion rate of 80% of those eligible for reinterviewing, including personal letters to reluctant respondents, the use of city directories to trace respondents, repeated visits to the old address and checks with neighbors and relatives; inquiries were made of employers or former employers and public agencies (e.g., welfare offices), checks were made of forwarding addresses at post offices, special delivery letters were sent to trace respondents wherever there appeared to be any possibility of delivery, and Retail Credit Bureau records were checked for those for whom no current address could be found.

C. *The National 3 Sample.* The N3 supplementary sample of men aged 21 to 59 was obtained with the same probability sampling principles used in N2, except that N3 was drawn afresh rather than being obtained by reinterviewing. The interviewing was conducted from February to December 1969.

TABLE 66.—*Completion Rates of the 1967 National 2 Interviews*

	N	%
Total selected for reinterview from 2746 in initial N1 sample	1810	101[a]
Excluded		
Deceased	52	3
Institutionalized, too ill or senile	29	2
Absent from the 48 states	34	2
Ineligible	*115*	*7*
Base of eligible respondents (selected minus ineligible)	1695	
Refused or unusable interview	218	12
Wrong person reinterviewed	29	12
Not found, never home	89	5
Eligible, not interviewed	*336*	*19*
Reinterviewed	1359[b]	75
Completion rate		80

[a] Percentages add to 101 because of rounding.

[b] Of these 1359 N2 respondents, all of the 583 men aged 21–59 were combined with the N3 sample (see Table 67) for the combined N2–N3 analyses reported in this monograph.

In N3 some oversampling of urban areas was resorted to in order to yield a larger number of men who had had drinking problems, since it had been established in earlier surveys that city size is one of the principal variables in problem drinking. Of the 100 primary sampling units covered in the N2 survey, the 60 rural or small-city (under 50,000) population units were subsampled at half-rate (i.e., 30 were selected), and thus 70 were sampled in N3 of the 100 which were sampled in N2. As will be noted below in the discussion of the sample weightings, it developed that this procedure made no important differences in the ultimate findings.

Table 67 shows the completion rates of the National 3 survey. Interviews were conducted in 73% of the occupied households which may have contained a man aged 21 to 59; because some occupants refused to give the ages of men, this completion rate is somewhat understated.

As in N2, intensive efforts were resorted to in N3 to bring the completion rate up to 73%. These included personal letters, telephone calls, repeated visits (as many as 15 or 20) to find prospective respondents, use of city directories, and inquiries to employers, public agencies and post offices, and special de-

TABLE 67.—*Completion Rates of the 1969 National 3 Interviews*

	N	%
Eligibility of Households		
Vacant units	222[a]	9
Occupied but ineligible (no men 21–59)	875	36
Eligible households	1339[b]	55
Total addresses	2436	100
Completion Rates		
Interviewed	978	73
Refused or unusable	253	19
Other nonresponse	108	8
Total	1339	100

[a] Includes a few addresses initially defined as "housing units" but found to have been demolished or otherwise not eligible as a housing unit.

[b] Includes housing units where eligibility could not be determined, usually because occupants refused to give ages of men. The completion rate would have been somewhat higher if it had been possible to determine eligibility in all these cases and exclude from the base all units without any men aged 21–59.

livery letters when it was believed these might help to complete an interview.

The exact completion rate for the N2 men aged 21–59 is unknown because this was a sampling of all men and women aged 21 and over, and separate completion rates by sex are difficult to compute. Since the completion rate for N2 for both sexes and all ages was 80%, however, and since men aged 21–59 are notably harder to find at home, it is estimated that the N2 completion rate may have been from 73 to 76%, comparable to the N3 rate.

The completion rate of three-fourths of the eligible men aged 21 to 59 is fairly high for this hard-to-get population, although few studies of this special population are available for comparison. To the extent that about one-fourth of the eligible population was missed, some underestimation of the proportions of problem drinkers in the base population (of men living in households) definitely did occur, because we know from the N2 follow-up that heavy drinkers are harder to find and interview than are other drinkers (19, *p. 174*). Thus the findings on the rates of problem drinking in this monograph are somewhat conservatively stated, and certainly not overstated.

D. Sample Weighting and Statistical Reliability. The sample plans called for oversampling of certain groups to ensure sufficient numbers of problem drinkers for analysis, with provision for obtaining adequate representation in all undersampled groups to permit later weighting of the sample if desired. Insofar as men were concerned, the N2 study undersampled only the "light" drinkers (half of the 162 men in this category) and households with more than 1 adult (only 1 was interviewed per household). The chief subsampling in N3 was (as already noted) taking half of the 60 primary sampling units from rural areas and small cities, thus having a total of 70 sampling units. Two relatively trivial additional types of subsampling in N3 involved handling a few large multiple-dwelling units which were built between the time of the initial enumeration of households and the interviewing (these were subsampled, with provision for later weighting the findings proportionately), and in handling the few households with more than 1 man aged 21–59 in residence (only 1 was interviewed at random, with provision for proportionate weight-ings to represent those not interviewed).

After the interviewing was completed, appropriate weights were assigned to compensate for these various subsampling processes. But, because there are a number of advantages to using unweighted data (e.g., ease in recombining findings and computations of statistical reliability) where there is no sub-stantial bias, results were tabulated separately on a weighted and unweighted basis. It was found, for the combined N2–N3 data, that in only 1 instance was the difference between weight-ed and unweighted aggregated findings on the 13 types of prob-lem drinking scores as much as one percentage point. When 60 independent variables or scores on intervening sociopsy-chological variables were tabulated, in only 3 instances was the difference as much as 3 percentage points. The three vari-ables were those of urbanization, urbanization change (di-rectly related to the chief subsampling variable of urbaniza-tion) and alienation, on which the "high" score was 3.9 percentage points higher on the weighted than the unweighted basis.

Since it was established that the weighting would make no practical difference in the results, the data in this monograph are all reported on an unweighted basis.

It should be added that this special sample of men aged 21–59 has lower variance than an equal-sized sample of the general adult population; that is, most of the heavy drinkers in the adult population will be concentrated within this group. This is the primary reason why weighted and unweighted data were not found to make much difference in the N3 sample. Weightings for size of household and undersampling of light drinkers, however, were found to make a considerable dif-ference in the N1 and 2 samples of all adults (men and women) 21 and older; consequently these findings for the general pop-ulation were reported on a weighted basis (20).

A note on statistical significance of differences in this mono-graph is in order at this point. This monograph contains many hundreds of comparisons of findings from various subgroups. Since the sample was a probability sample, all the findings can be subjected to tests of statistical significance. Formal tests of significance have not been presented here, however, because other important criteria, including independent replications of findings from comparing subgroups within this survey and between this survey and prior surveys, have been available for discussing the importance of the implications of observed differences. We have avoided drawing any conclusions or inferences on the basis of findings on isolated items which may have stemmed from chance. Summary Table 68 is provided in case any reader wishes to perform an approximate test of the statistical significance of the differences between any two percentages presented in this book.

2. The 1967–68 San Francisco Survey

The San Francisco sample was drawn according to the same general probability sampling principles as the national survey: that is, giving each male aged 21 to 59 in the household population a known chance of selection, through random sampling procedures, from the selection of the areas to be covered to the selection of the individual within the household.[2] The sample was defined as men aged 21–59 living in households (thus

TABLE 68.—*Approximate Sampling Tolerances for Differences Between Two Survey Percentages At or Near These Levels, in Per Cent*[a]

Size of Samples Compared	10 or 90%	20 or 80%	30 or 70%	40 or 60%	50%
750 and 750	4	5	6	6	6
and 500	4	6	6	7	7
and 250	5	7	8	9	9
and 100	8	10	12	13	13
500 and 500	5	6	7	8	8
and 250	5	8	8	9	9
and 100	8	11	13	14	14
250 and 250	7	8	10	11	11
and 100	9	12	13	14	14
100 and 100	10	14	16	17	17

(95 in 100 confidence level)

[a] Adapted, with permission, from a table published by ORC Caravan Surveys, Princeton, N.J., May 1965. The effect of clustering (selecting respondents in groups within primary sampling units) is taken into account in the formula used.

[2] Dr. Josephine Williams was responsible for the detailed sample design.

excluding transients, institutionalized persons and those living on military bases or college campuses) who were "Caucasian" (including those of mixed American Indian origin who had Spanish surnames), the non-Caucasians being omitted from the sample in order to control for variance stemming from the unusual ethnic mix in San Francisco.

Sampling procedures in San Francisco differed from those in the national sample in matters of detail rather than principle. A new (1966) Polk City Directory provided a more convenient sampling base than in the national sampling, where it was necessary to select segments at random and to prelist all households within those subdivisions. Instead, every Nth name was drawn from the directory through systematic random sampling, yielding an unclustered sample which provided proportionate representation to every census tract in the city. In addition, every 16th hotel, motel, residence club, etc., in the city directory was included and canvassed to determine if there were any permanent residents; from the list of rooms occupied by permanent residents every Nth room was drawn into the sample.

Another stratum was added to represent any homes that had been constructed or dwelling units converted during the time between the compilation of the directory and the 1967–68 survey. A subsample of 70 blocks was drawn and those of highest density were subsampled at a higher rate than other blocks to achieve the effect of drawing a sample from a list of blocks stratified by density.

For all sample blocks chosen, every dwelling unit in the block was enumerated. The revised lists were compared with the city directory; any dwelling units missed in the directory were subsampled at rates to represent appropriately all dwelling units existing at the time of the survey.

Interviewers checked at each chosen dwelling unit to determine whether it contained one or more Caucasian men aged 21 to 59. If more than one lived in the unit, a single respondent was designated for the interview (to avoid contaminating effects of interviewing more than one person per dwelling unit); in such instances, data were kept to permit weighting responses according to the total eligible persons in the household.

Actually less than 10% of the sample resided in dwelling units which had more than one eligible respondent. Thus the weighted findings differed very little from the unweighted results, so that for convenience the findings are presented in unweighted form.

Because of the length of the interview (from 2 to 2½ hours) and its complexity, only interviewers were utilized who had had extensive training through written instructions, briefings by supervisors and practice interviews prior to their formal assignments. Unlike the national surveys, which used men interviewers, women interviewers were used primarily in this San Francisco survey because most of the highly trained interviewers in the area are women. Also, reluctance to report drinking at all was judged to be less of a problem than, say, in rural Iowa.

TABLE 69.—*Completion Rates of the San Francisco 1967–68 Survey*

Eligibility of Households	N	%
Vacant units	93[a]	3
Occupied but ineligible (no men 21–59)	1669	61
Eligible households	976[b]	36
Total addresses	2738	*100*

Completion Rates		
Interviewed	786	81
Refused or unusable	177	18
Other nonresponse	13	1
Total	976	*100*

Distribution by Stratum	% Interviewed Cases (N = 786)	% Original Address List (2738)
Dwelling unit from directory	85	82
Rooms in hotels, etc. from directory	18	12
Supplementary sample of units not in directory	7	6

[a] Includes some addresses initially defined as "housing units" but found to have been demolished or otherwise not eligible as a housing unit.

[b] Includes housing units where eligibility could not be determined (usually because occupants refused to give ages of males); thus the completion rate would have been somewhat higher if it had been possible to determine eligibility in all these cases.

Intensive field supervision assured interviewing standards and, to get as high a completion rate as possible, repeated call-backs and rotation of interviewers were used for reluctant or evasive respondents. The field work was substantially completed between September 1967 and May of 1968. Table 69 shows that the completion rate was 81% which compares very favorably with the 73% of the National 3 survey, because it is traditionally more difficult to trace respondents in metropolitan areas of high transiency like San Francisco than in the nation as a whole.

Appendix B

The Drinking Problems Scores

1. The National Samples

In the analyses of the National data in the present monograph, three separate series of problem-drinking measures are used for different purposes: *(1) The N3 Optimum Scales,* the "best estimate" available from the full list of items scored on N3, are built on current and lifetime time frames. *(2) The N2–N3 Scales* are designed for exact comparability between the two studies. They differ from the optimum scales primarily by the omission of items not asked on N2 and are built on N2–N3 for current and lifetime time frames. *(3) The N3 Past–Current Comparable Scales* differ from the optimum scales by the exclusion of items for which full past information was not obtained. They were constructed from N3 for current, past and lfetime time frames.

In building the scales, the benchmark was the optimum scales, and the other series are matched to the optimum scales in form and differ only by omitting items as necessary. A summary of the current optimum N3 scales in the form they were finally used is presented here; detailed scoring procedures for all the scale series are available.

Respondents were coded into the highest-severity scale step for which they qualified; all respondents who did not qualify for any of the listed steps were coded into step 0 on that scale. "Minimal-severity problems" for each of the 13 specific problem areas includes all respondents in steps 1–4; "high problems" includes all in steps 2–4 (except for belligerence, where the "high" and "minimal severity" criteria were the same). The time period for current problems is the last 3 years; however, parts of heavy intake and psychological dependence are drawn from items simply phrased in the present tense.

Heavy intake. Step 3 (3.5%), 12+ drinks at a time at least once a week, or 8+ drinks at least nearly every day. Step 2 (9.5%), 12+ drinks at least monthly, or 8+ drinks at least weekly, or 5+ at least 4 times a week. Step 1 (10.8%), 8+ drinks at least monthly, or 5+ drinks or "high or tight" at least weekly.

Binge Drinking. Step 3 (1.8%), Stayed intoxicated several days at a time within the last 3 years, and high or tight for at least a day at a time 5+ times in the last 3 years. Step 2 (4.2%), Either of the items in step 3. Step 1 (1.5%), High or tight for at least a day within the last 3 years.

Psychological Dependence. Collapsed from an additive raw score constructed with 3 points for "very important," 1 point for "fairly important" for each of the following reasons for drinking: When I want to forget everything, Helps cheer me up when I am in a bad mood, Because I need it when tense and nervous, Helps me to forget my worries, Having a drink . . . helpful when I am depressed or nervous. Three points were added for an open-ended response to why drinking more (needed to relax, relieve tension, nerves, depression), 3 points for "Often drank in order to change the way I felt," and 2 points for open-ended response to why cut down or quit within the last 3 years (fewer problems, worries, tensions, responsibilities). Step 4 (3.3% scored 11-23 points; Step 3 (1.6%), 9-10; Step 2 (4.0%), 7-8; and Step 1 (15.3%), 3–6.

Loss of control. Partially constructed from an additive score, with one point for each of the following: Once I started drinking it was difficult to stop before I became completely intoxicated, Sometimes kept on drinking after I had promised myself not to, Tried to quit or cut down but failed, Worry about my drinking "a lot"; or any reference to losing control of drinking or fear of becoming an alcoholic in open-ended responses on reasons for cutting down, quitting, or trying to do either. Step 4 (0.7%), "I am/was an alcoholic" or lost control of my drinking, as an explicit open-ended response to reasons for cutting down or quitting or trying to; or trying and failing to quit or cut down at least twice in the last 3 years; Step 3 (1.3%), a score of 3–5 on the additive score; Step 2 (2.5%), 2; Step 1 (9.4%), 1.

Symptomatic drinking. An additive score constructed from one point for each of: Skipped regular meals while drinking, Tossed down several drinks to get a quicker effect, Had a quick drink when no one was looking, A few quick drinks before a party to make sure I had enough, Awakened the next day unable to remember what I had done while drinking, Often took a drink first thing in the morning, Hands shook a lot after drinking, Sometimes high or tight drinking by myself. Step 4 (2.6%), scored 5–8; Step 3 (1.8%), 4; Step 2 (3.8%), 3; Step 1 (6.3%), 2.

Belligerence. Step 2 (3.0%), Felt aggressive or cross, Got into a fight, Got into a heated argument while drinking. Step 1 (6.4%), any two of the experiences named in step 2 (this step is included in "high problems" on Belligerence).

Problems with wife. Step 4 (0.3%), Wife actually left respondent because of his drinking; Step 3 (1.7%), Wife threatened to leave; Step

2 (11.5%), Wife became angry over respondent's drinking, or respondent reports his drinking has been harmful to his marriage or home life; Step 1 (7.4%), Wife showed concern over respondent's drinking, or indicated he should cut down on his drinking.

Problems with relatives. Step 2 (8.2%), Respondent's drinking was very displeasing to a relative; Step 1 (3.9%), A relative indicated respondent should cut down on his drinking.

Problems with friends or neighbors. Step 3 (2.8%), Drinking was involved in losing a friendship; Step 2 (4.6%), Drinking has been harmful to friendships and social life or both friends and neighbors have indicated respondent should cut down; Step 1 (2.0%), Either friends or neighbors have indicated respondent should cut down.

Job problems. Step 4 (1.9%), Lost a job or nearly lost one because of drinking, or Drinking led to quitting a job. Step 3 (0.8%), Any two of the following three items: Drinking hurt my chances for promotion, People at work indicated I should cut down, Drinking harmful to my work and employment opportunities. Step 2 (3.2%), Any one of the items listed under step 3. Step 1 (4.5%), Have either gotten high or tight on the job, or Stayed away from work because of a hangover.

Police problems. Step 3 (0.9%), Trouble with the law both because of driving after drinking and about drinking when driving was not involved. Step 2 (3.4%), Either of the items listed under step 3; Step 1 (1.4%), Policeman questioned or warned respondent because of his drinking.

Health and injury problems. Step 3 (2.1%), Had an illness connected with drinking which kept me from working or regular activities for a week or more, or In a hospital or rest home for an illness connected with drinking. Step 2 (4.8%), Drinking contributed to my getting hurt in an accident; or Physician suggested I cut down on drinking, and at least one of the following: A liver ailment (doctor treated); Drinking had a harmful effect on health, or "Bad health, doctor's orders," etc., as open-ended reasons for cutting down or quitting or trying to. Step 1 (8.6%), Any one of the items mentioned under step 2.

Financial problems. Step 3 (3.7%), Spent money on drinks needed for essentials (e.g., food, clothing or payments); Step 2 (3.7%), Drinking was harmful to financial position; Step 1 (7.9%), Spent too much money on drinks or after drinking.

Full social consequences score. Constructed by adding together the face value of the respondent's steps on wife, relatives, friends or neighbors, job and police, except that the third step was scored as 4 for friends and neighbors and police. "High problems" scored 3+, "Minimal-severity problems," 1+.

Full tangible consequences score. Constructed by adding to the social-consequences score the face value of the respondent's steps on health and injury and financial problems, except step 3 scored as

4 for both these additional areas. "High problems" scored 3+, "Minimal severity problems," 1+.

Problematic intake scale. Composed of the highest-severity step the respondent attained on either heavy intake or binge drinking.

Current problems typology. Class 4 "high problems" (score 3+) on tangible consequences score; Class 3, not in step 4, but in Steps 1–3 on heavy intake, or steps 2–3 on binge drinking; Class 2, All others with *any* problem of at least minimal severity (steps 1); Class 1, All others who have been drinking within the last 3 years; Class 0, Abstainers throughout the last 3 years.

N2–N3 current over-all problems score.[1] Constructed only for the N2–N3 comparable scales by adding scores from each problem area, with 6 points for a "severe," 3 for a "moderate," and 1 for a "mild" problem. The "severe" level is generally set at or above the high problems level used in N3 and the "mild" level at or below the N3 minimal-severity level. A score of 7+ thus means problems in at least two areas with one of them severe, or mild problems in at least seven areas, or equivalent combinations.

2. The San Francisco Sample

The versions of the problem-drinking measures used for the San Francisco sample were adapted to bear a fairly close resemblance to the national sample measures. "High problems" includes all in steps 2 and above (there is no "high problems" group on financial problems). As in the national scale scores, respondents are coded into the highest applicable severity and into step 0 if they do not qualify for any listed step. Only the listed steps plus step 0 exist. The time period for "current problems" is 3 years for binge drinking, and wife, interpersonal, job, police and accident problems, and 1 year for the remainder of the problem areas. For wife, interpersonal and job problems, full information on the severity of problems in the period 1-3 years ago was not always available from the questionnaire, resulting in underestimates of severity.

Heavy intake. Step 4 (5.5%), 12+ drinks on an occasion at least once a week, or 8+ drinks at least nearly every day; Step 2 (7.0%), 12+ drinks on an occasion at least once a month, or 8+ drinks at least once a week, or 4+ drinks at least nearly every day. Step 1 (11.1%), 8+ drinks at least once a month, or 4+ drinks at least once a week.

[1] A close analogue to the score used in Cahalan (19, *p. 36*).

Binge drinking. Step 2 (7.4%), Drunk or high for more than a day at a time within the last 3 years.

Psychological dependence. Derived from an additive raw score defined as: 2 points for "very important," 1 point for "fairly important," for each of "Because I need it when tense and nervous" and "A drink helps me forget my worries" as reasons for drinking, and 2 points each for Getting drunk when upset, unhappy or tense, or Drinking more than usual when I just want to forget everything. Step 4 (2.0%), scores 6–8; Step 3 (5.6%), 4–5; Step 2 (4.2%), 3; Step 1 (18.7%), 1–2.

Loss of control. Constructed as an additive scale, 1 point for each of the following: Fairly or extremely hard to cut down or quit drinking, I sometimes get drunk even when there's an important reason to stay sober, When I have a drink I almost always drink until I pass out, There have been occasions when I kept on drinking after I promised myself not to. Step 4 (0%), score 4; Step 3 (0.6%), 3; Step 2 (2.5%), 2; and Step 1 (9.5%), 1.

Symptomatic behavior. Collapsed from an additive score, one point for each of the following: I sometimes take a drink the first thing in the morning when I get up, I sometimes wake up in the morning after drinking and cannot remember doing some things that I did even after people tell me about them, I sometimes take a few quick drinks before going to a party to make sure I'll have enough, I sometimes sneak drinks when no one is looking, I have taken a drink to get rid of a hangover, When I am drinking by myself, I tend to drink more. Step 4 (1.2%), scores 4–6; Step 3 (2.3%), 3; Step 2 (6.9%), 2; and Step 1 (13.8%), 1.

Problems with wife. Step 4 (1.4%), Wife left, separated, divorced, etc., because of respondent's drinking; Step 3 (1.2%), Wife threatened to leave; Step 2 (3.9%), Wife became angry at respondent for his drinking; Step 1 (5.6%), Wife showed concern over respondent's drinking.

Interpersonal problems. Collapsed from a score derived from reports of problems due to the respondent's drinking with all friends and relatives (other than wives) (combines the areas of relatives and friends in the national studies): 4 points for a break in relationship, 3 points for a threat of break but no break, 2 points for a person getting angry without threat, and 1 point for any other show of concern. Step 6 (0.9%) score 6+; Step 5 (1.5%), 5; Step 4 (0.9%), 4; Step 3 (2.5%), 3; Step 2 (4.5%), 2; and Step 1 (8.8%), 1.

Job problems. Step 4 (1.3%), Fired, laid off or quit job due to drinking; Step 3 (1.3%), Warned or complained to at the job about drinking, or Losing out on a promotion or pay raise due to drinking; Step 2 (4.7%), Going to work drunk.

Police problems. Step 3 (0%), both of items named in step 2; Step 2 (3.8%), Either arrested for drunken driving or other law trouble connected with drinking; Step 1 (1.9%), Police stopped, talked to, sent home, etc., because of drinking.

Accident problems. Step 2 (3.2%), Respondent's drinking caused him to have an accident or injury.

Financial problems. Step 1 (17.3%), Respondent felt he was spending too much money on drinking.

Social consequences score. Constructed by adding together the scores on wife, interpersonal, job, police, and accident problems. "High problems" is equivalent to a score of 3+.

Appendix C

Composition of Predictor Scores

Summaries of the items composing each score of the N3 and San Francisco surveys are given below. Except as noted, the score was constructed by allotting one point for each item.

1. NATIONAL 3 SCORES

A. *Childhood History*

Youthful rashness. Sent to the school principal for acting up, played hooky quite often, involved in fist fights more than once.

Childhood hardship. Changes in neighborhoods or schools were hardship, inadequate income, disadvantages because of race, religion or nationality when aged 5 to 21.

Family disruption. Did not live with both mother and father before age 16, parents were separated or divorced when respondent was aged 5–21.

Childhood unhappiness and family cohesion. Home was less peaceful than others, conditions around home often troublesome, no real friends of own age, parents admired another child more; happy as a child? (unhappy, 2 points, half-and-half, 1 point.)

B. *Personality Scores*

Somatization. All sorts of pains and ailments, fullness or clogging in head or nose, shortness of breath when not exercising.

Affective anxiety. Felt tense or nervous, worried, depressed; is the worrying type, bothered by nervousness; irritable, fidgety.

Physical depression. Often too tired even to do things he likes to do, periods of days or weeks or months when he can't get going, has hard time making up mind about things he should do.

Psychiatric symptoms. Feels he is about to go to pieces, have the same dream over and over, bothered by useless thoughts, feels as if something dreadful is going to happen, or as if he was going to have nervous breakdown.

Intrapunitiveness. Does things he regrets afterwards, has not lived the right kind of life, wishes he could be as happy as others seem to be, hardest battles are with self, hard not to give up hope of amounting to something, feel as though he has done something wrong or evil.

Alienation or paranoia. Feels people around are not too friendly, things are getting worse in spite of what people say, often feels left out, hard to know how to treat people, would live very differently if had choice, people often talk behind his back, his way of doing things is apt to be misunderstood.

Impulsivity. Often acts on spur of moment, changes mind rather quickly, spends more money than thinks he should, does not let risk of getting hurt stop him from having good time.

Tolerance of deviance. Not really bad not to work steadily, to have sex relations with several women when single, to get into fights, for a husband and wife to be separated, for a woman to have sex relations with several men when she is single, for a man to fool around with other women after marriage, for parents hardly ever to stay home with their children, for someone not to pay back money he owes, for a married women to fool around with other men.

Sociability. Likes to take part in social activities, likes to belong to as many clubs as possible, people think of him as a very social type, likes to be with people, people seem to enjoy being with him.

C. Social Situation, Habits and History Scores

Nonhelpfulness of others. The following people would not be helpful in an emergency: people at work, neighbors, wife, relatives, police.

Social activity. Gets together socially or visits friends several times a week; or all three of: often visits friends, often has visitors, and often goes out for entertainment.

Lack of neighborhood roots. Eight or more moves in the last 10 years (2 points), 2–7 moves in the last 10 years, never socializes with neighbors, conditions round neighborhood often troublesome (2 points), sometimes troublesome.

Drug habits. Smokes 2+ packs of cigarettes a day (3 points), 1–2 packs (2 points), smokes less than 1 pack a day; ever used pills to pep him up (2 points), to calm him down, to help him sleep at night, taking a tranquilizer when depressed.

Home-role friction. Conditions round home now troublesome—often (3 points), sometimes (2 points), rarely; how happily married—not very happy, less happy than average (3 points), just about average (2 points), a little happier than average (conditions round home weighted doubly for the unmarried).

Work friction. Conditions often troublesome at work, would prefer different occupation, worry a lot about not getting ahead in work.

Health problems. Health only fair or poor, serious health problems in last 12 months; problems requiring medical attention in last 3 years—migraine or severe headache, high blood pressure, heart trouble or stroke, liver trouble, stomach or duodenal ulcer, other serious stomach trouble, other serious internal trouble, nervous breakdown; same list of specific conditions for before 3 years ago.

D. Drinking-Context Variables

Heavy drinking context. Drinks served with close friends—nearly every time (3 points), more than half the time (2 points), at least once in a while; how many close friends drink quite a bit—nearly all (3 points), about half (2 points), only a few; how often goes to bar or cocktail lounge—at least once a week (3 points), less but once a month (2 points), more than "never."

Attitudes of others to respondent's drinking. Wife, father, mother, other "most important person" feels it is acceptable for respondent to drink 8 or more drinks (2 points), 4–7 drinks.

Respondent's attitudes to drinking. There are good things to be said about drinking; drinking does more good than harm; it is not a bad thing for a man to drink a lot; would miss drinking; it is all right to get drunk whenever you feel like it (2 points), once in a while; 2 points for "very important," 1 for "fairly important" to these reasons for drinking: to be sociable, because the people the respondent knows drink, to celebrate special occasions, because it is the polite thing to do.

2. SAN FRANCISCO SCORES

Childhood unhappiness–lack of family cohesion. Did not always live with both parents up to age of 16, unhappy childhood, parents' marriage was unhappy, members of family were not close, when a child home was less peaceful than homes of most other people, parents approved of another child more than they did of him.

Youthful hell-raising. Played hooky quite often, sometimes sent to the principal for acting up, as a young man got into fist fights fought in anger.

Moralism. Does not like people with very strict moral standards, less strict about right and wrong than most people, not in favor of very strict enforcement of all laws, sometimes enjoys going against the rules. (Score used in reverse form.)

Hotheadedness–belligerence. At times feels like smashing things, often said to be hotheaded, at times feels like picking a fist fight.

Happiness–euphoria. Respondent and wife are not well suited to each other, does not get a great deal of enjoyment from his work, does not often feel on top of the world, does not like his place of living, not very happy. (Score used in reverse form.)

Impetuosity. Often acts on the spur of the moment, often spends more money than thinks he should, does not usually stick at job or problem if not getting anywhere, unlikely to undo knots rather than cutting the string, more fun to see what turns up rather than plan ahead, rather enjoys it when something unexpected breaks routine, spends money on spur of moment for something that gives pleasure.

Psychiatric symptoms. Sometimes feels he is about to go to pieces, several times a week feels as if something dreadful is going to happen, has had feeling he was going to have a nervous breakdown, sometimes has same dream over and over.

Tension. Tension or strain in work, gets tense when feels others' disapproval, often gets tense, nervous, depressed, or a little blue.

"Macho." All young men should compete in sports, easier to understand hell-raiser than a sissy, a boy who spends much free time reading books should be encouraged to take part in manly activities, bookworms and eggheads usually accomplish less than a practical man, a little experience is worth a lot of theory.

Passive physical pleasures. Likes staying in bed late in the morning, hot milk, dozing by fire, ice cream sundaes with whipped cream on top; dislikes hard physical exercise.

Somatic complaints. Fairly often has trouble going to sleep or staying asleep, sometimes poor appetite, shortness of breath when not exercising or working hard, often upset or nervous stomach.

Guilt. Wastes time and spends it uselessly, does things he is sorry for afterwards more often than other people.

Interpersonal isolation. Lives alone, seldom gets together with friends, no religious affiliation, retired or unemployed, one of last in his crowd to hear what is going on, does not enjoy crowds just to be with people, worries do not seem to disappear when he gets into a crowd of lively friends.

Distrust. People often talk behind his back, if you get too friendly people will take advantage of you, has often found people jealous of his good ideas, the more one knows a person, the more often you find he lets you down.

Assertiveness. Likes to let people know where he stands, likes to boss other people around, likes to compete with others, can be hard-boiled if necessary.

Daring. Would like parachute jumping, does not let the risk of getting hurt stop him from having a good time, would like to drive a racing car.

Bibliography

1. ACHTÉ, K., SEPPÄLÄ, K., GINMAN, L. and COLLIANDER, N. Alcoholic psychoses in Finland. (Finnish Foundation for Alcohol Studies, Publ. No. 19.) Helsinki; 1969.
2. ADKINS, D. C. The simple structure of the American Psychological Association. Amer. Psychol. 9: 175–180, 1954.
3. ALLPORT, G. W. [Book review of The American Soldier.] J. abnorm. soc. Psychol. 45: 168–173, 1950.
4. ALLPORT, G. W. The nature of prejudice. Garden City, N.Y.; Doubleday; 1958.
5. ATTKISSON, C. Suicide in San Francisco's Skid Row. Arch. gen. Psychiat. 23: 149–157, 1970.
6. BAILEY, M. B., HABERMAN, P. W. and ALKSNE, H. The epidemiology of alcoholism in an urban residential area. Quart. J. Stud. Alc. 26: 19–40, 1965.
7. BAILEY, M. B., HABERMAN, P. W. and SHEINBERG, J. Identifying alcoholics in population surveys; a report on reliability. Quart. J. Stud. Alc. 27: 300–315, 1966.
8. BALES, R. F. Cultural differences in rates of alcoholism. Pp. 263–277. In: MCCARTHY, R. G., ed. Drinking and intoxication. New Brunswick, N.J.; Rutgers Center of Alcohol Studies; 1959.
9. BELSON, W. A. Measuring the effects of television; a description of method. Publ. Opin. Quart. 22: 11–18, 1958.
10. BELSON, W. A. Matching and prediction on the principle of biological classification. Appl. Statist. 8: 65–75, 1959.
11. BLALOCK, H. M. Theory building and causal inferences. Pp. 155–198. In: BLALOCK, H. M. and BLALOCK, A. B., eds. Methodology in social research. New York; McGraw-Hill; 1968.
12. BLOCK, J. The challenge of response sets; unconfounding meaning, acquiescence, and social desirability in the MMPI. New York; Appleton; 1965.
13. BOHRNSTEDT, G. W. Observations on the measurement of change. Pp. 113–133. In: BORGATTA, E. F. and BOHRNSTEDT, G. W., eds. Sociological methodology. San Francisco; Jossey-Bass; 1970.
14. BOUDON, R. A new look at correlation analysis. Pp. 199–235. In: BLALOCK, H. M. and BLALOCK, A. B., eds. Methodology in social research. New York; McGraw-Hill; 1968.
15. BRUUN, K. The actual and the registered frequency of drunkenness in Helsinki. Brit. J. Addict. 64: 3–8, 1969.
16. BRUUN, K. Finland: the non-medical approach. Int. Congr. Alcsm & Drug Dep., 29th, pp. 545–555, 1970.
17. CAHALAN, D. Correlates of change in drinking behavior in an urban community sample over a three-year period. Ph.D. dissertation, George Washington University; 1968.
18. CAHALAN, D. Correlates of respondent accuracy in the Denver validity survey. Publ. Opin. Quart. 32: 608–621, 1968–69.

19. CAHALAN, D. Problem drinkers; a national survey. San Francisco; Jossey-Bass; 1970.

20. CAHALAN, D., CISIN, I. and CROSSLEY, H. American drinking practices; a national study of drinking behavior and attitudes. (Rutgers Center of Alcohol Studies, Monogr. No. 6.) New Brunswick, N.J.; 1969.

21. CAHALAN, D. and MEIER, N. C. The validity of mail-ballot polls. Psychol. Rec. 3: 1–12, 1939.

22. CAMPBELL, D. T. Common fate, similarity, and other indices of the status of aggregates of persons as social entities. Behav. Sci. 3: 14–25, 1958.

23. CAMPBELL, D. T. From description to experimentation; interpreting trends as quasi-experiments. Pp. 212–242. In: HARRIS, C. W., ed. Problems in measuring change. Madison; University of Wisconsin Press; 1963.

24. CAMPBELL, D. T. and STANLEY, J. C. Experimental and quasi-experimental designs for research. Chicago; Rand McNally; 1966.

25. CARTWRIGHT, D. S. Ecological variables. Pp. 155–218. In: BORGATTA, E. F. and BOHRNSTEDT, G. W., eds. Sociological methodology. San Francisco; Jossey-Bass; 1970.

26. CASEY, R. L., MASUDA, M. and HOLMES, T. Quantitative study of recall of life events. J. psychosom. Res. 11: 239–247, 1967.

27. CHAFETZ, M. E. Alcoholism prevention and reality. Quart. J. Stud. Alc. 28: 345–348, 1967.

28. CHRISTIE, N. Scandinavian experience in legislation and control. Pp. 101–122. In: BOSTON UNIVERSITY, LAW–MEDICINE INSTITUTE. National conference on legal issues in alcoholism and alcohol usage. Boston; 1966.

29. CLARK V. A. and HOPKINS, C. E. Time is of the essence. J. chron. Dis. 20: 565–569, 1967.

30. CLARK, W. Operational definitions of drinking problems and associated prevalence rates. Quart. J. Stud. Alc. 27: 648–668, 1966.

31. CLAUSEN, J. A. and KOHN, M. L. The ecological approach in social psychiatry. Amer. J. Sociol. 60: 140–149, 1954.

32. CLINARD, M. B. The relation of urbanization and urbanism to criminal behavior. Pp. 541–558. In: BURGESS, E. W. and BOGUE, D. J., eds. Contributions to urban sociology. Chicago; University of Chicago Press; 1963.

33. CLOWARD, R. A. and OHLIN, L. E. Delinquency and opportunity; a theory of delinquent gangs. New York; Free Press; 1960.

34. COLEMAN, J. S. The mathematical study of change. Pp. 428–478. In: BLALOCK, H. M. and BLALOCK, A. B., eds. Methodology in social research. New York; McGraw-Hill; 1968.

35. COOPERATIVE COMMISSION ON THE STUDY OF ALCOHOLISM. Alcohol problems; a report to the nation. Prepared by Plaut, T. F. A. New York; Oxford University Press; 1967.

36. DE LINT, J. and SCHMIDT, W. The distribution of alcohol consumption in Ontario. Quart. J. Stud. Alc. 29: 968–973, 1968.

37. DE LINT, J. and SCHMIDT, W. Consumption averages and alcoholism prevalence; a brief review of epidemiological investigations. Brit. J. Addict. **66:** 97-107, 1971.

38. DOLLARD, J. Drinking mores of the social classes. Pp. 95-104. In: Alcohol, science and society. New Brunswick, N.J.; Journal of Studies on Alcohol; 1945.

39. DRAPER, N. R. and SMITH, H. Applied regression analysis. New York; Wiley; 1966.

40. DURKHEIM, E. Suicide. New York; Free Press; 1951.

41. EFRON, V. and KELLER, M. Selected statistics on consumption of alcohol (1850-1968) and on alcoholism (1930-1968). New Brunswick, N.J.; Rutgers Center of Alcohol Studies; 1970.

42. EWING, J. A. Notes on quantity frequency studies on alcohol intake. Drinking & Drug Pract. Surveyor, Berkeley, Calif., No. 1, pp. 8-11, 1970.

43. FARIS, R. E. L. and DUNHAM, H. W. Mental disorders in urban areas. Chicago; University of Chicago Press; 1939.

44. FINK, R. Parental drinking and its impact on adult drinkers. (California Drinking Practices Study, Rep. No. 5.) Berkeley; California State Department of Public Health; 1962.

45. FISHER, G. A discriminant analysis of reporting errors in health interviews. Appl. Statist. **11:** 148-163, 1962.

46. GLOCK, C. Y. Survey design and analysis in sociology. Pp. 1-62. In: GLOCK, C. Y., ed. Survey research in the social sciences. New York; Russell Sage Foundation; 1967.

47. GOFFMAN, E. Stigma; notes on the management of spoiled identity. Englewood Cliffs, N.J.; Prentice-Hall; 1963.

48. GOVE, W. R. Societal reaction as an explanation of mental illness; an elevation. Amer. sociol. Rev. **35:** 873-884, 1970.

49. GUSFIELD, J. R. Symbolic crusade; status politics and the American temperance movement. Urbana; University of Illinois Press; 1963.

50. HAYMAN, M. The myth of social drinking. Amer. J. Psychiat. **124:** 585-594, 1967.

51. HOLLINGSHEAD, A. B. Two-factor index of social position. New Haven, Conn.; 1957.

52. HYMAN, H. Survey design and analysis; principles, cases and procedures. New York; Free Press; 1955.

53. JACKSON, J. K. The definition and measurement of alcoholism; H-technique scales of preoccupation with alcohol and psychological involvement. Quart. J. Stud. Alc. **18:** 240-262, 1957.

54. JACKSON, J. K. Types of drinking patterns of male alcoholics. Quart. J. Stud. Alc. **19:** 269-302, 1958.

55. JAEGER, C. M. and PENNOCK, J. L. An analysis of consistency of response in household surveys. J. Amer. Statist. Ass. **56:** 320-327, 1961.

56. JELLINEK, E. M. Phases in the drinking history of alcoholics; analysis of a survey conducted by the official organ of Alcoholics Anonymous. Quart. J. Stud. Alc. **7:** 1-88, 1946.

57. JELLINEK, E. M. Recent trends in alcoholism and in alcohol consumption. Quart. J. Stud. Alc. **8:** 1-42, 1947.

58. JELLINEK, E. M. Phases of alcohol addiction. Quart. J. Stud. Alc. **13**: 673–684, 1952.

59. JELLINEK, E. M. The disease concept of alcoholism. Highland Park, N.J.; Hillhouse Press; 1960.

60. JELLINEK, E. M. Alcoholism, a genus and some of its species. Canad. med. Ass. J. **83**: 1341–1345, 1960.

61. JESSOR, R., GRAVES, T. D., HANSON, R. C. and JESSOR, S. L. Society, personality, and deviant behavior; a study of a tri-ethnic community. New York; Holt, Rinehart & Winston; 1968.

62. JONES, M. C. Personality correlates and antecedents of drinking patterns in adult males. J. cons. clin. Psychol. **32**: 2–12, 1968.

63. KELLER, M. The definition of alcoholism and the estimation of its prevalence. Pp. 310–329. In: PITTMAN, D. J. and SNYDER, C. R., eds. Society, culture, and drinking patterns. New York; Wiley; 1962.

64. KENDALL, P. L. and LAZARSFELD, P. F. Problems of survey analysis. Pp. 133–196. In: MERTON, R. K. and LAZARSFELD, P. F., eds. Continuities in social research. New York; Free Press; 1950.

65. KIVIRANTA, P. Alcoholism syndrome in Finland; a comparative analysis of members of the A.A. movement, outpatients of A-clinics and inmates of the institutions for the care of alcoholics. (Finnish Foundation for Alcohol Studies, Vol. 17.) Helsinki; 1969.

66. KNUPFER, G. Epidemiologic studies and control programs in alcoholism. V. The epidemiology of problem drinking. Amer. J. publ. Hlth **57**: 973–986, 1967.

67. KNUPFER, G., FINK, R., CLARK, W. B. and GOFFMAN, A. S. Factors related to amount of drinking in an urban community. (California Drinking Practices Study, Rep. No. 6.) Berkeley; California State Department of Public Health; 1963.

68. KNUPFER, G. and ROOM, R. Age, sex and social class as factors in amount of drinking in a metropolitan community. Social Probl. **12**: 224–240, 1964.

69. KNUPFER, G. and ROOM, R. Drinking patterns and attitudes of Irish, Jewish and White Protestant American men. Quart. J. Stud. Alc. **28**: 676–699, 1967.

70. KNUPFER, G. and ROOM, R. Abstainers in a metropolitan community. Quart. J. Stud. Alc. **31**: 108–131, 1970.

71. LANSING, J. B. and KISH, L. Family life cycle as an independent variable. Amer. sociol. Rev. **22**: 512–519, 1957.

72. LARSEN, D. E. and ABU-LABAN, B. Norm qualities and deviant drinking behavior. Social Probl. **15**: 441–450, 1968.

73. LAZARSFELD, P. F. The mutual effects of statistical variables. New York; Columbia University, Bureau of Applied Social Research; 1947.

74. LAZARSFELD, P. F. Problems in the analysis of mutual interaction between two variables. New York; Columbia University, Bureau of Applied Research; 1969.

75. LINDZEY, G., ed. Handbook of social psychology; Vol. 1. Reading, Mass.; Addison-Wesley; 1954.

76. LIPSET, S. M., LAZARSFELD, P. F., BARTON, A. H. and LINZ, J. The psychology of voting; an analysis of political behavior. Pp. 1124–1175. In: LINDZEY, G., ed. Handbook of social psychology; Vol. II. Reading, Mass.; Addison-Wesley; 1954.

77. LISANSKY-GOMBERG, E. S. Etiology of alcoholism. J. cons. clin. Psychol. **32:** 18–20, 1968.

78. LOLLI, G., SERIANNI, E., GOLDER, G. M. and LUZZATTO-FEGIZ, P. Alcohol in Italian culture; food and wine in relation to sobriety among Italians and Italian Americans. (Rutgers Center of Alcohol Studies, Monogr. No. 3.) New Brunswick, N.J.; 1958.

79. MACANDREW, C. and EDGERTON, R. B. Drunken comportment; a social explanation. Chicago; Aldine; 1969.

80. McCORD, W. and McCORD, J. A longitudinal study of the personality of alcoholics. Pp. 413–430. In: PITTMAN, D. J. and SNYDER, C. R. Society, culture, and drinking patterns. New York; Wiley; 1962.

81. McCORD, W., McCORD, J. and GUDEMAN, J. Origins of alcoholism. (Stanford Studies in Sociology, No. 1.) Stanford; Stanford University Press; 1960.

82. MacCORQUODALE, K. and MEEHL, P. E. On a distinction between hypothetical constructs and intervening variables. Psychol. Rev. **55:** 95–107, 1948.

83. McNEMAR, Q. Psychological statistics. 2d ed. New York; Wiley; 1955.

84. MÄKELÄ, K. Measuring the consumption of alcohol in the 1968–1969 alcohol consumption study. (Social Research Institute of Alcohol Studies, Rep. No. 2.) Helsinki; Oy ALKO Ab; 1971.

85. MALZBERG, B. The alcoholic psychoses; demographic aspects at mid-century in New York State. New Brunswick, N.J.; Rutgers Center of Alcohol Studies; 1960.

86. MANIS, J. G. and HUNT, C. L. The community survey as a measure of the prevalence of alcoholism. Quart. J. Stud. Alc. **18:** 212–216, 1957.

87. MERTON, R. K. Social theory and social structure. New York; Free Press; 1957.

88. MIZRUCHI, E. H. and PERRUCCI, R. Prescription, proscription and permissiveness; aspects of norms and deviant drinking behavior. Pp. 234–253. In: MADDOX, G. L., ed. The domesticated drug; drinking among collegians. New Haven; College & University Press; 1970.

89. MULFORD, H. A. Drinking and deviant drinking, U.S.A., 1963. Quart. J. Stud. Alc. **25:** 634–650, 1964.

90. MULFORD, H. A. Alcoholics, alcoholism and problem drinkers as social objects-in-the-making. Int. Congr. Alc. Alcsm, 28th, Vol. 1 (Abst.), pp. 96–97, 1968.

91. MULFORD, H. A. and MILLER, D. E. Drinking in Iowa. *I.* Sociocultural distribution of drinkers; with a methodological model for sampling evaluation and interpretation of findings. Quart. J. Stud. Alc. **20:** 704–726, 1959.

92. MULFORD, H. A. and MILLER, D. E. Drinking in Iowa. *III.* A scale of definitions of alcohol related to drinking behavior. Quart. J. Stud. Alc. **21:** 267–278, 1960.

93. MULFORD, H. A. and MILLER, D. E. Drinking in Iowa. *IV.* Preoccupation with alcohol and definitions of alcohol, heavy drinking and trouble due to drinking. Quart. J. Stud. Alc. **21:** 279–291, 1960.

94. MULFORD, H. A. and MILLER, D. E. Drinking in Iowa. *V.* Drinking and alcoholic drinking. Quart. J. Stud. Alc. **21:** 483–499, 1960.

95. MULFORD, H. A. and WILSON, R. W. Identifying problem drinkers in a household health survey; a description of field procedures and analytical techniques developed to measure the prevalence of alcoholism. (U.S. National Center for Health Statistics Ser. 2, No. 16.) Washington, D.C.; U.S. Govt Print. Off.; 1966.

96. NASATIR, D. A contextual analysis of academic failure. School Rev., Ithaca, N.Y. **71:** 290–298, 1963.

97. NETER, J. and WAKSBERG, J. Response errors in collection of expenditures data by household interviews; an experimental study. (U.S. Bureau of the Census Tech. Paper No. 11.) Washington, D.C.; U.S. Govt Print. Off.; 1965.

98. NEW YORK STATE MORELAND COMMISSION ON THE ALCOHOLIC BEVERAGE CONTROL LAW. The relationship of the alcoholic beverage control law and the problems of alcohol. (Study Paper No. 1.) New York, 1963.

99. ORFORD, J. Aspects of the relationship between alcohol and drug abuse. Int. Congr. Alcsm & Drug Dep., 29th, pp. 130–144, 1970.

100. PARRY, H. and CROSSLEY, H. Validity of responses to survey questions. Publ. Opin. Quart. **14:** 61–80, 1950.

101. PARTANEN, J., BRUUN, K. and MARKKANEN, T. Inheritance of drinking behavior; a study on intelligence, personality and use of alcohol by adult twins. (Finnish Foundation for Alcohol Studies, Vol. 14.) Helsinki; 1966.

102. PEARL, A., BUECHLEY, R. and LIPSCOMB, W. R. Cirrhosis mortality in three large cities; implications for alcoholism and intercity comparisons. Pp. 345–355. In: PITTMAN, D. J. and SNYDER, C. R., eds. Society, culture, and drinking patterns. New York; Wiley; 1962.

103. PEARL, R. Alcohol and longevity. New York; Knopf; 1926.

104. PELZ, D. C. and ANDREWS, F. M. Detecting causal priorities in panel study data. Amer. sociol. Rev. **29:** 836–848, 1964.

105. POPHAM, R. E. Indirect methods of alcoholism prevalence estimation; a critical evaluation. Pp. 294–306. In: POPHAM, R. E., ed. Alcohol and alcoholism. Toronto; University of Toronto Press; 1970.

106. PRESTON, J. D. On norm qualitites and deviant drinking behavior. Social Probl. **16:** 535–537, 1969.

107. REINERT, R. E. The concept of alcoholism as a bad habit. Bull. Menninger Clin. **32:** 35–46, 1968.

108. REISS, I. L. Premarital sex as deviant behavior; an application of current approaches to deviance. Amer. sociol. Rev. **35:** 78–87, 1970.

109. RILEY, J. W., JR., MARDEN, C. F. and LIFSHITZ, M. The motivational pattern of drinking; based on the verbal responses of a cross-section sample of users. Quart. J. Stud. Alc. **9:** 353–362, 1948.

110. ROBINS, L. N. Deviant children grown up; a sociological and psychiatric study of sociopathic personality. Baltimore; Williams & Wilkins; 1966.

111. ROBINS, L. N., BATES, W. M. and O'NEAL, P. Adult drinking patterns of former problem children. Pp. 395–412. In: PITTMAN, D. J. and SNYDER, C. R., eds. Society, culture, and drinking patterns. New York; Wiley; 1962.

112. ROBINSON, C. Straw votes. New York; Columbia University Press; 1932.

113. ROMAN, P. M. and TRICE, H. M. The development of deviant drinking behavior; occupational risk factors. Arch. environ. Hlth 20: 424–435, 1970.

114. ROOM, R. G. Amount of drinking and alcoholism. Int. Congr. Alc. Alcsm, 28th, Vol. 1 (Abst.), pp. 97–98, 1968.

115. ROOM, R. Cultural contingencies of alcoholism; variations between and within nineteenth-century urban ethnic groups in alcohol-related death rates. J. Hlth soc. Behav. 9: 99–113, 1968.

116. ROOM, R. Interrelations of state policies, consumption and alcohol problems in the U.S. states. Pp. 56–78. In: EWING, J. and ROUSE, B., eds. Law and drinking behavior. Chapel Hill, N.C.; University of North Carolina Center for Alcohol Studies; 1971.

117. ROOM, R. Drinking in the rural south. Pp. 79–108. In: EWING, J. and ROUSE, B., eds. Law and drinking behavior. Chapel Hill, N.C.: University of North Carolina Center for Alcohol Studies; 1971.

118. ROOM, R. Measures of heavy drinking; the difference it makes. Drinking & Drug Pract. Surveyor, Berkeley, Calif. No. 3, pp. 3–6, 1971.

119. ROOM, R. Law and drinking behavior. Drinking & Drug. Pract. Surveyor, Berkeley, Calif. No. 3, pp. 12–14, 1971.

120. ROOM, R. Survey vs. sales data for the U.S. Drinking & Drug Pract. Surveyor, Berkeley, Calif. No. 3, pp. 15–16, 1971.

121. ROOM, R. Alcohol-related urban mortality; a cross-national study. Drinking & Drug Pract. Surveyor, Berkeley, Calif. No. 5, pp. 11–13, 1972.

122. ROOM, R. Drinking patterns in large U.S. cities; a comparison of San Francisco and national samples. Quart. J. Stud. Alc., Suppl. No. 6, pp. 28–57, 1972.

123. ROSENBERG, M. Factors influencing change of occupational choice. Pp. 250–259. In: LAZARSFELD, P. F. and ROSENBERG, M., eds. The language of social research. New York; Free Press; 1955.

124. ROTTER, J. B. Social learning and clinical psychology. New York; Prentice-Hall; 1954.

125. ROZELLE, R. M. Causal relations in attitude change as demonstrated through the cross-lagged panel correlation. Evanston, Ill.; Northwestern University; 1965.

126. ROZELLE, R. M. and CAMPBELL, D. T. More plausible rival hypotheses in the cross-lagged correlation technique. Psychol. Bull. 71: 74–80, 1969.

127. SCHUR, E. M. Reactions to deviance; a critical assessment. Amer. J. Sociol. 75: 309–322, 1969.

128. SEELEY, J. R. The W.H.O. definition of alcoholism. Quart. J. Stud. Alc. 20: 352–356, 1959.

129. SEIFERT, A. M. Religious affiliation and problem drinking. Ph.D. dissertation, University of California; 1972.

130. SHEVKY, E. and BELL, W. Social area analysis. Stanford; Stanford University Press; 1955.

131. SIEGLER, M., OSMOND, H. and NEWELL, S. Models of alcoholism. Quart. J. Stud. Alc. 29: 571–591, 1968.

132. SMITH, T. Social stress and cardiovascular disease; factors involving sociocultural incongruity and change; a review of empirical findings. Millbank mem. Fd Quart. 45 (Suppl.):, 23–39, April 1967.

133. SNYDER, C. R. Inebriety, alcoholism and anomie. Pp. 189–212. In: CLINARD, M. B., ed. Anomie and deviant behavior. New York; Free Press; 1964.

134. SOKAL, R. R. and SNEATH, P. H. A. Principles of numerical taxonomy. San Francisco; Freeman; 1963.

135. SONQUIST, J. A. and MORGAN, J. N. The detection of interaction effects. (Institute for Social Research, Monogr. No. 35.) Ann Arbor; University of Michigan; 1964.

136. STRAUS, R. and BACON, S. D. Drinking in college. New Haven; Yale University Press; 1953.

137. SUTHERLAND, E. H. and CRESSEY, D. R. Principles of criminology. 5th ed. New York; Lippincott; 1955.

138. SWIECICKI, A. Alkohol, zagadnienia polityki spolecznej. (Alcohol, problems of social policy.) Warszawa; Spoleczny Komitet Przeciwalkoholowy, Zarzad Glowny; 1968. (Abst. in Drinking & Drug Prac. Surveyor, Berkeley, Calif., No. 5, pp. 1–8, 1972.)

139. THOMANN, G. Real and imaginary effects of intemperance; a statistical sketch, containing letters and statements from the superintendents of eighty American insane asylums, the history of five hundred inebriates, the history of . . . paupers, and statistics of drunkenness. . . . New York; United States Brewers' Association; 1884.

140. TOLMAN, E. C. Operational behaviorism and current trends in psychology. In: MARX M. H., ed. Psychological theory. New York; Macmillan; 1951.

141. TRYON, R. C. Identification of social areas by cluster analysis. Berkeley; University of California Press; 1955.

142. TRYON, R. C. Predicting group differences in cluster analysis; the social area problem. Multivar. behav. Res., Ft Worth 2: 453–475, 1967.

143. TRYON, R. C. Comparative cluster analysis of social areas. Multivar. behav. Res., Ft Worth 3: 213–232, 1968.

144. U.S. CONGRESS. SENATE. SPECIAL SUBCOMMITTEE ON ALCOHOLISM AND NARCOTICS. The impact of alcoholism; hearings before the Special Subcommittee on Alcoholism and Narcotics of the Committee on Labor and Public Welfare of the United States Senate, 91st Congress, first session on the examination of the impact of alcoholism. Washington, D.C.; U.S. Govt Print. Off.; 1970.

145. U.S. PUBLIC HEALTH SERVICE. ADVISORY COMMITTEE TO THE SURGEON GENERAL. Smoking and health. (U.S. Public Health Service Publ. No. 1103.) Washington, D.C.; U.S. Govt Print. Off.; 1964.

146. U.S. PUBLIC HEALTH SERVICE. NATIONAL CENTER FOR HEALTH STATISTICS. Reporting of hospitalization in the health interview survey. (U.S. Public Health Service Publ. No. 1000, Ser. 2, No. 6.) Washington, D.C.; U.S. Govt Print. Off.; 1965.
147. U.S. PUBLIC HEALTH SERVICE. NATIONAL CENTER FOR HEALTH STATISTICS. Health interview responses compared with medical records. (U.S. Public Health Service Publ. No. 1000, Ser. 2, No. 7.) Washington, D.C.; U.S. Govt Print. Off.; 1965.
148. U.S. PUBLIC HEALTH SERVICE. NATIONAL CENTER FOR HEALTH STATISTICS. Interview data on chronic conditions compared with information derived from medical records. (U.S. Public Health Service Publ. No. 1000, Ser. 2, No. 23.) Washington, D.C.; U.S. Govt Print. Off.; 1967.
149. VAN DER RYN, S. Amenity attributes of residential locations. (San Francisco Community Renewal Program Tech. Paper No. 3.) Boston; Little; 1965.
150. WEBER, M. The Protestant ethic and the spirit of capitalism. PARSONS, T., transl. New York; Scribners; 1958.
151. WINER, B. J. A measure of interrelationship for overlapping groups. Psychometrika 20: 63–68, 1955.
152. Quitting may be hazardous. Behav. Today 2 (No. 19); 1, 1971.
153. Powell v State of Texas. U.S. Sup. Ct Reports, Lawyer's Edition, Second Series, October term, 1967, (July 25), pp. 1254–1288, published 1968.

Index of Names

259

Index of Subjects

261